PENGUIN BO

AN EPIC LIFE

Prem Sagar began his career as a cinematographer with Ramanand Sagar's *Lalkar* (1972) soon after completing his education from the Film and Television Institute of India (FTII), Pune, where he received a gold medal for the best academic student of the year and a silver medal for the best photographed student film.

He was associated as a cinematographer and technical adviser with several popular and memorable films of Ramanand Sagar's production company, Sagar Arts, such as *Jalte Badan* (1973), *Hamrahi* (1974), *Charas* (1976), *Prem Bandhan* (1979), *Pyaara Dushman* (1980), *Armaan* (1981), *Baghavat* (1982), *Baadal* (1985) and *Salma* (1985). He then turned director with *Hum Tere Aashiq Hain* (1979).

In the eighties, Prem Sagar produced and directed Indian television's first fantasy serial, *Vikram aur Betaal*. Closely associated with the show *Ramayan*, Sagar went on to have an extremely successful career in television being associated with shows like *Shri Krishna* (1993–97), *Sai Baba* (2005–09), *Prithviraj Chauhan* (2006–09) and *Chandra Gupta Maurya* (2011–12) in various creative capacities. He also directed *Jai Maa Durga* (2007), *Mahima Shani Dev Ki* (2008–09), *Jai Jai Jai Bajrang Bali* (2011–15) and *Basera* (2009).

Prem Sagar has won fifteen awards as director of photography and has many accomplishments in the field of still photography. The honours include the prestigious associateship of the Royal Photographic Society of Great Britain and the Artiste Federation Internationale de L'Arts Photographique Paris.

Celebrating 35 Years of
Penguin Random House India

PRAISE FOR THE BOOK

'The book is essentially dovetailed around one man's saga, spilling out anecdotes that only an insider can have access to. What is amazing, however, is that despite keeping the father on a pedestal, he lets his story pulsate with humane facets intact'—Nonika Singh, *Tribune*

'The book is as much a biography as it is the chronicling of a changing India on celluloid—from the time of Partition to the success of the teleserial *Ramayan*, which changed the fortunes of Doordarshan, and how'—Rekha Dixit, *Week*

'Prem Sagar's narrative is simple and plain, shorn of descriptions or imagery . . . yet, the book is much more than just a biography. It is also a story of India's film history, from the 1930s and 1940s till the 1980s, when *Ramayan* would revolutionize television and change the fortunes of Doordarshan'—Devdan Mitra, *Telegraph*

'Ramanand Sagarji's famous *Ramayan* TV series and his striking literary precocity have left an indelible mark on us all!'—Amitabh Bachchan on Twitter on 10 January 2020

AN
EPIC
LIFE

Ramanand Sagar:
From *Barsaat* to
Ramayan

PREM SAGAR

PENGUIN BOOKS
An imprint of Penguin Random House

PENGUIN BOOKS

USA | Canada | UK | Ireland | Australia
New Zealand | India | South Africa | China

Penguin Books is part of the Penguin Random House group of companies
whose addresses can be found at global.penguinrandomhouse.com

Published by Penguin Random House India Pvt. Ltd
4th Floor, Capital Tower 1, MG Road,
Gurugram 122 002, Haryana, India

Penguin
Random House
India

First published by Westland Publications Private Limited 2019
Published in Penguin Books by Penguin Random House India 2023

ISBN 9780143459354

Typeset by SÜRYA, New Delhi
Printed at Replika Press Pvt. Ltd, India

www.penguin.co.in

MIX
Paper from
responsible sources
FSC® C016779

Papaji's grand children
JYOTI, MANISHA, GEETA, SEETA, SHAKTI, GAURI, AMAR,
MEENAKSHI, AMRIT, AKASH, RAJEEV, VISHAL and PARUL

Papaji's great grand-children
GAYATRI, VARUN, MALIKA, ARYAMAAN, SAKSHI
MAHANT, SIDHANT, ARJUN, ANNYA, VINAYAK,
ANYA, MYRA, ISHAAN and KIANA

all associated with Papaji's group of companies for their selfless seva
including RANGEEN SAHEB, PANDITJI, DHONDU,
KUMAR, HARISH, PINTO and JOHN
&
all friends, business associates and well wishers who were partners
in the life journey of Papaji,
Dr RAMANAND SAGAR, from a pauper to prince to a Maharishi

CONTENTS

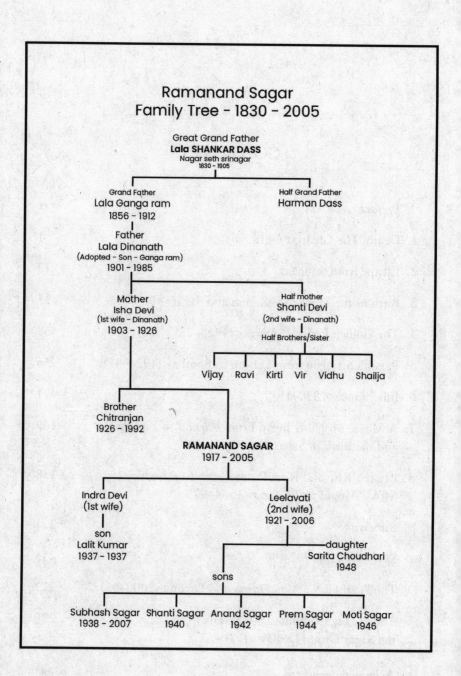

Ramanand Sagar
Family Tree - 1830 - 2005

Great Grand Father
Lala SHANKAR DASS
Nagar seth srinagar
1830 - 1905

Grand Father
Lala Ganga ram
1856 - 1912

Half Grand Father
Harman Dass

Father
Lala Dinanath
(Adopted - Son - Ganga ram)
1901 - 1985

Mother
Isha Devi
(1st wife - Dinanath)
1903 - 1926

Half mother
Shanti Devi
(2nd wife - Dinanath)

Half Brothers/Sister

Vijay   Ravi   Kirti   Vir   Vidhu   Shailja

Brother
Chitranjan
1926 - 1992

RAMANAND SAGAR
1917 - 2005

Indra Devi
(1st wife)

Leelavati
(2nd wife)
1921 - 2006

son
Lalit Kumar
1937 - 1937

daughter
Sarita Choudhari
1948

sons

Subhash Sagar
1938 - 2007

Shanti Sagar
1940

Anand Sagar
1942

Prem Sagar
1944

Moti Sagar
1946

PREFACE

Jai Shri Ram!
Would it be right to reveal the sensitive secret truths—political, personal or miracles—of Papaji's life journey and his divine mission of making the legendary TV serial *Ramayan* which was destined at birth and revealed as early as 1942?

I am not sure whether I should be penning these memoirs, as a biographical tribute to Papaji—my revered and respected father Padmashri Dr Ramanand Sagar.

In different yugs, the teachings of the greatest Indian epic Ramayana were brought to mankind by different people. At first, Shiv Bhagwan narrated to Parvati Maa with king of crows Kakbhushandi listening. Later, Brahmrishi Valmiki penned the Ramayana as a kavya (poetry). Sant Tulsidass wrote it in Awadhi language. In this kalyug—the age of vice and downfall—Papaji was perhaps born to revive and spread the message of the benevolent gracious Shri Ram to mankind through television, the most powerful audio-visual mass media of the previous century.

All of Papaji's years in journalism, as an author of stories, stage plays, books and films—he wrote the dialogues, story or screenplay of twenty-nine films—and his role as a producer and director of such blockbusters like *Ghunghat, Zindagi, Arzoo, Ankhen, Geet, Lalkar, Charas, Baghavat,* were only a step towards his final goal of bringing Ramayana to television viewers throughout the world.

We brothers—Subhash, Anand, Moti and me—and grandson Jyoti were sent to this world to assist him, almost like just like the vanar sena assisted Shri Ram. Subhash handled the production and direction, editing was handled by Anand and Moti and camera, technical and marketing was my forte.

To get his biography recorded in his voice, I chased him for two years to get two hours of recording. In some personal moments with me, he would unveil the iron curtain surrounding his scratched soul. Late at night in my bedroom I would note down these incidents and now all this has become the basis of these memories as a biographical tribute. He never wanted to show his pain and wounds to anyone. I was the chosen one and I feel I was the closest to him among my siblings.

The question still remains. Did Papaji give me permission to delve into his personal life—to reveal to seekers and his bhaktas, his journey from a prince to a pauper to a Maharishi to the maker of *Ramayan* and *Shri Krishna*?

I am not even a speck in this divine yojana. I am not a writer and do not have the capacity to encompass Papaji's life and times and work and mission. But I feel pitra bhakti has given me the courage to try to pen down the memorable life and times of Dr Ramanand Sagar, my reverend father and to me, Papaji.

I am indebted to my son, Shiv Sagar, for encouraging me to accept this missionary task.

With the blessings of my ancestors, Gurus and Gods and with Papaji's permission and Durga Maa's blessings, I am making this attempt. Please forgive me for any mistakes or shortcomings and for any revelations too personal, sensitive or spiritual. May Maa Saraswati be with me.

Om Dum Durgaye Namaha!

PREM SAGAR

Ramanand Sagar at the age of twenty-four when he was diagnosed with tuberculosis and sent to the TB Sanatorium in Tangmarg, Kashmir.

Photo collection: Ramanand Sagar Foundation

1

DEATH: THE GREATEST GURU

In May 1941, twenty-four-year-old Papaji lay on a bed in a sanatorium at Tangmarg, in the beautiful valley of Kashmir. Papaji—Ramanand Sagar to the world—was staring death in the eye in the prime of his youth. Tuberculosis (TB) had drained the life out of him. There was no cure for TB then, and the sanatorium was like a waiting room before death could take him away. Every week, every day, all the patients silently watched one corpse after another being taken away, all the time trying to guess who was next in the queue.

One day, standing at the window, Ramanand watched a young couple, very much in love, walking out of the sanatorium, disease-free and normal. Their love seemed to have conquered the dreaded disease and even death. Tears rolled down Papaji's eyes as he made a promise to himself—to live and endure! He didn't know then what lay ahead of him and that destiny had chosen him for something big—to bring the Ramayana to drawing rooms.

Maybe it was God's will that brought Papaji back from the clutches of death. Death taught him the tenets of Sakshi Bhava (looking at life as a detached witness).

So how did my father develop TB in the first place? During his period of struggle in Lahore, between the ages of nineteen to twenty-four, my father worked as a clapper boy in the film *Raiders of the Rail Road* (1936), starring Usha. He then worked as a leading man in Kamala Movies' 1940 film, *Koel*, opposite Neelam with director Roshanlal Shorey. Later, he also played Abhimanyu in Pancholi Studios' film, *Krishna*. Both films either failed at the box office or were never released but it was believed that Neelam had TB. My father may have caught the disease then.

The next two years (1940-41) of Papaji's life were full of hardship. He did odd jobs as an apprentice to a goldsmith, a peon, a soap vendor and a truck cleaner just so that he could earn a little to buy milk for his first-born, Subhash. He would work during the day and stay up nights to study for his gold medal and the title of Munshi Fazal at Panjab University, Lahore. Life was difficult and with no hope. Papaji was burning the candle of life at both ends in order to achieve success.

Meanwhile, TB ravaged Papaji's weary, fatigued body. One day, he spat blood! An X-ray by the family doctor, Dr Malhotra, revealed my father's disease-ridden body. My grandfather, Lala Dinanath Chopra, whom we called Payaji, was forced to take Papaji to the sanatorium in Kashmir. My ancestors were prestigious landlords there and held the zamindari of villages spread over 500 acres of land inherited from Papaji's great-grandfather, Lala Shankar Dass. He was the proclaimed Nagar Seth (the richest man of Srinagar), in the court of Maharaja Gulab Singh (1846-57) till the reign of his grandson Maharaja Pratap Singh (1885-1925). But, before Papaji could come into his inheritance, much of it had vanished.

While Papaji patiently waited to take his last breath, he started penning down his experiences at the sanatorium. He saw life inside a world where death was a permanent companion. Some resisted death, while others played along ... but the end was certain, sooner or later. He jotted down people's perceptions of death and learnt some hard life lessons from them. He saw the true love of the young couple who had defied death. He realised the beauty of nature he was leaving behind and the poignancy of death that gave meaning to his existence.

On one of those days, my father received a postcard from his family. It conveyed the news of the birth of his third son, Anand, on

3 September 1941. The postcard read, '*Budhwar ke din, tumhare ghar mein ek budhu paida hua hai!*' that literally meant, 'On Wednesday, a fool was born in your house.' This was actually a play on the word for Wednesday (budhwar) and the Hindi word for fool (budhu), which was often used light-heartedly. That night, all the inmates of the sanatorium celebrated the birth of a new life. Even though the whole world lay mottled with the blood from the Second World War (1939-45), the inmates of the sanatorium rejoiced, as one of their own had been blessed with fatherhood for the third time. His eldest, Subhash, was four now and Shanti, two.

Papaji recalled how his fellow inmates had broken into a celebration. That night they had, with blankets over their heads, barged into the sugarcane and corn fields, lit fires, roasted bhuttas (corn) and chewed on sugarcane for its sweet nectar of life.

Papaji started sending his writings to *Adab-e-Mashriq*, a famous Urdu literary magazine of the 1940s in Lahore, under the title 'Maut Ke Bistar Se' or 'Diary of a TB Patient'. The editor of the magazine was deeply moved by his writing and the paradox of a man destined for death in a sanatorium showing others the way to live. Unknown to my father, the column became a huge hit and caught the eye of several literary luminaries. He had now become a celebrated writer outside the sanatorium. Rising like the legendary phoenix from the ashes of death, Papaji was soon on his road to recovery. Maybe it was due to inhaling the elixir of the magical Himalayan air!

In one of the extracts from his testimonies in the sanatorium he wrote, 'The question is that why did this dangerous infection spread in the localities on a large scale, because we are unable to cure this disease. Hunger and poverty can only be solved by social groups or the politicians running this country. The big question in front of us is that what action is being taken in order to stop all these things?' (*Hamdard*, 11 October 1942).

In 2004, sometime in September, Papaji recounted an incident that was perhaps connected to his miraculous recovery. A hakim used to live in Tangmarg while Papaji was in the sanatorium. One of the inmates suffering from terminal TB used to go to a nearby sugarcane field and sing with wild abandon while chewing on sugarcane.

Dukh ke ab din beetat nahi
Na main kisi ka, naa koyi mera
Chayya charon aur andhera

(Days of gloom and agony now do not pass any more
I am nobody's and nobody is mine
Darkness has set in all around.)

The song was from director Kedar Sharma's *Devdas*, sung by K.L. Saigal. Since the sanatorium doctors had sentenced him to a long wait for death, he used to visit the local hakim in the hope of finding a Unani cure for his disease. A few days later, the hakim discovered to his shock that his patient's TB was miraculously gone! On probing about the patient's daily routine and finding out about the sugarcane consumption, the hakim went to the sugarcane field, dug it and found a huge black snake buried there. He started burying dead snakes in the sugarcane field and began research in Unani medicine for a cure for TB. Papaji must have been one of the recipients of this miraculous cure.

In ancient China, the venom of the cobra was primarily used to treat cancer and arthritis. In the Indian Unani system of medicine, the cobra's venom has been used as a tonic, an aphrodisiac, a hepatic stimulant and for revival in critical conditions. My father's cure could be attributed to this divine Unani medicine developed by the hakim in Tangmarg.

Healed and recovered, on his way back from Tangmarg to Srinagar, Papaji's horse stopped in front of another man's horse coming from the opposite direction. The two men looked at each other in bewilderment. 'Ramanand …?' the gentleman whispered.

'Krishan Chander …!' Papaji replied, with faint recognition. The two were meeting for the first time.

They hugged each other. 'You have been writing the column, "Diary of a TB Patient" from your deathbed!' said Krishan Chander incredulously. Papaji was speechless at being recognised by a literary giant like Krishan Chander. This was the first time someone had acknowledged my father as a writer. After that, he never looked back.

Ramanand Sagar also wrote an article in the Urdu newspaper *Hamdard* on 11 October 1942, titled 'Kashmir mein Tap-e-Dique', about TB in Kashmir, under the name Ramanand Kashmiri. In the article, he stated vehemently, '... if the State Government thinks that building a sanatorium and a hospital for a few TB patients is completion of their duties, then it is a mistake as huge as the Himalaya mountains.'

My father began his career as a journalist in *Daily Milap* and *Daily Pratap*, two leading Urdu dailies of Lahore (1940-46). He later went on to write twenty-nine short stories, three novellas and two plays, *Gaura* and *Kalakar*, for Prithvi Theatres in 1948 and was associated with twenty-nine films between 1949 and 1985, either as producer, director or writer. Six of his films celebrated silver jubilees in a row—*Ghunghat, Zindagi, Arzoo, Ankhen, Geet* and *Lalkar*. Another two—*Charas* and *Bhagawat*—were huge hits in this period. He became a leading figure in the Indian film industry, with distribution offices across India, and in London.

Papaji also went on to create over 2,000 hours of television content, including the legendary series *Ramayan* (1987) and *Shri Krishna* (1992). *Ramayan* has been telecast in fifty-three countries, with a viewership of 650 million people, as estimated by the BBC. With his production of the Ramayana, Ramanand Sagar became the Tulsidas and the Valmiki of the Kalyug. He was nothing short of a Saraswati Putra, always brimming with ideas and finding creative ways to express them.

Initially, Papaji originally wrote under the name Ramanand Bedi, assuming the name of his mother Isha Devi who belonged to a Bedi family from Lahore. He also wrote as Ramanand Kashmiri, since four generations of his family were rooted in Kashmir. He adopted his father's surname and wrote as Ramanand Chopra, as the Kshatriya family on his paternal side was the original Chopra family that had migrated from Peshawar to Kashmir. However, he settled on the name Sagar and then came to be known as Ramanand Sagar.

At a very early stage in his life, my father was inspired by Maa Saraswati (Goddess of Knowledge) to write under the pen name

موت کے بستر سے

تپ دق کے ایک مریض کی ڈائری

DIARY OF A TB PATIENT
BY RAMANAND SAGAR
PUBLISHED IN URDU NEWS PAPER "PARAS" (LAHORE) 1942

MAY 1940

ab se yeh oata chala hai key main TB ka mariz hoon, ek
ajib si halat hai. Maazi(past) apnea daaman me mer adhoori
arzooyen liye badi be-dardi se muskura raha hai. Aisa
aaloom hota hai jaise kisi anjaan kissan ne apni tamam
enat ek aise maidan kop sairab karne(Paany dene) me
arf(spent) kart di ho jis me hasrat key paudon key aiwa
uchh nahi ugta.

austaqbil(future) kid taraf aankh utha kart dekhta hoon to
iss jaan lewa aue halak kiye bagair nana chhodhne wali
imaari key baim me main aaj tak jo kuchh padhu ya suna,
ho saara ilm(knowledge) pareshan khyalat kid soorat me
autaqbil(future) ko tareek(dark) kiye huye hai. Na-ummidi
o siwa kuchh dikhayee nahi deta. Lekin wah ri ummid! Usney
bhi tak ek nanha sa chiragh wahan jala rakha hai. Lekin
kela chiragh raat ki tareeki(darkness) ko zyda khaufnak
ana deta hai. Isi tarah bach rahne ki yeh ummid
ustaqbil(future) ko zyda pareshan karne wala bana rahi
ai. Agar Tap-e-dique(TB) ka mariz waqti taur par bach bhi
ahe toh kya, umar bhar ke liye toh dagh-daar ho jata hai.

oon kaho ke Qudrat ne ek ek "Teer-e-neem kash" chhodha
ai. (Less effortly targeted Arrow). Jiski Khallsh(pain) ob
indagi bhar na jaa sake-gi. Ek ajib halat hai, jaise meri
tar, zindegi aur maut ke bheech hichkole kha rahi hai.

aj hamaze college ke vice Principal janab Ahmed Gharib
awaz ne sare gharib khann par bhi tashrif laaye. Bahut
achh dilasa diya jis se girti huyee ummis phir sanbhal
yyee. Baher-hal duniya bar ummid qayam ast.(Ummid par
iniya qayam hai).

MAY 1940

May ko Lahore se chal kar aaj raat Srinagar pahuncha.
hore ue rawangi ka nazara tasawwur(Imagination) me aatey
aansu dabdaba astey hain. Doston ka hujoom(crowd) aur
ir yeh khyal ke shayad yeh hamari aakhri mulaqat ho. Isn
zba(feeling) ki maujoodgai me yeh andaza kiya ja sakta
i ke kis tarah aasre ka saara majma(crowd) mujhe aansu-on
lada hua ek baadal dikhayee de raha tha. Woh doston ka

بہار

جنبشِ موسمِ بہار ہے آج   غنچۂ برگ پر نکھار ہے آج

آرزو دل میں بیقرار ہے آج   دامنِ ہوش تار تار ہے آج

ذرے ذرے سے حسن پھوٹا ہے   جلوۂ دوست آشکار ہے آج

جو نہار حسیں ہے مست خرام   نغمہ زن موج آبشار ہے آج

ہائے کس طور سے ترنم ریز   سازِ قدرت کا تار تار ہے آج

ہمنوا لالہ زار کی کیا بات   رشکِ گلزار خار زار ہے آج

روح پر دہ سرور طاری ہے
ذکرِ فردوس ناگوار ہے آج

جگن ناتھ آزاد

Photographs of 'The Diary of a TB Patient' published in *Adab-e-Mashriq* (top left and bottom right), 'Maut de Bistar Chon' published in a Punjabi magazine and handwritten notes of Ramanand Sagar written in the sanatorium (top right). 'The Diary of a TB Patient' in Roman script which mentions that it was published in *Paras* (bottom left).

Photo collection: Ramanand Sagar Foundation

Letter of appreciation for Ramanand Sagar on *The Daily Milap* (head office at Anarkali, Lahore) letterhead dated 16 July 1940, signed by Managing Editor Ranbirji.

Photo collection: Ramanand Sagar Foundation

'Sagar'. An evolved soul, my father did not want to be tagged to his affluent family or limited by religion, caste, creed or geographical boundaries. Like the sagar (sea) that flows unrestricted, without boundaries, and is vishal (endless), my father chose to be a 'Sagar'. His works belonged to all humankind. This was clearly reflected in his texts as noted by Ishtiaq Ahmed, professor of political science at Stockholm University, who said with reference to one of his famous works, '*Aur Insaan Mar Gaya* (And Humanity Died) enjoys the reputation of being the most humane and politically neutral novel on the Partition. I was told this by two of my close friends in Stockholm: Sheikh Jawaid who is a voracious reader and an authority on the history and legends of Lahore and Syed Siraj ul Salakeen who is perhaps the most ardent Pakistani patriot in my close circle. They acknowledged that *Aur Insaan Mar Gaya* was a product of pure humanism in which the author had been fair to everyone.'

Ramanand Sagar revisited, in the late '60, the TB sanatorium in Tangmarg District Hospital.

Photo collection: Ramanand Sagar Foundation

At the behest of Krishan Chander, Papaji worked at Shalimar Pictures in Pune from 1942-45 even as he continued to be associated with *Daily Pratap* and *Daily Milaap*. Under the patronage of film producer W.Z. Ahmed (Wahiduddin Ziauddin Ahmed) and his actor-wife Neena (Shahida), celebrated writers, poets and artists such as Faiz Ahmed Faiz, Rajinder Singh Bedi, Saadat Hasan Manto, Akhtar-ul-Iman and Prithviraj Kapoor worked and contributed.

In the late 1940s, Krishan Chander and Manto encouraged Papaji to go to Bombay to meet filmmakers like Mehboob Khan. While in Pune, his friendship with Prithviraj Kapoor blossomed, that later led to Papaji joining Prithvi Theatres in 1948. This resulted in him writing the script of *Barsaat* for Raj Kapoor in 1949. He continued writing till the making of *Zindagi* (1964) for Gemini Studios in Chennai, starring Prithviraj Kapoor, which he also directed.

Manoj Panjnani, a film journalist and researcher from Dehradun, says in a personal communication to me: 'Sagar sahab worked as publicity manager in Shalimar Studios, Pune. Shalimar Studios was owned by W.Z. Ahmed. He wanted to raise the standard of films in India and therefore he employed literary persons in the studio. Besides Sagar sahab, Krishan Chander, Josh Mahilaabadi, Sagar Nizami and Bharat Vyas were other literary people on the payroll of the studio. These facts were given to me by Akhtar-ul-Iman, who joined the studio in 1944. After Partition, W.Z. Ahmed went away to Pakistan.'

The Birth of 'Sagar'

While on a visit to Bombay, Papaji went to Chowpatty beach. He had never seen the sea. He stood in the centre of the Queen's Necklace and closed his eyes in reverence to the astonishing power of the ocean. He prayed to Varun Dev (God of the oceans), to Ratnakar and to the mighty sagar for acceptance in this nagri of opportunities, dreams and aspirations. He looked at the golden city of Bombay that had the Midas touch. The city that unconditionally accepted everyone and provided food, shelter and opportunities to anyone who came to her with folded hands. Nobody remained hungry or jobless.

A tidal wave gushed through the sand and onto the nearby road. In joyful mirth, the wave mysteriously made a whirlpool of foam, a circle of faith and acceptance, making the sound of Om, blessing him. Stunned and delighted by the acceptance of this Kuber Nagri, Ramanand Sagar realised why he had been inspired, and decided his pen name would be 'Sagar'. He named his five sons in reverence to Sagar Dev—Subhash Sagar, Shanti Sagar, Anand Sagar, Prem Sagar and Moti Sagar.

At the Natraj Studio in 1975. Standing (left to right), Subhash Sagar, Shanti Sagar, Anand Sagar, Prem Sagar and Moti Sagar with their father Ramanand Sagar (seated).

Photo collection: Ramanand Sagar Foundation

While standing at Chowpatty, he felt like a puppet in the hands of the Almighty. In spite of his sincerity, diligence, ambition and dreams, all that he could achieve so far were brief stints in the Lahore, Pune and Bombay film industries.

Papaji's first film as a writer, *Barsaat*, released in 1949, was directed by Raj Kapoor and established the RK banner in the film industry. It was also the debut film of Shankar Jaikishan, Shailendra, Hasrat Jaipuri, Nimmi and Prem Nath. *Barsaat* was a big hit at the box office and made Papaji one of the most sought-after writers in Hindi cinema. The film ran for a hundred weeks and became a landmark in the history of Indian cinema.

Soon after, Prithvi Theatres staged Papaji's play *Kalakar* one morning at the Royal Opera House in Bombay. Prithviraj Kapoor decided to introduce his second son, the future 'yahoo' superstar, Shammi Kapoor, as a child artiste in the play. This created a conflict of principles, ethics and interests between Prithviraj Kapoor and my father since it involved tampering with my father's original script and so they both ended up sharing credits for writing the play. It was dedicated to all artistes who revered art and devoted their lives to it. Prithviraj Kapoor had laid the foundation of Prithvi Theatres with the same principles and ethics.

Silence—the language of the dead, unheard by the living—Papaji heard it the loudest. It reminded him of the silent deaths in the sanatorium that had left a lasting impression on his mind. His past defined the road map of his life's journey with the philosophy of Sakshi Bhava. He believed in complete surrender to the merciful hands of Bhagwan. Ramanand Sagar remained involved in every sphere of his life and found joy in them. The philosophy suggested that one ought to be patient and an outsider to one's experiences. Nothing should affect one's life balance. 'Sampoorn samarpan' or complete surrender into the graceful, merciful hands of God was needed to witness the power of the Almighty. One should be involved in all aspects of life, be it marriage, parenthood, struggle, fame, money or love, but one should stay subjective and objective at the same time.

'*Karta hote huye bhi dharta hona. Dharta hote huye bhi karta hona.*'—'Live subjectively and still be objective. Live objectively and still be subjective.' Papaji portrayed this in his classic TV serial *Ramayan* in the scene where Sage Valmiki gave the same advice to Shri Ram in the gurukul.

Papaji believed in Amma Mata Amritanandamayi Devi's preaching that asked one to look at the world as a 'sakshi' or witness.

Be it success or failure, the goal is to look at emotions, sadness, and happiness from a distance so that they do not affect you. This 'witness consciousness' as termed by Acharya Rajneesh (Osho) made sakshi bhava enrich Padmashri Ramanand Sagar's life.

My father's entire life was based on the idea of witness consciousness. No questions were asked and no answers were sought. Death taught him the principle of sakshi bhava. Having understood the ephemeral nature of human existence and the power of divine intervention, Ramanand Sagar started his journey into a new life.

Death had become my father's greatest guru.

2

ESCAPE FROM SRINAGAR

Papaji was thirty when he and his thirteen family members, including my mother, five children (including me), mother-in-law, brothers-in-law and their wives, sat huddled together at the old Srinagar airport, waiting like lambs to be led to the slaughter. From the other side of the airport, we could hear gunshots. The tribal Lashkar jihadis were only 500 metres away from us on the kuccha airfield.

Pakistan's Operation Gulmarg was on. The day was 26 October 1947. Pakistan was laying claim to the princely state of Jammu and Kashmir. The 10,000 jihadi Muslim tribals supported by the Pakistan army had reached Baramulla on 24 October. They cut the power lines to Srinagar, plunging the royal capital city into darkness. Then they lost two crucial days as they got greedy and looted and plundered the rich Baramulla town, raping women and abducting them to sell them off to the brothels of Rawalpindi, forcing them to convert to Islam or face death.

The tribal Lashkars from Waziristan had still not reached the heart of the city, as per plan, but were near the airport, trying to cut across the unpaved airstrip to attack and take over the royal city of Srinagar. That was their final mission. Barely two kilometres away from them were Papaji and his family, stranded on the Srinagar airstrip with other refugees.

In the early hours of 27 October, helplessly stranded at the airstrip, the Sagar family and the others feared for their lives. Stony silence reflected on frozen faces. Babies, children, women and men were in despair as their anxious eyes stared at the blood-red sky of sunrise. Cutting off the Srinagar airstrip would mean victory over the city followed by the fall of the Dogra dynasty-ruled kingdom of Kashmir. To save Srinagar and Kashmir was going to be an uphill task, what with all land routes being blocked. With the tough mountainous landscape and time running out, reaching Srinagar by air was the only route for the Indian military to invade, airdrop troops and evacuate people.

I remember it was Diwali. According to local legend, Major Somnath Sharma of 4th Kumaon regiment, along with two platoons of state forces, had hidden Diwali firecrackers in the paddy fields. The crackers went off periodically, acting as a decoy for gunshots.

It seemed as if the Indian soldiers were firing back at the invaders and also acted as a barricade between the butchers and innocent refugees. Unaware of the trap, the invaders, armed with automatic weapons, mortars and flame-throwers, waited for the Indian ammunition to get exhausted before attacking with full force. This lifesaving tactic of Major Somnath Sharma bought us a few hours to cross the bridge between death and life, though, as per military records, Major Sharma's company was airlifted to Srinagar only on 31 October.

The faint sound of the Dakota engines gave us hope. The Dakota DC-3, piloted by Biju Patnaik, landed with roaring engines at 8.30 a.m. on the short unpaved empty airstrip. This was the Douglas Dakota DC-3 of no. 12 squadron of the Royal Indian Air Force under Wing Commander K.L. Bhatia which had taken off at 6 a.m. from Delhi's Palam airport.

Seventeen soldiers of the 1st Sikh regiment under the commanding officer Lt. Col. Dewan Ranjit Rai, along with 500 pounds of personal arms equipment and bed rolls, jumped down and charged the enemy. Lt. Col. Rai manned the first line of fire, but just before darkness he was shot dead by a Lashkari militant lurking in the paddy fields. Lt. Col. Rai was posthumously awarded the first Maha Vir Chakra.

Papaji, my mother, Leelavati, my four brothers—Subhash, Shanti, Anand and Moti, my Nani, Suhagwati, my maternal aunt, Bimla, my three maternal uncles, Ram Lubhaya, Om and Shyam and my mami (maternal aunt), Rooprani and I sprang to life and dashed to the airfield.

Papaji was carrying a big trunk on his head, my naani had tied some silver jewellery and gold bangles around her waist while my mother, four months pregnant then, wore five to six gold bangles on her wrists and carried a godri (a bundle) on her head, whereas we were stuffed in double layers of shorts and shirts, not knowing what our lives had in store for us.

My younger brother Moti was barely three years old, while I was around five, and my eldest brother must have been eleven or twelve. All of us ran frantically with the crowd and reached the doors of the Dakota DC-3. The crowd was surging and there was total confusion as we tried to board the plane. Our family reached the door, which was about eight feet above the ground.

The crew was shouting, 'Only refugees! No baggage!' The refugees were discarding their meagre belongings so as not to miss the flight to life. On seeing the big trunk on Papaji's head, the crew refused to let us in. Amidst high drama, Papaji shouted, 'The trunk will go with me or none of my family will board this plane.' He then managed to put the trunk in the transport plane, disregarding the crew's orders.

Patnaik stared at Papaji and shouted angrily, 'You are a greedy man! Taking your wealth with you at the cost of a human being.' Saying that, he tried to push the trunk out. That was enough for my sturdy and strong Punjabi Jatni Nani, 'Chaiji' (a Jatni belongs to the headstrong Jat community and in Punjabi, grandmothers are affectionately called Chaiji), to not only push the trunk inside but also help my thirty-year-old Papaji and the rest of us inside the plane. That was not all. Patnaik stood there, shocked, watching all that, when Chaiji hollered, 'You have no shame and no ethics. Ramanand is the only bread earner we have. None of us have eaten or slept for four days. If you speak a word more, my tabbar (a joint family in Punjabi) and I will eat you up!'

The engine bellowed while military boots nudged Papaji. Patnaik kicked the trunk open and out came reams of handwritten pages and notes. He demanded to know what Papaji was carrying. My father, who was now in tears, said, 'These are notes for my novel *Aur Insaan Mar Gaya*, my crushed feelings, my sentiments about the futility of war and the need for peace. This is the only wealth I am carrying with me!' Biju Patnaik then recognised him as the Ramanand Sagar who had written the 'Diary of a TB Patient' from a sanatorium bed. Feeling guilty and overwhelmed, Patnaik touched Papaji's feet and hugged him. The doors closed and we took off to a new sunrise! Biju Patnaik was a multifaceted personality—a pilot, journalist, Sanskrit scholar, writer of several books, a literary giant of his time, two-time chief minister of Orissa and also governor of Assam.

Even before the border defined the Partition of the Indian subcontinent into India, with a Hindu-majority population, and Pakistan, with a Muslim-majority population, Papaji, being a journalist, had got a whiff of what was to come and knew the fate of Lahore was uncertain. He decided not to wait for the last two months of the Partition that was to take place on 15 August 1947. He wanted to move away from the bloodshed, the communal riots and mass massacres. With his faith and trust shaken, Papaji decided to shift his entire family to his father's house in Srinagar, Kashmir.

Meanwhile, Muslim jihadis were trying to occupy Kashmir and so Papaji took the familiar safe old Rawalpindi-Kashmir salt route. In the dead of the night my family boarded a bus from Rawalpindi to Srinagar.

On arriving in Srinagar, Papaji had a feeling that even if his father Dinanath wished to offer shelter to his family, Bhabhiji, my step-grandmother, with her own family to feed, may not embrace us. And he was right, for there would be angry arguments at night between Dinanath Chopra and his wife Suhagwati. Six days later, Dinanath shifted the whole tabbar to the family-owned farmhouse in Shalteng on the outskirts of Srinagar. Close to the bungalow lived Madhavlal, a respected man and a close family friend. He owned a couple of shops in Tangmarg and Gulmarg.

Looting had begun in remote areas due to the rising India-Pakistan Partition tension. At times it was difficult to sell even a gunny bag of kahwa, Kashmir's famous tea. Still, Madhavlal took care of the large family. He would get a sack full of apples from his shops and all kinds of eats and specialties of Kashmir—Pampore kulchas, telvora and chuchvora—which till date remain a family favourite. Papaji would manage to get some other snacks from shops in Srinagar, especially from a Kashmiri naanvahi shop that later shifted to Delhi when Muslim atrocities on Kashmiri Pandits were on the rise in the '90s.

Papaji taught us how to dip the small kulcha in kahwa, make it soft and salty, and then savour it. To this date, I remember that taste. Pampore, a historic town situated on the eastern side of the river Jehlum on the Srinagar-Jammu National Highway, was known for its baked delicacies, and both Hindus and Muslims owned bakeries there.

Baldev Sahai, or Chachaji, who was Dinanath's half-brother, had a hidden radio set in the Chopra family's Wazir Bagh residence in Srinagar. In the tension-filled circumstances, this was a prized possession. Papaji had quietly packed in this radio before moving to the farmhouse at Shalteng. The radio was his daily connect to India and the world. Late at night he would listen to it and update himself on the current situation. Be it Pakistan's training of Wazirstan tribals to invade Kashmir and capture Srinagar or the conspiracy being hatched in London to divide the continent, he would be informed about it all.

In the middle of all the tension and drama, a memorable incident took place. Having heard of the rich jagirdari stories of the Chopra family inheritance, my brothers Subhash, Shanti and Anand used to argue about who was the most important and influential Lala, since the suffix 'Lala' denoted prestige. Hearing the stories of the super-rich Lala Shankar Dass, Lala Gangaram and their grandfather Lala Dinanath, the boys, aged ten, eight and six, would go around looking for their Lala to prove to their cousins that their Lala was the most prominent of them all.

Ramanand Sagar's three sons, Subhash (right) Shanti (middle) and Anand (left), in search of their Lala at the farmhouse in Shalteng on the outskirts of Srinagar in 1947.

Photo collection: Ramanand Sagar Foundation

One day, as they roamed around the streets, a police patrol picked them up. They were taken to the chowki. On realising that they were children of the famous Chopra clan, they were treated royally to sumptuous local food and sweets!

But back home everyone was worried, and Madhavlal put all his contacts on red alert, looking for my three brothers who were busy savouring biryani in the police chowki, still arguing about whose Lala was richer. Later, the thaanedaar brought them home. Dinanath was all set to cane my brothers. Little Anand ran away and hid under the bed. Dinanath realised the kids were petrified of him and threw the cane away.

Madhavlal, who used to tell us stories about the haveli on the banks of the Jhelum river, would also narrate incidents about Papaji's stay in Srinagar and Jammu. Dinanath's half-brother, Baldev Chachaji, was very proud of the rich inheritance of the Chopra clan. Lala Shankar Dass was the Nagar Seth, the richest man of Srinagar, whose son Gangaram had inherited half his empire. Chachaji was Gangaram's only biological son.

But with the death of Papaji's mother, Isha Devi, in 1926, everything changed. The downfall began and the empire crumbled. Dinanath and Chachaji shifted to the Hindu-dominated city of Jammu. The super-rich spoilt brats started working as insurance

The super-rich spoilt brat Lala Dinanath. Ramanand Sagar was Lala Dinanath's jyesth putra (oldest son) from his first wife Isha Devi.

Photo collection: Ramanand Sagar Foundation

agents, going around selling life insurance policies. The two brothers, who had once enjoyed their breakfast in bed and slept for four days straight, were now roaming the streets of Jammu in torn shoes.

Despite their circumstances, Chachaji, known for his angry outbursts, kept his poise, joked and laughed about, making everyone around him happy. Chachaji was married to Shanti Devi, the daughter of a general manager of a spinning mill in Udhyani, in today's UP. They had two sons. The elder Rajinder Kumar became an IPS officer and the younger Santosh Kumar was a Deputy Superintendent of Police in the Jammu Police Force.

Madhavlal also remembered an incident of Papaji's bravery as a young man when he lived in Jammu. He and his friends were once sitting on the banks of a canal. Suddenly, they heard the screams of a man drowning. Even as his friends chose to ignore it, Papaji swiftly jumped into the roaring waters, swam with the tide and pulled the man out to safety. Interestingly, the writer Ved Rahi remembered this incident too. The same has been recorded in *Rozana Ranbir*, Jammu, dated 10 June 1947.

Rahi was very closely associated with Papaji. In 1924, Rahi's father Lala Mulkraj Saraf started the first daily Urdu newspaper, *Ranvir aur Ratan,* from Jammu. Rahi's real name was Ved Saraf, whereas 'Rahi', meaning a traveller, was his nom de plume. Saraf sahib wrote a letter to Papaji sometime in the '50s, introducing his son, a budding writer, who desired to learn screenwriting and filmmaking from him. He worked closely on all of Papaji's films in the '60s and '70s, including his stint in Madras with Gemini Studios. A Sahitya Akademi awardee, Ved Rahi has several literary laurels credited to him. He also wrote and directed the film *Veer Sawarkar*. He revered Papaji.

During our evening walks, sometime in September 2004, Papaji mentioned to me how Faiz Ahmed Faiz, a literary giant of his time, had once visited us at our farmhouse in Shalteng. He had come sometime in October 1947 when Sheikh Abdullah was in jail. He wanted to discuss Papaji's novel *Aur Insaan Mar Gaya* on Partition with him. The novel was a firsthand account of the immense human tragedy and one of the largest migrations in the history of mankind due to the bloody line drawn by the British barrister Sir Cyril Radcliffe who had never visited the land he was given the responsibility to divide, but sealed the fate of millions of people living in it. With incorrect census data and taking only seven weeks to do the job, the British changed the destiny of millions. Playing a clever trick, the British government, in a diplomatic move of divide and conquer, made the border public on 17 August 1947, two days after India gained its Independence.

Major Somnath Sharma, the first Param Vir Chakra awardee and a hero of the 1947 Kashmir War. According to local legend, Major Somnath Sharma of 4th Kumaon regiment, along with two platoons of state forces, set off Diwali firecrackers in the paddy fields, thus saving Ramanand Sagar and his thirteen family members from certain death at the Srinagar airstrip.

(Image sourced from the internet)

The Hindustan Times dated Tuesday, 28 October 1947.

(Image sourced from the internet)

While still at the Shalteng farmhouse, Papaji, being a journalist, after his meeting with Faiz Ahmed Faiz, had anticipated 'Operation Gulmarg' (invasion of Kashmir by the Pathan tribals from Waziristan). So, overnight, he decided to shift his family to the kachha airfield in Srinagar where we huddled together with other refugees for four days, waiting for help to escape to India.

The life-saving decision gave rise to many other such acts, including that of Major Somnath Sharma and his supposedly quick-thinking decision to use Diwali firecrackers to hoodwink the enemy. The Major continued to fight till his last breath. When he was engaged in the battle of Badgam near Srinagar City, a mortar shell exploded near him. His last message to the Brigade HQ received a few moments before he was killed was, 'The enemy is only fifty yards from us. We are hopelessly outnumbered but I will not withdraw one inch but will fight to the last man and the last round...' He was awarded the first Param Vir Chakra posthumously for his sacrifice. The man who single-handedly saved Kashmir!

Besides the invasion, there was also a political scramble. Maharaja Hari Singh, the ruler of the state, had not accepted the conditions of the Instrument of Accession to the Union of India. He also wasn't willing to release Sheikh Abdullah as per Pandit Nehru's wish. V.P. Menon, Sardar Patel's able lieutenant, was sitting in the Srinagar Palace Dussehra Durbar of the spendthrift Maharaja Hari Singh and negotiating. The popular belief of Sheikh Abdullah not wanting freedom for Kashmir and wanting to join Pakistan and not India may not have been true. From available records, namely, the book, *The Kashmir of Sheikh Abdullah* by C. Bilquees Taseer, a top Muslim League leader, it seemed that the Pakistani Left leaders championed the two-nation theory and were strategising to trap Sheikh Abdullah, the biggest mass leader of Kashmiri Muslims, hailed as 'Sher-e-Kashmir' and annex Kashmir for Pakistan. And if they failed to trap Abdullah or hold him captive, they would finally formulate a tribal invasion.

While all this was going on, Kashmir looked indefensible. As the mujahideen were rampaging like pirates, it was a minute by minute operation. As stated earlier, the military couldn't be sent by land, and so the only route available was the air route. Once the agreement (Instrument of Accession) was signed on 26 October 1947 between Maharaja Hari Singh in Jammu and the Government of India, the Dakota DC-3, full of military personnel, took off at 6 a.m. on 27 October from Delhi's Safdarjung airport and landed at 8.30 a.m. as our saviour![1]

Meanwhile, the local gossip was that the Maharaja was watching a mujra and as soon as the electricity of Srinagar was cut off in Baramulla town, he sat in his eighty-five vehicle cavalcade and escaped to the safety of Jammu city on 24 October, leaving Kashmir and its people, also the stranded refugees, at the mercy of the 10,000 local tribal militia and irregular Pakistani forces.

The records however maintain that V.P. Menon had advised Maharaja Hari Singh to shift to his safe summer capital Jammu where finally the accession deed was signed.

In 1846, the Dogra king Gulab Singh formalised the Treaty of Amritsar with the British for 75,00,000 Nanakshahi rupees. This

---

1. The Maharaja signed the Instrument under pressure, owing to the tribal invasion.

was in effect the sale deed of Kashmir. Gulab Singh was then declared the Maharaja of Jammu and Kashmir.

The hand of God that saved Papaji and his large family, the princely kingdom—the Indian state of Kashmir, and Maharaja Hari Singh was in the form of the greedy tribesmen who were not professional soldiers and spent two extra days in the town of Baramulla just fifty kilometres northwest of Srinagar, looting, plundering and exploiting women.

A local hero, Maqbool Sherwani, delayed the tribesmen by confusing their guide in the strategic town of Baramulla. He was nailed to a tree on 25 October 1947.

The bravery of some locals like Maqbool Sherwani and people like Major Somnath Sharma and Lt. Col. Dewan Ranjit Rai saved Srinagar and Kashmir, rightly known as 'heaven on earth' after the Persian couplet by Amir Khusrau which described Kashmir thus:

> *Agar firdaus bar roo-e zameen ast,*
> *Hameen ast-o hameen ast-o hameen ast...*

(If there is a paradise on earth, it is here, it is here, it is here!)

Later, W.H. Auden, in his poem, *Partition*, wrote:

> Unbiased at least he was when he arrived on his mission,
> Having never set eyes on this land he was called to partition.
> ...
> We can give you four judges, two Moslem and two Hindu,
> To consult with, but the final decision must rest with you.
> ...
> But in seven weeks it was done, the frontiers decided,
> A continent for better or worse divided.

As Jawaharlal Nehru said in his 'Tryst with Destiny' speech, 'At the stroke of the midnight hour, when the world sleeps, India will awake to life and freedom.'

That Papaji was brought here to the land of Ram after all that he and his family endured that fateful day in 1947 showed that God had something special in his mind for him. It seemed in a way fitting that he was the one who brought Ramayana to the screens of millions.

3

BIRTH OF THE MAHARISHI
RAMANAND SAGAR

It was a stormy day. Torrential rains had lashed the whole town. The small town, about forty kilometres away from Lahore, named after the house of a guru—Asal Guruke—shuddered, with its sparse brick-and-mud houses about to give in. In the small town was a small room where a child was born to a young, tender fourteen-year-old Ishwari (Isha) Devi Chopra (née Vidya Devi Bedi) on 29 December 1917, half an hour after sunrise. Ishwari was the wife of Dinanath Chopra.

Strangely, the newborn refused to cry or even open his eyes. The raging storm outside couldn't break the resolve of the newborn as he lay silent. The mother was waiting to hear her baby's first cry.

Vidya's father Raliya Ram Bedi and her brother Lala Niranjandas were convinced that the baby was stillborn. However, the local midwife, refusing to believe the worst, instantly picked up the stubborn newborn and placed him above a chulha or a fireplace made of bricks and cow dung. As if the fire had stirred him, the baby finally opened his eyes and wailed! Instantly, the whole room lit up.

His cries made his fourteen-year-old tired, exhausted mother weep tears of joy. Ishwari was happy to see her baby cry and gasp for his first breath. Lala Raliya Ram, my maternal great-grandfather, felt this was a divine act of Lord Shiva, the Maha Mrityunjay Mahadev,

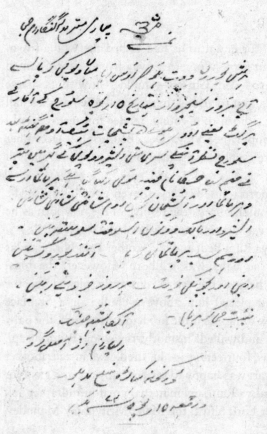

Postcard dated
1 January 1918,
announcing the birth
of Ramanand Sagar on
29 December 1917.

Photo collection:
Ramanand Sagar
Foundation

who could even revive the dead. The daimaa or the midwife smiled, for her instinct told her the child was like no other. He was special. Convinced of Mahadev's leela, they believed the newborn was God's own child and was destined to fulfil a divine order. Lala Raliya Ram, the baby's maternal grandfather, named him Chandramouli, one who holds the crescent moon on his forehead, one of the many names of Lord Shiva. He did this to gain the everlasting blessings of Lord Shiva and the creative genius of Chandra Dev for the baby. Chandramouli was to be later called Ramanand.

Lala Raliya Ram then sent a postcard to the child's paternal grandfather, Lala Ganga Ram, in Srinagar that read, 'My dear friend Gangaramji, by the mercy of Mahadev, on Saturday, 29 December 1917, half an hour after sunrise, a child was born to Ishwari Devi. He was named Chandramouli. Let the Lord bless him with a long life. Om shanti shanti shanti. Your well-wisher, Raliya Ram Bedi.'

Since Vidya Devi's mother was from Asal Guruke, a small town on the outskirts of Lahore, the teenage bride had gone to her maternal home for her first delivery where her brother Lala Niranjandas also lived. Vidya Devi's father Lala Raliya Ram Bedi was also present in Asal Guruke at the time of delivery. Her mother was no more. When my father, at the age of five, returned from Srinagar to Lahore to stay with his nanaji, he actually lived in a palatial house in Lahore and not at Asal Guruke.

Lala Raliya Ram originally belonged to Jalandhar where he owned a massive haveli in an area called Chak Bediyan or Kila Bediyan. The haveli exists even today. My father had visited that place once. During the reign of the Sikh Maharaja Ranjit Singh, the governor of Jalandhar was a Bedi. The Bedis were originally the Vedis who went to Benaras to study the Vedas and over a period came to be known as Bedis. Even Guru Nanak, the founder of Sikhism, is said to be from the Bedi lineage.

Historically, Lahore is around 2,000 years old. However, some travellers' accounts and legends have claimed that it is approximately 4,000 years old. Named after Lav (sometimes spelt Luv), one of the sons of Shri Ram, the Lahore fort still has a temple in its premises dedicated to him. Hence, Lahore—Lah and Awar—meaning the fort of Lav. In the past, it may have also been called Lavpuri, city of Lav, located on the banks of the river Ravi, named in honour of Maa Durga.

Lala Raliya Ram had married twice, and his second wife, Bhagwati, was also known to everyone as Bhagoshahi. She was childless. Desperate and despondent, the childless woman developed severe psychological issues. She had become so bitter that she would vent out her frustration on young, unaware, innocent children in the vicinity. Lala Dinanath Chopra, her stepson-in-law, pitied her deteriorating condition. In an understanding between Lala Dinanath Chopra and Lala Raliya Ram Bedi to help Bhagoshahi out of her mental condition, the young, reckless father promised to give his firstborn to them.

Lala Raliya Ram Bedi, Ramanand Sagar's nana and the father of his mother Isha Devi.

Photo collection: Ramanand Sagar Foundation

Sealed and signed, the agreement was a family secret. It was decided that Dinanath Chopra would portray himself as the child's elder brother and his wife as the child's bhabhi or sister-in-law. For the longest time, my grandfather was addressed as Bhaiyaji, meaning elder brother, which in course of time changed to Payaji. The child's maternal grandparents became his real parents to everyone concerned. Against her will, Isha Devi was forced to become her child's sister-in-law, oblivious to what fate held in store for her.

In that era, to adopt a child was an acceptable practice if one couldn't conceive. It was believed that the parents would be blessed abundantly for their selflessness. Hence, her own father and husband forced Isha Devi, my grandmother, a naive, innocent mother, born to the first wife of Lala Raliya Ram Bedi, into giving up her firstborn to her stepmother Bhagoshahi. Isha Devi never really accepted this situation. Her silence had become like the proverbial lull before the storm. It was waiting to wreak havoc and destruction.

The seeds of the unborn child's future were already sown. A life full of hardships and lack of motherly love coloured Ramanand's future writings much before he had taken his first breath in this world. The tragic death of his real mother, Isha Devi, at the young age of twenty-five filled my father's writing with imminent shades of pathos. His works defined the divine and sacred bond between a mother and her child. Now when I look back, it seems that my father's adverse fate made him deeply understand life's hardships.

As soon as my grandfather got the news of the birth of his first son, he remembered the promise he had made to Lala Raliya Ram and Bhagoshahi. Stubborn and unyielding, the sixteen-year-old Dinanath Chopra went down to Lahore and did the baby's naamkaran (naming ceremony). He named him Ramanand.

The naamkaran was followed by a reluctant mother giving away her child to Bhagoshahi. Dinanath had separated a mother from her child.

This was the beginning of Ramanand Sagar's long, tumultuous journey of life. Unknown to the torturous fate his boyhood held, my father's golden years of childhood began to unfold. His turbulent journey to manhood, filled with both unconditional love and cruelty, struggle and sacrifice, were like seeds sown that would eventually lead him to make *Ramayan*.

The events in Papaji's life were like divine interventions that were slowly paving the way for him to fulfil his destined role—that of creating *Ramayan* for TV. Even his initial name, Chandramouli, was a coincidence, since it was Lord Shiva, the Chandramouli, who had first narrated the story of the Ramayana to Maa Parvati while Kakbhushandi (an enlightened crow sage) secretly listened to it. It was another coincidence that my father had got a crescent moon-like scar on the left side of his forehead. It had so happened that his stepmother had thrown a gadvi (a metal pitcher) at him for not washing utensils properly.

In 1941, when my father was only twenty-four and he did not know where his next meal would come from, the Chopra family's mystic Pandit Nityanandji visited Lahore from Kashmir. It was then that he predicted the making of the *Ramayan* in the late 1980s.

He asked Papaji if he had ever seen the place of his birth. After asking him for some details like the presence of moles on his body and if he had a servant with one artificial eye, Nityanandji started describing the place of my father's birth in detail as if he was actually seeing everything in his mind—like the size of the room, the direction of the chulha, the trees, the beauty spot between the two eyes of the local midwife blessed with divine vision, and then went on to narrate the events around Papaji's birth, predicting his long journey into cinema and the making of *Ramayan* in the late '80s.

When my father could not even afford a cycle, Nityanandji accurately foresaw the accident of three co-passengers in Papaji's yellow-brown car.

As a child, I, too, have witnessed the magical powers of Nityanandji. Once, he held out both his arms outstretched and asked my elder brother Anand and me what we wished to eat. A sceptical Anand asked for aaru (a yellow pear-like fruit from Kashmir) and out of nowhere a fresh aaru appeared in his empty palms!

The events in Papaji's life kept pointing towards a divine destiny. In the early '50s, Papaji and I were sitting in the drawing room of our flat at Mahim, Bombay, when Nityanandji visited us. He was the kul pandit of our family in Kashmir and was very close to my father. He asked Papaji, who was sitting opposite him, to write a question on a piece of paper, fold it and place it under an inverted glass tumbler through which the folded chit was visible. After a minute, he asked Papaji to read the answer. The paper that had not even moved out of the tumbler had the answer written in Nityanandji's handwriting! We were never told what the contents of the note were except that it indicated a glorious future.

Papaji believed Nityanandji knew bhoot vidya (black magic), the ability to use and control the supernatural. He also felt that those who practised it would pay for it. Perhaps an anxious Payaji had sent for Nityanandji to know where his son was headed. After many years, Nityanandji died a torturous, unreal death.

Not only Nityanandji but many others who seemed to have a gift of foreseeing the future predicted Papaji's glory. Mohla Saheb, father of film producer Madan Mohan, who made blockbusters like *Dus Numberi*, gave one such push that directed Papaji towards his fate. A self-taught astrologer, Mohla Saheb closely studied Papaji's horoscope and prophesised that Ramanand Sagar would bring a spiritual awakening in the entire world through cinema. He promptly announced *Yogeshwar Krishna*, with my father as its director. Veteran political leader L.K. Advani was at the grand muhurat held in Natraj Film Studios in the presence of Shashi Kapoor, who played Krishna, and other eminent film personalities.

However, Mohla Saheb passed away before he could see his prediction for Papaji come true.

One could well call my father the maharishi of the electronic era, much like Rishi Valmiki who composed the great Sanskrit kavya of 24,000 verses in the Treta Yug, or Goswami Tulsidas who brought the grand narrative to the people in vernacular Awadhi, the language of the masses in the fifteenth century.

Coincidentally, in 1990, L.K. Advani, the then president of the Bharatiya Janata Party (BJP), took out a Ram Rath Yatra to Ayodhya for the construction of the Ram Lalla Temple that seemed to fan the fervour the TV series had created.

Ramanand Sagar with producer Mohla Saheb (extreme left), Raj Kapoor (extreme right), L.K. Advani (second right) who gave the mahurat clapshot and Shashi Kapoor (middle) as Krishna.

Photo collection: Ramanand Sagar Foundation

Papaji's experience as a journalist, author and a dramatist led him to make many films and explore the mass medium. He trained in the language of audiovisuals that helped him reach a global audience. My father was able to digitally adapt the great epic and reach a viewership of 650 million people.

Another incident that motivated my father to make his destiny come true was related to Shri Maha Avtaar Babaji, a spiritual, ageless guru who first came to light in the *Autobiography of a Yogi* by Paramhansa Yogananda. I feel reluctant in revealing details but my intentions are pure and my aim is only to create awareness and pay tribute to my revered father.

In 1970, Papaji and I were at Guwahati to scout for locations for his film *Lalkar* for which I was director of photography. Our

Maha Avtaar Babaji was introduced to Ramanand Sagar and clan by Dev Dutt Shastriji from Allahabad (above).

Photo collection: Ramanand Sagar Foundation

The isht guru of Ramanand Sagar—Maha Avtaar Param Guru Babaji.

(Image sourced from the internet)

family friend and distributor, Shankar Lal Goenka, owner of Kelvin Cinema, took us to the Kamakhya Temple, a prime shakti peeth. A staunch devotee of Devi, Papaji had performed Durga Saptashati Ashtami Havan every year from 1954 to 2005. He could never miss paying his obeisance to Maa Kamakhya.

Home to the famous bleeding Goddess, the Kamakhya Temple is one of the oldest of the fifty-one shakti peethas dedicated to the Hindu goddesses. It is an important destination for worshippers, mystics and pilgrims. According to mythical legends, Sati's yoni (vagina) fell at the spot after an enraged Shiva danced with her corpse in his arms. The temple holds a sculpted image of a yoni fed by a nearby spring that the pilgrims highly revere. A three-day festival called the Ambubachi Mela is held annually to celebrate the menstruation period of Goddess Kamakhya during which the temple is closed for all visitors. During this time, the Brahmaputra river turns red, for which no scientific reason has been found. Wrapped in mystery and mythical legends, the temple became a crucial turning point in Papaji's path to his destiny.

After doing the puja, when Papaji and I were taking pradakshina (doing the rounds of the temple), a small girl came to Papaji and said, 'There is a Baba sitting under a tree. He wishes to see you.' We walked up to the tree where the Baba sat. He looked at my father with a piercing gaze and blessed him with a silent gesture. My father asked him if he could be of service to him or he had any message for him, but Babaji just smiled. We paid our respects and left, forgetting the incident completely.

In 1982, while my father and his unit were shooting for the film *Kohinoor*, they were caught in a rainstorm. Drenched and shivering, Papaji and his unit desperately looked for shelter and came upon the small hut of a sadhu. Papaji quickly sent his assistant to request the sadhu for temporary shelter.

The sadhu initially got angry when the assistant requested for help, saying, 'He is a filmmaker from Bombay and is stuck in the storm with his unit including some women. Can you give us some shelter?'

The sadhu refused, but when the assistant blurted out the filmmaker's name, he exclaimed, 'Maa Durga! Please forgive me! It is Ramanand Sagar!' What followed next was a big surprise for the unit as the sadhu ran behind the assistant and told him to call Papaji and his crew inside. He then rustled up a humble meal for everyone. The sadhu then looked at Papaji curiously and asked, 'You are Ramanand Sagar? You had once visited the Kamakhya Temple in Guwahati where you met a sadhu. That was Maha Avtaar Babaji. You are one of the very few people who has seen and met Babaji in flesh and blood. He gives darshan only to the chosen ones. You are born for a divine mission, which you will soon find out.' The sadhu's name was Swami Ramanuj Saraswati and he was an atomic scientist-turned-spiritual seeker. He was researching the impact of atomic energy present in the waters of the river Ganga.

Papaji's second meeting with Maha Avtaar Babaji was sometime in the '80s while on a trip to Badrinath Temple in the Himalayas.

Badrinath is the first dham among the four dhams established by Adi Shankaracharya. After the aarti, Babaji mysteriously came to Papaji and requested for prasad. The prasad fell, but Babaji picked it up and ate it. He again looked at my father with the same kind, piercing gaze and a divine smile. My eldest brother Subhash Sagar was with my father then, and after some time, they realised it was Babaji! They tried to look for him but he had disappeared. Papaji's spiritual friend later conveyed that Babaji attends the last aarti of the evening at the Badrinath Temple, teleporting between his unseen home between Kedarnath and Badrinath. Having mastered the siddhi of disappearing and appearing instantly, no one ever sees him entering or exiting the temple!

When my father came out of the temple premises, still dazed about the divine darshan, he came across Ram Baba, as he was popularly called. He knew my father was a famous filmmaker. He looked straight into my father's eyes and said, 'Leave the dream world of cinema. Why don't you make the Ramayana for TV?' And then, Maha Avtaar Babaji's divine face flashed in front of Papaji's eyes.

As predicted by Ram Baba, the filming of the *Ramayan* for TV started the following year. The Badrinath Temple is situated on the banks of the river Alaknanda, a tributary of the Ganga. According to popular legend, Maa Lakshmi turned into the badri tree herself while protecting Lord Vishnu from scorching sunlight when he sat in penance amidst the badri bushes. Since Vishnu is her Lord (her Nath), the temple was named Badrinath. All this led me to believe that Papaji was indeed here on a divine mission. He was to revive the tenets of Sanatana Dharma through the Ramayana for the benefit of mankind—manas kalyan.

Maha Avtaar Babaji's real name was believed to be Nagraj, and he was a siddha yogi. Some books say he was born in Parangipettai, a village in Tamil Nadu in AD 203. He joined a small group of wandering sanyasis when he was only five and finally found his tapasthan or a spiritual penance spot at Katrigana, a sacred shrine, now in Sri Lanka. He gained many siddhis that blessed him with a complete understanding of paranormal power.

Babaji was connected to the entire lineage of eighteen siddha purushas from Agathiyar Kumbakonam, Valmiki and Patanjali to Dhanvantri and Courtallam. Babaji could thus appear at two places at the same time. It is believed that he is still alive. He has his guptsthan, a mysterious, hidden abode between Kedarnath and Badrinath, a Shangri-La where you age very slowly, a fictional land of eternal youth and peace, supposedly in the Himalayan mountains.

Some foreigner had once sketched a portrait of Maha Avtaar Babaji while doing penance in Badrinarayan. The head priest or Rawal of the Badrinath Temple, a Namboodiri from Kerala, had shown the sketch to me. He had let me take a photograph of it. No one knew how long the sketch was in the custody of the Rawals.

I must now narrate an incident related to Babaji in the Sagar family. My brother Shanti's wife, Poonam, was once in deep meditation and went into a trance. A communion with the divine had left her tired. My wife, Neelam, was present in the room. She used to visit the Anandpur Ashram in Delhi's Karol Bagh, where many disciples went into dizzy spells, singing ecstatically and then fainting. It was a common occurrence in spiritual experiences. Slowly, Neelam brought Poonam back to consciousness. Poonam then shared her subconscious experience of having visited Babaji's forbidden mystic abode in the Himalayas. She could see Babaji in a cave surrounded by a translucent curtain of frozen ice and mist. When she tried to enter to take Babaji's darshan, a guardian snake bit her in the forearm and she regained consciousness. Her arm was still paining and there was a slight mark in the shape of a snake's fang on her forearm. The pain lingered for a few days.

Many people around my father had names associated with gods like Shiva, Vishnu or Maa Shakti. His mother's name at birth was Vidya Devi, another name for Goddess Saraswati or the goddess of knowledge. After marriage, her name was changed to Ishwari Devi, another name for the goddess of wishes. His father Lala Dinanath's name was inspired by Lord Shiva that meant a benevolent father. His wife was Leelavati. Leela meant God's play with a man's destiny. Papaji's name Ramanand and my mother's name Leelavati when combined form 'Ramleela', the theatrical adaptation of the Ramayana played during Dussehra. Papaji's childhood companions from Lahore and the production manager for his company Sagar Art was Jagdish Chandra alias Panditji alias J.C. Bhakri. Jagdish is a name associated with Lord Vishnu, which means giving direction to the world, much like God.

Another name with god-like connotations, of a person close to Papaji, was that of his lifelong mentor, associate, companion and friend, the general manager of his company, P.N. Rangeen (Pashupati Nath Rangeen). His name meant 'father of the animals', and Pashupati was an incarnation of Lord Shiva. Rangeen was his nom de plume, as he was a writer and a lyricist. The name of my father's first servant after he arrived in Bombay during Partition was Devi Ram, a combination of Maa Devi and Shri Ram. He refused to accept a salary and worked free during the period of extreme struggle for the family in the early '50s. His great-grandfather's name was Ganga Ram while his great great-grandfather's name was Shankar Dass, both of which are derived from the names of gods. Even his brother's name, Chitranjan, means 'pleasing to the soul'. Papaji was surrounded with people whose names were inspired by gods and they kept him company. Some way or the other, Papaji was always uttering names of gods and goddesses even when he was not praying or doing a puja. The spiritual coincidences in Papaji's life left no doubt that he was destined for a divine mission.

29 December 1917 will always be an important date in the history of the Sagar family and that of Indian television, for that was the day when destiny's child, Ramanand Sagar, was born. Many years later, he brought the Ramayana to millions of households and finally completed his life's mission!

4

THE GOLDEN PERIOD: SRINAGAR
(1918–23)

Fourteen-year-old Isha Devi, my grandmother, arrived at Srinagar, grief-stricken. She pined for her infant son whom her husband had promised to give away to Bhagoshahi, his stepmother, who couldn't bear a child. Isha Devi would get hysterical, not eat her food and had just one plea: 'Do not send Ramanand to Lahore to that barren woman!' She could just not accept the reality that her infant son belonged to someone else now. Dinanath, her husband, who was just sixteen then, was stubborn as well, and was determined to send his son to Lahore. Helpless, yet defiant, Isha Devi went on a hunger strike and finally decided to undergo 'icchamrityu' or death by will, as she refused to drink even water. For Dinanath, the choice was tough, but he was hell bent upon upholding his honour. Fatherhood couldn't soften his stance. He was keen on keeping his promise made to Bhagoshahi.

However, Payaji relented and they made a truce. He would let Isha Devi experience the joy of motherhood for five years and after that her son would be sent to Lahore, where he would be then legally adopted by his maternal grandfather, Lala Raliya Ram Bedi, and step-grandmother, Bhagoshahi, although officially Ramanand would always be projected as the real son of his adoptive parents.

A sixteen-year-old naive and stubborn Lala Dinanath at the birth of his firstborn son Ramanand Sagar.

Photo collection: Ramanand Sagar Foundation

Nagar Seth, Lala Shankar Dass, the great-grandfather of Ramanand Sagar built this mansion in approximately 1854. It stands in ruins today.

Photograph courtesy: Shiv Sagar

My father, a baby then, was oblivious to the turmoil his mother was going through. It was the golden period of his life. He took Payaji to be his elder brother and Isha Devi to be his bhabhi (sister-in-law). His bond with his real mother strengthened even under the guise of a bhabhi. A happy Isha Devi would make the choicest Kashmiri food for him and not let him out of her sight even for a moment.

Meanwhile, his father Dinanath never took young Ramanand into his lap or carried him in his arms. In those days, it was considered beneath the dignity of men (read less masculine) to demonstrate affection for their children. Once he tried to pick up his son in a loving embrace, when suddenly a senior family member walked in and a sheepish Dinanath dropped Ramanand on the floor! Isha Devi had to rush to pick up her child.

Ramanand was awestruck and fascinated by the magnificent haveli (palace) built by his great-grandfather Lala Shankar Dass, the then Nagar Seth of Srinagar. Lala Shankar Dass was employed in the courts of three Maharajas, namely, Maharaja Gulab Singh, Maharaja Ranbir Singh and Maharaja Pratap Singh from 1845 to 1905. The family owned hundreds of acres of land in Chadat Ramji Ka Pura Chak (the complete estate) and a village named Shadipur on the outskirts of Srinagar. The haveli reflected his status in society. The three-storeyed mansion had marble and tiles specially brought from Tashkent and Samarkhand. In the basement there was an enormous wood-fired furnace of the same size as the ground floor above it. The furnace kept the huge palace rooms on the ground floor warm, much like the heating systems used in hotels and homes today.

On one side of the palace, there was the zenana that housed only women of the family, while the other part had the mardana, which belonged to the men. Only close male relatives were allowed to enter the zenana. Below, there was a hammam that had bathrooms on both sides where more than fifty people could bathe at once. Customarily, the children bathed with the women of the household. There was no flush system but a deep, empty well-like structure was dug up and covered. A water tank was placed at the top that functioned like a flush. No one knew where the water discharged from the flush went.

Once, one of the guests tried to retrieve his undergarments that had fallen into the well through a hook tied to an open turban. Unaware of how deep the well was, as he lowered the long cloth down into the well, over thirty feet of fabric was swallowed by the darkness of the pit, but its bottom was never found. Some said the well was two to three hundred feet deep, but there was no way to confirm their story.

The zenana section also housed a dining hall with a long table that was large enough to serve over twenty guests at a time. It was plastered daily with mud or cow dung. Every day the mansion held a feast for at least twenty guests who also stayed overnight. Villagers from Chak Charit Ram near Tangmarg would be seen feasting and sleeping overnight as guests of one of the richest families of Srinagar. In winter, the men and women occupied two different sides of the warmer ground floor and the first floor, while everyone shifted to the second and third floors in the summer to escape from the heat of the furnace burning below.

Papaji gave this royal description of the royal lifestyle of his ancestors to me a few days before his eighty-fifth birthday, on 29 December 2002. The flashback to the golden period of his life in the years between 1918-23 had faded, yet held an unforgettable charm, much like old photographs in the lost albums of memory.

A pampered child, little Ramanand would not eat his food sitting at one place. He would run around, with the loyal family servant Kashiram running with a plate behind him. Sometimes the kid would run to the banks of the Jhelum, hop from one boat to another, while Kashiram would struggle to keep pace.

In Kashmiri, 'kadal' means a bridge. It was across Zaina Kadal that the palace was built, just hundred yards away from the river. The first bridge on the river Jhelum was called Amira Kadal, later followed by other bridges like Habba Kadal, Fateh Kadal and Zaina Kadal. The bridges connected two different areas of the city with distinctive lifestyles, customs and traditions. The Zaina Kadal joined the Bohri Kadal area of old Srinagar to the Nawab Bazaar area. The ninety-metre-long bridge was the lifeline of old Srinagar and one of the oldest of seven bridges constructed on the river in the city. The bridge was built by Sultan Zainul Abidin, also known as Badshah, in the year 1427, and provided a splendid view of the old city. The bridge was a gift from Badshah to his people. It was symbolically built as a return gift to the pandit-hakim, Shri Bhat, who had cured the Sultan of a life-threatening disease. The hakim had asked for a gift 'as precious as life', and the Sultan, impressed by the doctor's humility, had gifted the city with its lifeline. It connected the two halves of Srinagar and provided the citizens with access to both parts. The wholesale markets of Srinagar were located at the Zaina Kadal. The marketplace was filled with wooden huts that sold spices, garments, dry fish and grains.

Ramanand Sagar spent his childhood in and around Zaina Kadal, the fourth bridge on the Jhelum river in Srinagar, where the Chopra family's ancestral house was built.

Photo collection: Ramanand Sagar Foundation

The area became the centre for every religious and business activity and prospered for many decades. Maharaja Ranbir Singh founded another market in the area, known as the Maharaj Gunj, a retail market. It is believed that he got traders from Punjab to settle in the area. They had shops on the ground floor and lived on the upper storeys. Papaji remembered that Maharaja Ranbir Singh was thought to be a soft-hearted man, and that when Ranbir Singh's father, Gulab Singh, bought Kashmir, the Punjabi traders helped him with the money.

The bridge was the centre of trading in those days and many shops in Maharaj Gunj flanked the old bridge to sell their wares. Maharaj Gunj eventually became an exclusive market on the banks of the river, with access stairs to the ghat, for people, mostly the influential, coming in boats.

Later, the bridge was dismantled and reconstructed by Pratap Singh in 1897 and again by Hari Singh in 1926. Zaina Kadal was known for spreading rumours and fake news and came to be rightly called the Khabr-i-Zaina Kadal. It was said that news reached the fastest in Zaina Kadal.

The marriage of Lala Dinanath and Isha Devi, the biological parents of Ramanand Sagar, in 1916.

Photo collection: Ramanand Sagar Foundation

The family had two loyal servants—Madh Bhatt and Kashiram. Kashiram was an opium addict and also consumed charas (cannabis) every day. However, no marriage proposal took place or major decision was taken without consulting these two. Even Lala

Dinanath's marriage to Isha Devi was approved by them. Papaji's grandfather, Lala Ganga Ram, had decided to get daughters-in-law from outside Srinagar since there were very few kshatriyas in the valley. Hence, Punjab became a natural choice for brides. Isha Devi was from Lahore. The two faithful servants had wholeheartedly approved of her.

They took care of the daily expenses. Kashiram was in charge of buying the kitchen necessities. He would buy vegetables for the entire family for only one paisa that had five damdis or dimes. A one-rupee note was quite big in size (8 inches by 10 inches approximately) then. For one dime, he would buy about ten to fifteen nadrus (lotus stems) and about fifteen baingans (brinjals) for another dime.

Although the servants were treated like family, they were not given cooked meals. They had to cook their own meals and eat only from earthern plates. They were not allowed to use the expensive metal plates that were kept for family and guests. The Bhats were originally Kashmiri Pandits who were converted to Islam by Muslim invaders over centuries. It is believed that it was Adi Shankaracharya, who, to preserve the genes of Kashmiri pandits, prudently had them migrate to Kerala where, in due time, they became the Namboodiri pandits of Kerala.

Papaji, as a child, usually ate from the plate of Kashiram, a Hindu turned Muslim. Young Ramanand would even go to Kashiram's home where he would eat with his family. This was enough for the gossipmongers to wag their tongues. They wondered how a kshatriya Hindu was being allowed to eat at a Muslim servant's house.

The palace contained a huge toshkhana (a treasure room). All silver and gold coins of the toshkhana were stored in big canvas bins, much like the ones that store wheat in the farmhouses of Punjab today. Ten to twelve feet tall and five to ten feet in diameter, these bins had an outlet at the bottom where you could put your hand in and take out gold and silver coins. In those days, coins were not counted, but weighed and poured into the treasure bins from the top. These bins were kept at the toshkhana with other precious items like jewellery, artifacts, vases, gold utensils, and so on.

Ramanand would secretly get inside the treasure bins and take out a handful of gold and silver coins. Kashiram was a part of this innocent conspiracy and took pleasure in the royal game. Isha Devi would watch them from her balcony or from her ornate jharokha and laugh at their childish pranks. Kashiram would follow Ramanand to the river where he would play tapli with the coins. Holding a coin between his index finger and thumb he would skilfully throw it on the surface of the water, counting the number of taplis (skims) the coin took before sinking in the water. The locals played this game with round and flat stones. Even his father Lala Dinanath was very fond of playing tapli with gold and silver coins in the Dal Lake. Every evening he would specially go to the lake and play tapli with ten to twenty silver coins, watching them skim on the water before they sank. After two decades, when he lost everything, he would joke, saying, 'I do not know how many silver coins from our family's lost treasure are still lying at the bottom of the Dal Lake!'

Kashiram was the longest surviving loyal servant of the family. He lived with his sister in the village owned by the family and would say, 'I will die here only. I will be with this family my whole life...' He proved his loyalty till he died at the age of ninety, having seen and lived through almost four generations of the family. He had seen them going from riches to rags.

We were among the very few kshatriya Chopras who had migrated from Peshawar at the time of Ramanand's great-grandfather Lala Shankar Dass. All our successive generations were Shiva bhakts and the clan's kuldevi was Kheer Bhavani. The holy shrine of Maa Kheer Bhavani is a temple constructed over a sacred spring—fourteen miles east of Srinagar—near the village of Tula Mula. The brahmins of Tula Mula are known for their spiritual prowess. Many mystics are found in the area around Shakti Peeth and they are popularly called muthus (there are fifty-four shakti peeths in India including Kamakhya in Assam and Kheer Bhavani in Kashmir).

It was believed that Ma Bhavani could predict the future. The Muslim invaders destroyed the holy shrine multiple times but Maharaja Pratap Singh, a disciple of the goddess, rebuilt it in the

1920s. Legend has it that Raavan, after worshipping the goddess, offered her kheer or rice pudding that she graciously accepted, and since then she is called Kheer Bhavani. Even Swami Vivekanand, while worshipping Kheer Bhavani, is said to have had a spiritual experience. Devi Maa had telepathically ordered him to return and do 'sansarseva' (service to society) and 'manas kalyan' (social welfare), instead of becoming a sanyasi in the hills. The holy spring surrounding the temple is known to change its colour to hues of red, pink, orange, green, blue and white. A black or blood-red shade of the spring water is believed to be inauspicious, indicating famine or war.

The family used to visit their villages and lands in Victorian style-carriages, though Dinanath had his own personal white horse named Nebra. It was believed to be prestigious in the tradition of the family to wander around one's estate on a horse. Twenty-one-year-old Dinanath would don his royal clothes and tour around his jagir while young Ramanand watched him, transfixed. The whole act of riding on a horse while people looked on admiringly tickled his childlike fancy.

One day, Ramanand made a plan with Kashiram. He sneaked into the stables and jumped on a horseback without using a saddle. Kashiram ran along with the horse as it galloped to Hari Parbat, a few kilometres away, with little Ramanand on its back. The subjects along the path bowed down and paid obeisance to the person they called Chotte Lalaji as he sat proudly with barely-controlled glee. However, riding a horse without a saddle wounded little Ramanand's backside, but he was so happy living in the moment that he did not realise he was bleeding. On reaching the haveli, his father Dinanath confronted Kashiram about taking the little boy on a horse ride without a saddle. Isha Devi, who was watching him from a jharokha in the zenana, was happy about her son's first horse ride. Dinanath beat up Kashiram with a cane for taking Ramanand on a horse ride without a saddle. Dumbfounded, Ramanand was unable to understand his father's anger as he watched him cane Kashiram mercilessly.

Dinanath's anger was legendary. It was mercurial and sometimes uncontrolled. He was usually very calm but once he beat up his youngest son Vidhu Vinod Chopra, born from his second wife Suhagwati, with a cane. Vidhu, as he was affectionately called, could never forget his father's thrashing. He even attributes his success in becoming a famous film producer in India with films like *Munnabhai MBBS*, *Lage Raho Munnabhai* and *3 Idiots* to this thrashing. Ironically, the name 'Dinanath' meant 'merciful'.

Ramanand was shocked to see this side of his father and a paralysing fear would grip his body on seeing his father angry.

When Dinanath was thrashing Kashiram, Isha Devi immediately ran down, gathered her son and tended to his wounds. However, little Ramanand was traumatised for life and went into a state of shock. He hugged his mother and never left her side, even in the last days of his stay at Srinagar. Terrified, he would cry endlessly at night, sleeping next to Isha Devi, with Madh Bhatt sitting outside the room. At times, Madh Bhatt would forcefully take the child with him to his room and put him to sleep, as if he was his own son, giving Isha Devi some time with her husband Dinanath.

One day while coming back from school, accompanied by Madh Bhatt, Ramanand wanted to buy something from the bazaar. He saw his father Dinanath sitting with his mother through the jharokha. On his request, Dinanath threw a one-rupee note down to where the young boy was standing, unaware of a mule that was slyly standing below. As the note fluttered down from the second-

Five-year-old Ramanand Sagar wearing an English suit, laced socks pulled up to his knees, English boots and a matching English shirt.

Photo collection: Ramanand Sagar Foundation

storeyed window, it was caught by the animal in his mouth and chewed away before anyone could react. Dinanath shouted at Madh Bhatt for his carelessness while Isha Devi laughed uproariously. The loyal servant beat the mule mercilessly but the one-rupee note was gone as one expensive meal!

In the 1920s, Srinagar had small schools and students were admitted at around four years of age. Ramanand had also joined school at the same time and soon became the class monitor. The teachers would cane the mischievous students in class by using a stick of the khugli bushes, an itching plant. Once Ramanand was also caned with the stick. He refused to go to school for days.

Ramanand Sagar spent the first five years of his life growing up in his great-grandfather Lala Shankar Dass's palace mansion, built in 1854. This is a photograph of the three-storeyed mansion with its jharoka windows and a basement with a woodfire furnace, in its present state.

Photograph courtesy: Shiv Sagar

Such anecdotes stayed with Papaji throughout his life—moments frozen like silent photographs—till his death on 12 December 2005. I tried noting down most of what he told me between the years 2002-2004.

Five years of Ramanand's golden childhood were coming to an end. Those years just flew by and the sword of separation hung over Isha Devi's head. The tragic moment of departure had finally arrived. In stony silence, Isha Devi stood on the second-floor balcony, hesitant to come down. The separation from her only son was unbearable to her. Clutching the photograph of little Ramanand dressed in an English suit, laced socks pulled up to his knees, English boots and a matching English shirt, tightly to her chest, her eyes were brimming with tears.

Below, in the driveway, Dinanath and three men were getting the tonga ready for the journey. Ramanand kept looking at Isha Devi. The confused boy could perhaps sense that she was his real mother. Her unconditional love, the way she would pamper him, hug and kiss him, tend to his wounds, look at him longingly or the way she would feed and dress him, said it all. He wanted to run back and surrender himself into Isha Devi's tender arms, into the loving embrace of his mother, whom he would never see after this moment.

Once Isha Devi had even confided in him that she was his real mother but at that time he did not believe her. The faint memory of that moment still lingered in Papaji's memory somewhere, as he sat there, recalling those happy moments with his mother.

Ramanand suddenly felt a man's iron grip on his shoulder, which ended his reverie. Dinanath was waiting for him to climb on to the tonga that was ready to take them to Lahore via Rawalpindi, accompanied by three Kashmiri men. Dinanath stood there as a lonely spectator, while Isha Devi watched her boy go away. Ramanand kept looking at her, his little heart believing that she was indeed his real mother.

Unsuspecting of the journey ahead, the dark clouds of gloom, despair and uncertainty had already begun to cast their dreary shadows on Ramanand's future. It took four to five days for the tonga to reach Rawalpindi. They then boarded a train from Rawalpindi to Lahore. On reaching Lahore, the three unknown Kashmiri men from Srinagar casually handed over the custody of Ramanand to his paternal grandparents. Papaji had a clear memory of this moment, as if it was imprinted in his memory and refused to fade with time. I remember Papaji telling me about this on 9 August 2004.

Back in Srinagar, Isha Devi was devastated. Lost and forlorn, she could not accept the injustice meted out to her and Ramanand. And all this for keeping a promise made without her consent. The grief-stricken young mother started slipping into the final stages of insanity.

Unable to see her suffering, two years later, Dinanath, on the pretext of a business trip, took Isha Devi to Lahore just so she could have a glimpse of her son. She saw a crescent-shaped scar on the left side of his forehead. Bhagoshahi had flung a pitcher at seven-year-old Ramanand for not doing his chores properly. She saw Ramanand being ill-treated and he looked undernourished. He washed clothes, cleaned utensils and swept the floors. Her tender heart could no longer take it.

Even after returning to Srinagar, Isha Devi could not shake off the memory of her son's bruise. She was angry and bitter and refused to eat till her son was brought back to her. On seeing her deteriorating condition, Lala Ganga Ram's only biological son, Baldev, who we fondly called Chachaji, took it upon himself to reunite the mother and son.

The stories of the two brothers and their rich lifestyle went back a long way. Baldev Chachaji and his stepbrother Dinanath used to read many books rented from the Pratap Library at Zaina Kadal. Their favourites were books by Arthur Conan Doyle. They lived in a make-believe world, full of mysteries and adventures.

Like a character from one of these detective stories, wearing a moustache, headgear and goggles, Chachaji went to Ramanand's school. The little boy recognised his Chachaji despite his disguise. It was decided that the next day Ramanand would carry his books, a pair of his best clothes and other necessities and go back to Kashmir.

Chachaji then made him sit in a bus from Rawalpindi and changed into a tonga to go further. Foolishly, Chachaji made Ramanand write a postcard that was to reach Bhagoshahi the next day, saying that he had to attend a marriage and would be away for two to three days. They took the tonga across the bridge at Sipayan, a small town nearby. Once across the bridge, Chachaji burst into triumphant laughter, reaching Srinagar in James Bond style.

Dinanath was shocked to see Ramanand and sent an urgent telegram to Lala Raliya Ram Bedi wondering how the little boy had landed in Srinagar. Ramanand was immediately sent back to Lahore and was not ever allowed to see Isha Devi again.

This final separation from her son drove Isha Devi to total insanity. On seeing her miserable condition, Kashiram felt morally responsible since he had approved of her as Dinanath's bride. Out of pity, he would give her some opium tablets to relieve her of the unbearable pain. Soon, Isha Devi turned to drugs to escape her pain, and became an addict. She started falling sick and became a hunchback. She could never forget the last moments she had spent with her little son. She was dying every day. The grief soon took its toll as she gave up her life at the age of twenty-six.

While in Lahore, sleeping alone in a dingy room in Bhagoshahi's house, Ramanand woke up from a bad dream. As fate would have it, that night Bhagoshahi beat him up for disturbing her sleep and threw him out into the courtyard. The whole night Ramanand could not sleep a wink and got flashes of his mother. The golden period of his life flitted across his eyes, as he recalled Isha Devi's happy face and the moments he had spent with her.

A year before her death, when Isha Devi's madness had reached its zenith, Dinanath had decided to have a second child in the hope of giving her the motherhood she longed for, wishing that she would be sane again. Chitranjan Chopra was born in 1926 at Lahore and was Ramanand's only biological brother. But it was too late. Isha Devi had already lost her will to live. She died a year after.

In the sixty-one years that I have known my father, only once, towards the last few months before his death, he had confided in me, 'I can never excuse my father Dinanath ... How could he abandon me? How could he give his own son away as an adopted son? How could my mother have borne this?'

Ramanand Sagar's grandfather Lala Gangaram with wife Ratan Kaur seated with ten-year-old adopted son Lala Dinanath on the right and her two-year-old biological son Baldev on the left.

Photo collection: Ramanand Sagar Foundation

It was very uncharacteristic of Papaji to talk like that about his father because he revered him and was always his devoted son, but perhaps venting it out once gave him the peace he needed before he died.

Isha Devi's death was like a curse and struck a fatal blow to Dinanath and the future of the wealthy Chopra clan. Nothing was ever the same again. Fortunes had started to dwindle. My grandfather was very young, just fourteen, and Baldev Chachaji was six when their father Lala Ganga Ram died in 1912.

Ill-advised by a coterie of greedy, selfish and self-centred advisers, the chief one being Bansilal, Lala Dinanath reached a stage when the soles of his shoes bore big holes and he had to put a cardboard shoe tongue inside to prevent the stones from hurting him while walking.

On the advice of his diwans, Sansar Chand and Amarchand, he bought four Rolls Royces, which, after leaving Peshawar, could not climb even 6,000 feet let alone the blizzard-hit Banihal pass at 12,000 feet ('banihal' means 'blizzard' in Kashmiri). Young Dinanath was fooled into believing that he would be the first in Kashmir to own a fleet of Rolls Royces in Srinagar after Maharaja Hari Singh. They assured him that people would not only salute him but he would also make a lot of money. In reality, the two diwans had connived with the fraudulent employees of Bombay Motors opposite the Royal Opera House, Bombay. They had replaced the new engines with old ones in a brand-new body and palmed them off to an unsuspecting twenty-six-year-old Dinanath in Srinagar. The cars were abandoned and were later sold piece by piece as spare parts.

As time elapsed, Dinanath tried to set up a few factories and silk mills that shut down, thanks to his scheming friends and relatives. All the profits were received by the munims and cashiers, which they pocketed, while Dinanath made every payment. Everyone knew that Dinanath and Baldev Chachaji had poor business sense. The boys were raised in a prosperous household and were groomed to be rich, spoilt brats. They would sleep for days at a stretch and tea and food would be served to them in their beds. A game of chess was their preferred pastime and sometimes the game extended to weeks, with continuity charts being kept with the help of diagrams.

The two diwans worked out a big plan to dupe the brothers by taking advantage of their blind superstitious beliefs. They brought a fake alchemist to Dinanath and Baldev Chachaji who boasted of converting any metal into gold by touching it with the mythological paras stone (a wishing stone). As per plan, they took Dinanath on Amarnath yatra, a popular pilgrimage to the holy cave of Amarnath, where he saw a copper-skinned man who had a burning sensation in his body. The man told them that he had met a sadhu and seen him making copper ash and on touching the ash with his tongue, his whole body had started burning and his skin had turned copper in colour.

A sadhu standing nearby heard their conversation but they paid no attention to him. Dinanath bought the story and went back the next day to help the man as per the diwans' advice. They told him that his act would bring him good fortune. Accompanied by the two diwans, Dinanath saw the same strange sadhu whom they had seen the day before. The sadhu then asked the man if he had touched the copper ash. He said 'yes'. The sadhu then started applying different herbs on his skin and bathed him while reciting some verses, and voila, cured him!

Actually, all the sadhu had done was give the man a bath, and the 'copper' was gone! But Dinanath, naïve that he was, was amazed at his abilities. Having gained Dinanath's confidence, the sadhu slyly asked the man to make some copper ash. He also said that he knew to make only parabhasm (mercury ash), and if the two types of ash were mixed and applied to any iron object and then rubbed with the paras stone, it would turn the iron object to pure gold. Once the fake bhasm (ash) was made, the sadhu mixed both the types of ash and applied it to a big, black iron lock. He took out the 'magic' paras stone from his satchel and rubbed it onto the iron lock while reciting a few mantras. He rinsed it in a bucket of water so that the iron paint and bhasm were washed away instantly and the iron lock turned into 'pure gold'. The now-cured copper-skinned man, along with Dinanath and his two diwans, went to the bazaar and sold the gold lock for a high price. The goldsmith confirmed the lock was of gold but on applying the same paras stone on an iron object smeared with the two bhasms, it did not work. The strange sadhu had vanished. The diwans were in cahoots with the goldsmith, the sadhu and the sick man. Dinanath had bought the stone for an exorbitant price.

The diwans pocketed a substantial amount of that money paid for the stone. The stone never worked after that. On finally realising that he had been cheated, Payaji hunted for the sadhu up to Rangoon in Burma but it was a wild goose chase, as this gave the cunning diwans enough time in his absence to dispose of valuable properties in Lahore, Rawalpindi and Srinagar. No one could ever catch their lies and deceit while they continued to cheat the unsuspecting family.

Dinanath's affluent, spoilt upbringing, tender age and foolish actions led to his downfall. He had to take on a job as a general manager of an insurance company called Ruby Insurance, which later became National Insurance, owned by the Birla family.

Payaji insisted that he be taken to the family temple of Kheer Bhavani. There he recognised a spiritually enlightened Muthu Mahatma, a mystic whom everybody dreaded. Putting his head at his feet, he told him what he had lost.

The mystic smiled and said, 'Dinanath, *tu yahin hain!* (You are still here!) From now onwards you belong to Jammu. Leave this city!' Suddenly changing his stance, the Mahatma scolded Dinanath: 'You foolish man, the mother and child bond is like your bond with God. Respect the bond. Do not break it. Respect the divinity of motherhood, its sanctity!'

The mahatma then went into a trance and said, 'Throw away all the hundis and the promissory notes your ancestors have left behind. That is your only way to repent!'

It was clear that the Trikal Darshi Muthu, who could see the past, present and future, was referring to Isha Devi.

Dinanath was stunned by the mystic's revelation of the hundi papers (loan money documents) and his indirect reference to Isha Devi's death and the torture she underwent. Following the mystic's advice, he went to Jammu to his small office room and for a whole week ransacked the safes, cupboards and rummaged through all the drawers. Like a man possessed, he tore and set fire to all the papers and legal documents detailing loans worth millions. Perhaps Isha Devi's curse had taken its toll.

My grandfather Lala Dinanath Chopra was also Lala Ganga Ram's adopted son and had never experienced mother's love. He could not understand Isha Devi's pain of separation. Lala Ganga Ram could not have a child from his first wife and so he had adopted Dinanath, the son of his first wife's sister. After the first wife's death, Ganga Ram remarried and fathered Baldev Chachaji. Dinanath therefore did not understand the value of motherhood. Lala Dinanath's story was one of riches to rags.

5

PAPAJI'S STRUGGLE FROM
LAHORE TO BOMBAY
(1924–47)

Five-year-old Ramanand was standing all alone in the one-storeyed house of his Nana-Nani. He had reached there after a four-day-long trip by tonga and train. He was told all along by the people who had brought him from Kashmir to Lahore that this was his parents' house and that Lala Raliya Ram was his Bauji (father) and Bhagoshahi, his Maaji (mother).

The big house was situated in a lane in Lahore. The backyard had buffalo sheds while the front door opened into the gully, in front of which there was a courtyard. A small room in the centre of the courtyard served as a kitchen. There was a well too. Further into the courtyard was the one-storeyed house of Ramanand's foster parents who lived on the first floor. In earlier times, people in north India used to dig wells in the courtyards of their houses from where water was daily pulled up and drawn by a rope and bucket. The well in Bhagoshahi's house was approximately twenty to thirty feet deep and four to five feet wide. The water level would drop down to seven to eight feet in summers and every year the bottom of the well had to be thoroughly cleaned up.

When Papaji was about seven, he would climb down the well with the help of a rope and clean the sludge from the bottom using a bucket. Papaji would descend into the well with his back pressed to one edge and feet to the opposite edge and scale downwards with a rope. He would then come up the same way. He would pour potassium permanganate into the water left in the well, turning it a deep red. It would remain that way for at least two days, after which it again became clear and potable. This exhausting process would take multiple trips in and out of the deep well which would take up almost half his day.

Bhagoshahi had a waiting room built in the disguised kitchen, touching the outer periphery of the well. At the back of this room, there were concealed steps leading down to the hidden treasure room that lay ten feet below the courtyard floor. One wall of the treasure room coincided with the outer periphery wall of the well which had a secret window opening into the room from the well. Since the secret window was also ten feet below the courtyard, it brought in cool, fresh air to the underground room to beat the summer heat. The temperature of this room remained cooler than the air-conditioned rooms of today.

Bauji and Maaji had aptly named this secret room 'gufa' or cave. It was a code word that only they used. In summers, they would walk from the courtyard into the waiting room and slyly slip down to the gufa for their afternoon siesta.

Papaji would go to the gufa which he would call his Maaji's 'maal room'. They were in the business of moneylending on interest, and Bhagoshahi would hide the money earned using unscrupulous means in this room. Hence, the entire 10 by 10 square feet secret gufa was filled with silver utensils, pearls, diamond necklaces, gold jewellery and other expensive items. It was a room built on the backs of the needy borrowers whose wealth she had extracted in the name of interest through unfair means. Sometimes Bhagoshahi would take Papaji with her to this secret chamber. He remembered every little detail of that room. If there was any default in the payment of the interest or principal amount, she would seize gold bangles, necklaces and other ornaments from the borrower. At times she would grab a poor farmer's goat and send her henchmen to break his house down. To her, money was everything.

Whenever a borrower came to her house, she would make him sit in front of the waiting room and would grab his gold jewellery brought as security. She would then go to the secret room to stash it away and bring the cash in return. Over and above the security deposit, she would also make the borrowers sign promissory notes. All this had hardened her, and the stigma of being a childless woman had only made her insensitive and harsh.

My father's life had become devoid of all colour. The shades of motherhood were absent and there were no feelings, affection or love coming his way. But since he was a positive and sensitive person, he poured all his life experiences into his writings and enriched it. His character was rock solid. He truly believed in the values of dharma and fought for justice for which he could even have sacrificed his life.

Bauji had married again after the death of his first wife from whom Isha Devi was born. She was my grandmother. Bauji's second wife was Bhagoshahi (Maaji). Parmanand, son of Lala Niranjandas, who was Isha Devi's nephew, also stayed with my father in the same house. He was treated quite differently from Papaji. After all, he was the grandson of Lala Raliya Ram and Bhagoshahi and was Mama (maternal uncle) to my father.

Ramanand's first day in the new city was something he remembered very clearly. Maaji took Papaji to the bazaar to buy some household items. As he had had an affluent upbringing in Lala Dinanath's palatial mansion in Kashmir where he would play on the shikaras, eat luscious fruits, lose silver coins in the Dal Lake, sneak into the toshkhana or treasury and ride his father's white horse Nebra, it was a different and peculiar experience for the little boy to have to leave all that behind and walk in the narrow lanes of Lahore. The gullies and small shops of the city seemed strange to the five-year-old. Like any other curious boy of his age, Ramanand darted from one shop to another, ran across showrooms and stalls from one side of the street to the other, looking at the oddly-dressed people, while Maaji kept walking forward without looking back. When she finally reached home, she realised that the boy was not trailing behind, and was nowhere to be found. She could never imagine that the young boy would lose sight of her in the new surroundings.

There was a hue and cry as the entire neighbourhood gathered around her. Bauji was left dumbstruck. A small boy had got lost in the strange, new city and would be unable to find his way through the cramped lanes and gullies of Lahore.

Since the market was not very far away, and there were only two bends in the narrow gully between Maaji's house and the bazaar, Ramanand, who was very sharp, returned home very calmly, having memorised the way. He couldn't believe the drama that was unfolding at the house. He innocently said to the shocked people, 'I came back the same way I had gone. There was a gurudwara...'

Once settled in the new home, Maaji sent Ramanand to a public school but not before she made him do all the household chores like washing utensils and clothes, cleaning the floor with a broom, milking buffaloes in the backyard, drawing water from the well, and so on. Every day she woke Ramanand up in the early hours of the morning so that he could finish the chores before he left for school. At times she would shout and scream at the little boy for not doing his work properly. She treated him like a servant. Once she flung a metal pitcher at him, leaving a lifelong scar on his forehead. That crescent moon-shaped scar reminded Papaji of his painful childhood. There would be days when he would sleep on an empty stomach, with no warm bedding or blankets, penniless, and forced to study hard so he could get the scholarship grant to continue his education.

His childhood incidents were like a whiplash for him, haunting and hurting him. In October 2002, he narrated to me an incident frozen in his memory even at eighty-five. Once when he was six, he was walking on a railway track, collecting colourful, round pebbles lying there. He started playing with them and since he was not privileged enough to get toys, he put some of the pebbles in his pocket to play with later. Seeing this, Maaji raged with anger, and in an uncontrollable fit, slapped him, and threw the pebbles out of the window. The young boy cried bitterly and begged his mother to let him keep the pebbles, but Bhagoshahi showed no mercy as she dragged him back home. The little boy wondered what wrong he had done to be beaten up like that. This incident, even though he was merely six years old, never faded from his memory. Even remembering it brought tears to his eyes. His childhood affected the way he treated his six children later. He could never deny any child's desire or wish but never made it look easy so as to spoil them. He was a hard taskmaster to his children but in case of his grandchildren and great-grandchildren, he never imposed his opinions or methods of parenting.

The entire extended family of Ramanand Sagar at the inauguration of the Sagar Tourist Resort in Manali in 1992.

Photo collection: Ramanand Sagar Foundation

He drew an iron curtain on all aspects of his life; no one was allowed to peep in except at certain times when he would share his pain and bare his deep wounds; wounds that had never healed. I felt it was my duty as his son that I never slept before he did or ate my meal before he had his. Only after massaging his feet and hearing him snore would I leave his bedside. Sometimes it would be way past midnight and I would wait for him to fall asleep, not making him conscious of my presence.

I feel I was the Ram to his Dashrath. This continued even after my marriage, and my wife Neelam was very accommodating of our rituals. She respected my actions. My time with my father seemed like an unbelievable fairytale. My selfless devotion towards him perhaps softened him and eased his pain. Sometimes he would show me these gashes of time, still bleeding, still fresh. Owing to his cursed childhood, he could never scold any child or get irritated even after having thirteen grandchildren and nine great-grandchildren in his lifetime. He did not want the joy of any child to remain unfulfilled. He wanted to fulfill every child's wish and revel in their happiness.

Lost in the fantasy world of dreams and aspirations, my father would sleep like a child, always at peace.

Bhagoshahi was a crude woman. In their home located at the Shalimar Darwaza area of Lahore, she stayed in a bedroom on the first floor. Once a thief climbed up the window of her bedroom while she was sleeping. Always on alert about the ill-gotten wealth she possessed, she woke up instantly and caught the thief by his hair and beat him with her iron fists. The thief struggled to get away but she had him in her clutches. He managed to jump out of the window but she held on to his hair while he hung midair. Finally, in pain and having lost a clump of his hair, the thief fell to the ground and fled for his life.

After the death of Lala Raliya Ram, the atrocities of Bhagoshahi crossed all limits. Her insanity and frustration on account of being childless had reached its zenith. One day, unable to bear it any more, my father, a very young boy then, decided to run away. He woke up as usual the next morning, completed the gruelling chores of the day, picked up his school bag, and left without raising anyone's suspicions. Wandering aimlessly in the narrow gullies of the old city, he suddenly came across a big Jesus Christ statue. The nails in his hands and the pain on his face made Ramanand connect with him on a personal level. He could identify himself with the crucified God. For hours, he was lost, looking at the statue, fascinated and spellbound. He instantly decided to convert to Christianity. Lost in the excitement and enthusiasm of having finally found happiness in his life, he started walking towards the church across the lane.

Just as he was about to cross the iron gate of the church, a soft voice called out his name. He turned to see a sadhu standing behind him. Surprised, he went to the sadhu with folded hands. The sage blessed young Ramanand, and asked him, 'Are you lost? Where are you going?' On hearing his tragic story and his decision to convert to Christianity, the sadhu looked deeply into his eyes and said, 'It's fine to change your path, change your religion, but first at least wait to see where your present path takes you; maybe it's swarg (heaven). Understand your religion and try to live happily with what you have. Do not take your destiny in your hands but realise the eternal "searcher" philosophy of Hinduism. Accept God's will...' The sadhu had simply explained to the young boy the fundamental tenets of Sanatan Dharma. The sadhu's philosophy of 'living without questions asked' hit Ramanand like a sledgehammer. He turned to go back home, pretending nothing had happened.

Next day in school, he narrated the incident to his friend Shishupal studying with him in the same class. The incident and the philosophy of Sanatan Dharma for all mankind made such an impact on Shishupal that he, in the years to come, would become a sadhu and be initiated by the name of 'Ramanand'.

That night Papaji could not sleep a wink. He had taken the first step to fulfilling his life's mission of bringing the idealism of the Ramayana to every religion, be it Hinduism, Islam, Christianity or Zoroastrianism. Life continued for the young boy. Work. Study. Sleep. Survive.

In his early teens, before Ramanand's encounter with the sadhu, when Lala Raliya Ram was still alive, Ramanand got swept up by the wave of patriotism engulfing the country. India was awakening to the possibility of freedom from British rule. The name of the young martyr Bhagat Singh was popular among people, especially teenagers. Once, on his way to school, he came across a frenzied mob singing the praises of Bhagat Singh and giving speeches on nationalism and martyrdom.

Ramanand jumped on to the soapbox and started shouting, 'Bhagat Singh zindabaad! Inquilaab zindabaad!' Seeing such a small boy caught in nationalist fervour, the crowd went wild with excitement. They made him stand on a wooden soapbox with a flag in hand. The elated boy started shouting the slogans with the mob joining his cries. 'Inquilaab zindabaad!' was one of the most common slogans echoed in every corner of the streets of Lahore and India. Bhagat Singh himself had coined the slogan as he rebelled against the oppression of the British. The Urdu slogan meant 'Long live the revolution' and evoked passion and dedication in the people to fight for their country. Slowly the British soldiers with lathis closed in on the frantic mob.

Ramanand was prepared to sacrifice his life, and the mob had gone mad. Suddenly, a strong hand slapped Ramanand across his face and pulled him away from the maddening crowd. Lala Raliya Ram, on learning that Ramanand had not returned from school, had arrived at the right time to save his adopted son from imminent danger. He dragged the little boy home. Ramanand's enthusiasm had vanished into thin air.

This incident and the influence of Bhagat Singh was so great on Ramanand's life that he made a film on the young martyr. Unfortunately, two other films on Bhagat Singh, one starring Ajay Devgan and the other Bobby Deol clashed with it at the box office on the same release date.

In October 2002, Papaji, while drinking his whisky at night, narrated to me a very interesting incident about Shishupal. My father spoke of Shishupal's brilliance, and the competition he faced because of him for scholarship grants and other monetary benefits. Due to these continuous competitive fights, the school authorities shifted them to separate divisions so that both students could benefit. This continued till the eighth standard. Shishupal, after graduating from Lahore with a first division, became a sadhu. He decided to become an ascetic by renouncing worldly and material pleasures.

Many years later, in 1982-83, while shooting for the film *Kohinoor* in the Himalayas, we arrived in Haridwar. We were looking for a dharamshala. In one of the lanes, there was a board that read 'Ramanand Dharamshala'. A surprised Papaji and I went inside and met the manager who was also my father's classmate from Lahore. The manager revealed that 'Ramanand' of 'Ramanand Dharamshala' was none other than Shishupal! The manager had joined Shishupal after the latter had decided to become a sadhu.

Both the Ramanands realised that they were classmates from Lahore. While one became a sage, the other was a famous filmmaker who had delivered superhit films like *Ghunghat, Zindagi* and *Arzoo*, among others. The two met like Krishna and Sudama, hugging each other, with tears of joy rolling down their faces. They went down memory lane as they shared their life stories.

After completing school, Ramanand shifted to Srinagar to his ancestral home to go to Pratap College for higher studies. While in Srinagar, sixteen-year-old Ramanand met his only biological brother, five-year-old Chitranjan Chopra (Chitu), born in 1926 to Isha Devi, for the first time. Not much is known about the next four years of Papaji's life as there is no recorded information.

The cover of the Pratap College magazine, in Srinagar (1933), which carried Ramanand's first mature love story, 'Pritam Pariksha'.

Photo collection: Ramanand Sagar Foundation

A significant incident of his life in 1933 as a sixteen-year-old college student in Srinagar was the publication of the short story 'Pritam Pariksha' (Testing the Beloved) in his college magazine. The story was a mature divine love story with a twist at the end.

The story and the editor's note.
Photo collection: Ramanand Sagar Foundation

'An orphan was waiting for Krishna in Vrindavan. Time was ticking away as he looked for him in the depths of the jungle. Suddenly there was lightning and darkness surrounding the place. Was he testing his love? Where was the sound of the flute coming from? He totally surrendered to the lord and willed to walk to eternity in search for him. The leaves rustled … had he come? Waiting for his lover…'

The editor of the magazine was in a state of disbelief. The college principal summoned Ramanand and demanded to know if he had copied the story from someone. Ramanand replied that it was an original story. The editor, still suspicious, wrote a disclaimer, 'The editor is not responsible for the originality of this story.'

The divine love story written then reconfirmed that there was a seed of Krishna and Shri Ram embedded in his soul. In the TV serial *Shri Krishna* on Doordarshan, the entire scene of Uddhav being tested with the gopis waiting for Shri Krishna, delicately portrayed in 'Uddhav Prasang', is a reflection of the story 'Pritam Pariksha'. The TV series was a mega blockbuster and topped the television charts for over 120 weeks. 'Pritam Pariksha' was the beginning of establishing Ramanand as a sensitive, romantic writer who knew to portray the power of true love. In later years, he gave superhits like *Insaniyat* (1955), *Paigham* (1957), *Raj Tilak* (1958), *Ghunghat* (1960), *Zindagi* (1964), *Arzoo* (1965), *Ankhen* (1968), *Geet* (1972), *Lalkar* (1972), *Charas* (1976) and *Bhagawat* (1980), among others. Whatever be the theme, love was always a dominant factor in his works.

After finishing college in Srinagar, Ramanand was back in Lahore. He saw the power of cinema after the screening of *Seeta*, starring Prithviraj Kapoor and Durga Khote, and directed by Debaki Bose, and *Chandidas*, starring K.L. Saigal, directed by Nitin Bose. Crowds surged to cinema halls, crying, weeping and identifying with Maa Seeta and her fate and dharma.

Chandidas's father cut off both his arms because of his supposed desire for the younger second wife of his father after which saint Gorakhnath came to Chandidas's rescue. Ramanand felt these stories mirrored his own life with Maaji and Bauji and the intervention of the sadhu under the sacred cross of Christ.

Filled with a burning desire to express his writing through cinema, a young, ambitious Ramanand joined films at nineteen in 1936. He became a clapper boy for the silent film, *Raiders of the Rail Road*, starring Usha, and thus began his illustrious film career.

Throughout his career in cinema, Ramanand never forgot to express his gratitude to the great director Debaki Bose who was a big influence on his filmmaking. Similarly, P.C. Barua was one such personality who shaped his creativity and technique.

Seeing Papaji's rise in the film industry and expecting that he would eventually come into his inheritance from a wealthy family, Bhagoshahi laid a trap for him in the guise of a marriage proposal.

Ramanand Sagar started his film career as a clapper boy in the silent film *Raiders of the Rail Road* in 1936.

Photo collection: Ramanand Sagar Foundation

Without his knowledge, she fixed his marriage with the daughter of a leading cloth merchant. She had apparently demanded a huge dowry from the bride's father Bhavani Das who had readily agreed to the match. Maaji kept it a quiet affair, lest her ulterior motives were exposed.

Bhavani Das was a reputed wholesale and retail cloth merchant and conducted his business from a shop named Kripa Ram Bhavani Das, located at a prime spot in Shalimi Darwaza, a landmark of the old Lahore city, which exists till date. Kripa Ram was Bhavani Das's father's name. Visitors from across India went to his shop to buy cloth. Bhavani Das had a son named Ayodhyanath and a daughter Baikunthi from his first marriage, after which he married Suhagwati, who would be Ramanand's future mother-in-law. She gave birth to three daughters and three sons. The name of Ramanand's first wife is not known; maybe it was Indra Devi. Then there was Leelawati, alias Kaulaa, my mother, Bimla Devi, my future maasi, and my future mamas—Ram Lubhaiya alias Panju, Om Prakash and Shyam Sunder. Panju Mama used to manage the business 'Bhavani Das di Hatti' and was an expert in the Landa accounting system in which one needed to know multiplication tables for fractions. The cloth was measured in a particular manner and then sold.

Mahajani is a Landa (also called Lahnda) mercantile script—a merchant script popularly used in north-western India (now Pakistan). 'Mahajani' is a Hindi word for bankers, also called sarafs, and 'landa' means without tail, and is written from left to right.

My mother's family surname was Bery and the entire clan lived in a three-storeyed house at Kattayanwali Gully, so called because it was very narrow, as if someone had cut a normal lane into half—kattayan (one which is cut). In front of the three-storeyed house, a huge Beriwala Baba's temple was located. The temple had a significant following, and every Thursday many people thronged its doors to pay obeisance to the deity. Many of their wishes would come true. My Nani Suhagwati was an ardent follower of Beriwala Baba and had a strange spiritual connection with him. After Partition, this connection reached a different level of intensity when every Thursday Beriwala Baba would possess her body in our refugee quarters in Daryaganj, Delhi.

Inside the house, below the staircase on the ground floor lived a black snake coiled under the steps. Everyone going up and down the stairs would pay respect to the naag devta (snake God) and believed that it was the protector of the house. Like a family member, it was fed milk every morning. No one was ever scared of the huge, ten-foot-long snake which never hissed at anyone. It was a seemingly gentle, docile creature settled comfortably in its nest, loved and worshipped. It was a big joint family with Bhavani Das, his second wife and their six children, together with two children from the first wife.

Immediately after his marriage to Bhavani Das's first daughter, Ramanand felt suspicious of the whole arrangement. Bhagoshahi never let him know the truth, and welcomed the bride home. A year later, the new bride got very ill when she was in the last stages of her pregnancy. Her younger sister, Leelawati, was by her side. The mother died during childbirth. A baby boy was born. He was named Ratan Kumar. Leelawati took to her sister's son as her own child, but fate had other plans, and Ratan died as an infant.

A frustrated Bhavani Das did not want to face the reality of the situation. When Ramanand found out about the dowry, he was shattered. Dowry was against his principles. He saw the selfless love with which Leelawati took care of her sister and Ratan Kumar. He decided to make up for the ghastly sin he had unknowingly committed. He accompanied my Nani, whom we affectionately called Chaiji, to Haridwar to perform the last rites of her infant grandson. The innocent soul was born to die; born to change the course of Ramanand's life. My father performed the last rites as per the Hindu tradition and surrendered his ashes in the holy river Ganga, praying for his son's salvation. Chaiji saw Ramanand's grief-stricken face. Ramanand asked her to join her hands and make a chalice of her palms. He gathered the sacred water from the river and poured it into her hands, imploring her, requesting and begging her, to get Leelawati married to him without any dowry. Chaiji immediately agreed to it and a divine plan unfolded in the presence of the sacred Ganga.

Bhavani Das rejected the proposal, while Bhagoshahi refused to even consider the offer of a dowry-less marriage, but Chaiji was bound by the promise she had made to Ramanand with Ganga Maiya as witness.

Kaulaa, as my mother was affectionately called at home, was a free bird, flying kites, stealing them and breaking the manjha (glass thread) used in kite-flying games played on the roofs of Lahore. She ran in narrow, winding lanes in her kachcha or shorts, chasing kites. Her most prized possessions were the pinis of the manjha, that is, the glass thread rolled in balls.

Ramanand had seen the devotion with which Kaulaa had cared for her sister and her infant son. He was determined to marry her without any dowry; he had found in her his soulmate. One ratan (gem) had been snatched from his life but he was blessed with another invaluable one in the form of Kaulaa. Without involving Bhavani Das or Bhagoshahi, Ramanand and Chaiji took a bold step. He married Kaulaa in a temple in the cantonment of old Lahore city. His childhood friend, Prithviraj, posed as the father of the bride and did her kanyadaan. Their match was made in heaven. Their names, when combined together, spelt 'ramleela'. The union of my parents was thus like a happy indication of the things to come, the divine mission which my father had embarked upon—the making of the TV serial *Ramayan* in 1987. In retrospect, and hearing the story of their marriage from my Mama Om Prakash, and Prithviraj, it seemed that it was God's plan, a divine yojana that led my father to his destiny.

Ramanand and Kaulaa, alias Leelavati, in their earlier days.

Photo collection: Ramanand Sagar Foundation

Papaji also refused to accept dowry for the marriages of any of his five sons. He took only a shagun (ceremonial amount) of one rupee and four annas. In fact, some proposals had to be refused since the girls' parents insisted on giving dowry. They believed dowry to be a safety net for their daughters' lives. One such proposal came for my brother Shanti, from a royal family of Rajasthan. Another such proposal came for Anand, my third brother. However, it was finally accepted, as the dowry money went into a trust to honour Indian scientists and their achievements.

Chetram Patuwar, the kul purohit of the Chopra khandaan in Haridwar, was a Kashmiri Pandit. At pilgrim centres, as per tradition, details complete with their family genealogy and history, are put down in the records. All kul purohits carry forward this tradition from one generation to another and continue the lineage.

The last sanskar or antyesti sanskar of Ramanand's first son has been recorded in the Thakre language prevalent in Peshawar and the North-West Frontier by our family purohits. Chetaram Patuwar's son, Gopal Krishna Patuwar, and his grandson Chajjuram Patuwar have continued to record everything in their house in Jwalapura, a few kilometres before Haridwar.

Meanwhile, the newlyweds, Kaulaa and Ramanand, left in a tonga for Bhagoshahi's mansion. It started pouring as if the heavens had opened up to shower their blessings over the young couple. On reaching the house, Ramanand realised he had no money to pay the tongawala. Pandit Jagdish Chander Bhakri, who was also a part of the wedding ceremony, had accompanied the couple. He paid five annas for the ride.

The fully-drenched bride and groom stood outside, knocking at the door of Bhagoshahi, but she didn't open it. They begged with folded hands, but after an hour or so, had to give up and spend the night in the tiny house of Pandit Bhakri, who was also a childhood friend of Ramanand's and had a cycle repair shop attached to his humble abode.

Papaji never forgot Pandit Bhakri's gesture. The debt of those five annas could not be paid back; it was priceless. When Papaji started his own company, Sagar Art, in 1950, he traced Panditji in Jalandhar who lived with his four sons and two daughters, still struggling to make ends meet by repairing cycles. Papaji requested him to join his film company and Panditji was made in-charge of the production of all the films ever made by him. No one ever questioned Panditji. All his sons were raised in the company. My father also bought a three-room flat for Panditji and his family in Bombay, where he later breathed his last surrounded by his entire family. Papaji's friendship with Panditji reminded me of Sudama who had brought a handful of rice for his friend, the king of Dwarka, Lord Krishna, and in return, the lord gave the poor brahmin all the riches and comforts of life.

After considerable persuasion, Maaji finally, though reluctantly, let Ramanand and his bride Leelawati enter the house. Leelawati was shocked to see her husband doing household chores. True to her traditional upbringing and being the dutiful wife that she was, she soon took over all the housework.

The very next year, in 1937, Ramanand became the proud father to Subhash, my eldest brother. In 1938, there was a Kumbh Mela held in Haridwar where several Hindu pilgrims gathered peacefully to celebrate the victory of gods over demons in a battle for the elixir of life. The Kumbh Mela is held every twelve years when, as per Hindu astrology, Jupiter is in the zodiac of Aquarius and the sun enters Aries. The Indian National Congress wanted to use this platform to spread their mission of Independence, and Pandit Jawaharlal Nehru was to attend the fair. Ramanand joined the Indian National Congress Youth Brigade to fight for the country's freedom.

Hence, Papaji started the tiny Ganges Publicity Bureau Company, keeping in mind the Kumbh, and went to Haridwar with his wife and son and his only biological brother Chitu. A day before they left for the holy city, Ramanand found Chitu standing in front of him. Twelve-year-old Chitu had run away from Srinagar and managed to reach Lahore on his own. He was holding a photo of Isha Devi sitting on a shikara in the Jhelum. He had heard whispers and rumours of Isha Devi being his and his elder brother's mother, but the truth was kept a secret.

A picture from 1938—
Ramanand Sagar, wife
Leelawati, Subhash on his
mother's lap and Ramanand
Sagar's brother, Chitu.

Photo collection: Ramanand
Sagar Foundation

Ramanand shifted to a small room, with the nameplate 'Publicity Tower', in a white hexagonal tower on the Railway Station Road which connected Haridwar station to Hari ki Pauri ghat of the Ganga. The tower was on the banks of a nullah or a rivulet flowing through the centre of the city near the Lalita Rao bridge.

This hexagonal white tower belonged to Bhagoshahi. It was her place to hide all her ill-gotten gains. She was hell-bent on Ramanand divorcing Leelawati. She was only interested in getting him married again so that she could ask for a bigger dowry. My father was a man of principles and never heeded her selfish advice, although he kept telling her, 'I will always look after you, but only Leelawati will be my wife. I will never ever accept dowry.'

After Partition, in her last years, Bhagoshahi moved to this hexagonal tower of sin, into its dark and negative energy. Parmanand shifted with her to take care of Maaji in her old age, since she had promised to give him some of her enormous wealth. She, till her last breath, tried to persuade Papaji into the maya trap, but he didn't budge. He even visited and stayed with her for a few days before she died a terrible death.

Ramanand was a part of the Kumbh mob on the platforms of Haridwar station when Pandit Jawaharlal Nehru stood at the entrance of the rail coach, waving at the pilgrims in the fair. Ramanand ran up to the door and managed to shake hands with Panditji as a kar sevak of the Indian National Youth Brigade.

Due to poor sanitary conditions, cholera had spread in epidemic proportions in the Kumbh Mela of 1938. Hundreds of dead bodies were strewn on railway platforms—it is believed that 70,622 deaths were officially recorded due to this epidemic. Ramanand became a selfless service worker—picking up corpses and loading them onto trains, burning dead bodies in makeshift cremation pyres, administering medicine, food and clean water to over four million stranded pilgrims.

Ramanand wound up all operations of the Ganga Publicity Bureau procured by him as a business assignment from the Indian National Congress. The entire business plan was a major disaster. Finally, he returned to Lahore to pursue a career in films again. Chitu was sent back to Srinagar to their father Dinanath Chopra.

Once, Papaji narrated to me a funny incident that happened during Haridwar's Kumbh Mela. While wandering on the ghats one day, he met a group of ascetics who offered him panch charnamrut, a holy drink made of five sacred offerings—milk, Gangajal, curd, honey and ghee. Unknown to him, the prasad was laced with bhang, a preparation of cannabis. Ramanand drank it readily, not realising the hallucinatory after-effects of the intoxicant. When he reached the publicity tower room, he could not behave normally. In a bizarre way he felt he had lost his hand. He picked up his toddler son Subhash and placed him on a four-foot-high sideboard and asked the toddler who had had just learnt to walk to jump! He was 'seeing' more than one Subhash. While he managed to hold his son the first few times when he jumped, at one point, Subhash fell on the floor with a thud. Leelawati ran to her wailing son and was aghast seeing her husband's condition. She caught his hand and forced him to sleep, covering him up with multiple blankets as a dazed Chitu was told to look after his elder brother. She then calmed her son down. Ramanand slept for many hours, and when he got up later, he was shocked to hear about the amusing incident.

Between the period of 1938–41, Papaji was signed as a leading man for a film titled *Koel* opposite actress Neelam. Roshan Lal Shorey, a trained cinematographer from the United States (US), under the banner of Kamla Movie Tones, directed the film. The film flopped miserably and the company closed down after the failure of films like *Koel* and *Nishan*. Ramanand was assigned the role of Abhimanyu in a movie titled *Krishna* under the banner of Pancholi Studios, but the film never released. His struggle in the film industry had started.

Unable to bear the atrocities of Bhagoshahi, Leelawati forced Ramanand to leave her house and become independent. He also started his scholarly studies, and in 1942, was awarded the prestigious title of Munshi Fazal (PhD in Persian) by Punjab University. He won two gold medals and topped in the highest degree examinations for Urdu and Persian, and was conferred the title of 'Adib-e-Alam'.

Papaji's life was taking him to unknown shores. He held multiple jobs, developed himself as a writer from a journalist and entered films. In 1939, his second son Shanti was born, and two years later, in 1941, while he was in the sanatorium, the third son, Anand, arrived.

To survive, Ramanand worked as a goldsmith's apprentice, washed cars and trucks early in the morning, worked as a peon during the day, and despite holding these menial jobs, he could barely afford milk for his family. He even bought a chemistry book on how to manufacture soaps and perfumes. Both husband and wife would stay up late into the night and make scented soaps and perfumes. Five such items were packed in a gift basket and Ramanand would sell them to office-goers, mill workers and rich ladies in the bazaar for one rupee and four annas. He would target the office-goers and workers at the beginning of the month because it was then that they would have received their salaries. He would palm off a few products to them with some sweet sales talk.

Tirelessly working the whole day and studying for his degree and writing stories at night, Ramanand overexerted himself. It was during this time that the dreadful disease of TB ravaged his body. His immune system had weakened and his body was unable to fight back. It was a miracle that he escaped from the jaws of death lying in a TB sanatorium at Tangmarg, Kashmir. But even in these difficult times, he pursued his goal and earned two gold medals from Panjab University.

In twelve years, Papaji had written plays for All India Radio, twenty-nine short stories, one book and a collection of short stories, *Taaziyane*, in Urdu, a novel, two serialised stories and two stage plays. He also published *Jwaar Bhata* in 1943 in three editions, *Aainey* in 1944, two collections of short stories which included the stories 'Aabhe Hayat', 'Bakshish', 'Ek aur Toshkhana', 'Dil Ko Khush Karne Ki Fursat Nahi', 'Tangmarg Ke Aade Par', 'Pyaasi', and 'Jab Pehle Roz Baraf Giri', among others.

In *Naya Daur*, a literary magazine from Bangalore, in 1945, he published 'Mera Humdam Mera Dost'. 'Radha' was published in the annual edition of *Saqi*, a leading literary magazine of that time. In 1948, his play *Gaura* was enacted by Prithviraj Kapoor and it introduced Shammi Kapoor, while his second play *Kalakar* was written for Prithvi Theatres. In 1949, he wrote another story, 'Phool aur Kaante'.

Interestingly, a short story from this time, 'Kalank', published in 1948, though narrating an incident that occurred during the Partition, appears to have the seed of the Ramayana in it. During the Partition riots, a Hindu girl is kidnapped and is forced to live as a slave in a Muslim village across the river Ravi. When she manages to flee and finds her husband and father-in-law, she is not accepted by them. The reason and logic given is that even in the Ramayana, Shri Ram banished Sita to the forest because of the 'kalank' (blemish) on her chastity after having stayed in Raavan's Ashok Vatika.

In 1949, 'Phool aur Kante' was serialised in *Sargam*, a leading literary magazine. Similarly, 'Kalank' was published in *Naya Samaj*, Calcutta, in August 1948, and 'Aur Ladka Ho Gaya' in the Diwali special edition.

Ramanand worked without rest from a first-floor room attached to a balcony covered with a flimsy tin roof. The house was owned by a mentally unstable landlord who was given the name 'Sap Di Khodi' (mare or mount of a snake). The one-room apartment was opposite Kattayanwali Gully, where Leelawati had grown up in her parents' three-storeyed house.

At the beginning of the gully was a sweet shop. The animal-friendly owner had constructed a trough for storing water for the wandering cows and camels. Next to the trough, he had placed a huge slab of rock salt for all street animals, especially cows, to lick. Below Ramanand and Leelawati's single-room apartment there was a courtyard which skirted the boundary of the shop and the gully. All children played in the courtyard including Subhash, Shanti, Anand and me.

There would be days when suddenly one could hear the sound of a metal utensil being flung out on the playground. The wife of the deranged Sap Di Khodi would be standing at the door of their ground floor residence, screaming and shouting, with her husband running outside, trying to dodge the utensils. Sometimes my parents would come down and calm her, and at times, Papaji would run behind Sap Di Khodi, trying to save him from the utensils.

The children would sometimes form a train, hold Sap Di Khodi's torn shirt from behind, and chug around the yard, shouting, 'Sap Di Khodi! Hai Hai!' Sap Di Khodi would play along, feeling important.

But, how did the landlord get the curious name Sap Di Khodi, one might wonder? There is an interesting story behind it. Sap Di Khodi had a camel in his possession which he would load goods with while travelling to Lahore for business and trade. He was very harsh to the docile camel. One day he beat the helpless creature black and blue for no reason. The animal had suffered enough to promise revenge.

On his way back to Lahore, the camel threw him on the ground and started attacking him. To escape the camel's wrath, Sap Di Khodi ran and finally took shelter inside a dried well. The revengeful camel, unable to get inside the few feet deep well, parked itself on its outer dried wall with its gaze fixed on his master. The camel lurked around angrily, waiting to attack. From morning till late in the evening the camel showed no remorse to its master. Hours passed. Hungry and thirsty, Sap Di Khodi cursed his destiny and prayed to his ancestors, begging for forgiveness.

As if he wasn't frightened enough, Sap Di Khodi suddenly saw a family of snakes coming out of one of the walls of the well and gliding towards the outer wall of the dried well. After many snakes had come out, he saw a strange sight. A black cobra came out of the wall, balancing on his erect hood a white, one-foot-long snake standing on its tail. It seemed that the white snake was the king of the den. Sap Di Khodi was dumbfounded at the mystical sight. At last, he gathered courage and prayed to the white snake with folded hands to save him from the enraged camel. The snakes disappeared into the hole in the wall on the other side of the well. Sap Di Khodi stood there, dazed, but suddenly realised that the deranged camel was not moving. He slowly crept out of the dried well to see the camel dead. The snakes had bitten the camel. He kicked the dead camel in anger but his entire foot went inside its stomach. The snakes seemed to have turned a live camel into a hollow body. Sap Di Khodi returned to Lahore but was never a normal man again, as he seemed to have lost his mental balance.

Many of Leelawati's childhood friends staying in Kattayanwali Gully asked her about her husband's profession. Leelawati would shake her head and reply innocently that she herself didn't know what he did. 'All the time he sits on the floor bedding and keeps writing all day and night.' Her friends would wonder how someone could write so much. They could not understand what a writer did, since none of them had a formal education in a school. Their parents felt that education would ruin their chances of a marriage.

When my mother was in class IV in school, the teacher pulled her pigtail for making mischief. Her parents decided not to ever send her to school again. And so, Leelawati remained uneducated for the rest of her life in contrast to my father who was a scholar, a prolific writer and a philosopher. Even after fifty years of marriage, Leelawati could only sign her name in Hindi, but she raised her six children strictly and did not compromise on their education and principles.

Chaiji, on witnessing her daughter's mediocre social status, secretly gave her an expensive sari. When Leelawati wore it to go to her parents' home, Ramanand did not go to bring her back. Finally, after several attempts by Chaiji, an understanding was reached between the two. Papaji told his mother-in-law, 'Either your daughter stays with me in my condition and earnings or...' He, for the rest of his life, never bought anything for himself that was more expensive than what he could buy for his wife. Chaiji was so happy to see Papaji live by his principles that she admired him even more.

Papaji narrated to me an incident in October 2002 about my mother. Leelawati, while sending her two sons, Subash and Shanti, to school would dress them up as neatly as possible. Shanti would go to his nana's shop (Leelawati's father) and ask for a few coins. Like all doting grandfathers, he would readily give him a small amount with which he could buy enough chana (chickpeas) or other little tasty snacks popular on the streets of Lahore.

Then, Shanti would find a comfortable place and sit there the whole day to watch the world go by. In the evening, he would join other kids returning from school and reach home without arousing suspicion. Leelawati soon realised something was not right and one day followed her son. She then told Papaji what had happened. Papaji, having had a rough childhood laughed at his son's mischief and soon after, wrote a series of stories in a book titled *The Adventures in Space* for his children.

On the day he had to appear for his final exam for the title of Munshi Fazal, four-year-old Subhash got lost in the narrow lanes of Lahore. Leelawati created a scene. She hollered, 'Final exam or not, get my son back! Where will my little one sleep? Who will give him food? He cannot even speak properly or remember his house. How will we find him?' After some tense moments and with time running out for the final exam, Ramanand left everything to destiny. From nowhere, a bunch of children came in with Subhash, shouting, '*Yeh baccha kiska hai?*' (Whose child is this?) Tears rolled down Leelawati's face on seeing her little boy and Ramanand hugged him and put him in his mother's lap. He hurriedly left for the university exam and managed to reach there just in time to pass with flying colours.

Papaji always believed in the power of destiny, which is beyond our control. On one hand, there was his life's biggest achievement awaiting him, his literary degree, and on the other was his son's life; but he never underestimated the power of fate or destiny. He would later, in many scenes in his films and stories, bring out the role destiny plays in one's life by putting the characters in fateful situations.

Across the courtyard of Kattayanwali Gully lived a family of Kapoors, one of the wealthiest families in Lahore. The four brothers and their father had multiple business interests—cinema, theatres, restaurants, loans and cigarette agencies, among others. The cigarette agency was a flourishing one and was a virtual cash cow. The second eldest brother Krishna Kapoor and his wife Kusum Lata were very fond of my parents. S.K. Kapoor knew the famous lineage and rich inheritance of Papaji and my mother's affluent background.

During the early 1940s, Kusum Lata, in order to flaunt her social status, would go to college in a horse-drawn carriage. She was a matriculate—a rare achievement for a woman in those days. Even with the contrasting financial conditions of the two families, a verbal promise was made that if Ramanand and Leelawati's next child was a boy and the Kapoor couple's next child was a girl, they would get both children married when they reached the appropriate age. This is exactly what happened twenty-five years after Partition. Papaji kept his promise when the Kapoors approached him with their daughter Neelam's hand for his son Prem. This is how I found my life partner and soulmate. Today's generation might never believe my story.

After twenty-five years, destiny had turned the tables for both the families. Ramanand Sagar had become a common name all over India with superhits like Raj Kapoor's *Barsaat*, *Arzoo*, *Ankhen*, *Geet* and other films. On the other hand, the Kapoors had lost a lot of their wealth and businesses in family disputes.

In a dilemma over a verbal promise made years ago, the Kapoors approached Papaji with the proposal, and Papaji sent Anand with his friend, philosopher and guide, Rangeen Saheb, to me in Pune where

Prem and Neelam Sagar at their wedding.

Photo collection: Ramanand Sagar Foundation

I was studying cinematography at the Film and Television Institute of India (FTII). They quietly whisked me away to Sambhaji Park on Jungli Maharaj Road, seated me below Rani Lakshmibai's statue, and gently enquired if I had a girlfriend who I would like to marry or had promised to marry. Then they told me about Papaji's dilemma and his promise to the Kapoors. The clash was between his promise and his son's right to choose his life partner, but for me my father's word meant everything.

I never felt the need to question my father's decision. It was my duty as a son that I never questioned him and followed all that he said. My father was still following his dharma and was sensitive to the promise he had made despite the change in his social and economic status. He need not have kept his word, but he did.

Once my son, Shiv, asked me if I would jump off a cliff if my father asked me and I said, 'Yes.' He thought I was lying.

In 1944, I was born, the fourth son of Ramanand Sagar. In the early '40s, Papaji struggled to pursue his profession in Pune and Bombay. He worked hard to find his roots, start a profession and survive with his family. I learnt to take my first steps in Pune holding two pups as support. Papaji also worked as a publicity manager at Shalimar Studios owned by W.Z. Ahmed. He stayed in a small, rented bungalow named Pinky Villa on Shankardas Seth Road where Shalimar Studios was also located. Since I was only a few months old, my mother insisted on taking me along with her to Pune while her three elder sons remained with Chaiji in Lahore.

During this brief time, I had hernia and pneumonia. I was miraculously saved by the godsent wonder drug, penicillin, which, even though discovered earlier by the Scottish scientist Alexander Fleming, was commercially used in India only in 1944. I was one of the first guinea pig patients in India on whom the drug was tested. I had to be injected with it every two hours as its effect only lasted for two hours. The hernia was operated by a cut made in my right groin. It was nothing short of a miracle. Papaji and Mummyji were striving day and night to keep me alive. Finally, I was saved.

During his stay in Pune, my father came into contact with well-known writers like Rajinder Singh Bedi, Sadat Hasan Manto, Krishan Chander, Josh Mahilabadi, Bharat Vyas, Sagar Nizami and actors like Prithviraj Kapoor, Chandrashekhar and other eminent personalities. Once, during Holi, Krishan Chander brought pakodas for everyone to feast on. After everyone had polished them off, Krishanji mischievously announced that they were pakodas of bhang. Everyone promptly got on their cycles and ran off to safe spots before they could start experiencing nasty hallucinations. Papaji straightaway went to producer W.Z. Ahmed who sat there with his actor wife Neena, whose real name was Shahida. Under the influence of bhang, Papaji felt that Ahmed saab had robbed him of his Ray-Ban sunglasses, and kept them on his table. Ramanand would slyly pick up the goggles and put them in his pocket. Ahmed saab would softly tell him, 'Ramanand, these are mine.' This went on for an hour. Finally, Ramanand passed out completely and woke up in bed in Pinky Villa with a worried Leelawati nursing him. Papaji had bought Ray-Ban sunglasses from his meagre earnings and always felt that Ahmed saab was jealous of his glamorous goggles and wanted to steal them. The sunglasses were Papaji's prized possession as they were the first thing he had bought for himself in his life. The twist in this funny incident was that both Ahmed saab and Papaji had identical sunglasses.

After Partition, Mr W.Z. Ahmed, like many other Muslims of that period, preferred to migrate and settle in Karachi in Pakistan. He continued to make films as one of the leading filmmakers in Pakistan, as reported in *Dawn*, a leading daily of Karachi. He died there on 1 April 2007 at the ripe age of ninety-one. There is no doubt about W.Z. Ahmed's contribution in introducing multitalented people to Hindi cinema.

I came across one incident of Papaji's period of struggle in Pune in the late 1940s while I was studying at the FTII in 1966. As students of FTII, we would sit under the wisdom tree the whole day and in the evening, we would walk to Maharishi Karve Road and sit in a makeshift tea stall named Asha Tea House. Every Wednesday, it was packed with FTII students glued to the radio set listening to Binaca Geet Mala. The Marathi owner of the shop never asked us to pay for the endless cups of tea consumed. Most students paid their dues but owing to economic struggles, some students put their unpaid amounts in a notebook. Tea was on loan. The owner would just smile and let them go without a question. It was a strange act of kindness. On learning who my father was, the owner showed me an account notebook. Rustling through a few pages, he came to the year 1948 and began scanning the names of the people who owed him money. One of the names was my father's, who owed him five rupees for the tea. Guru Dutt and Dev Anand also owed him money. Dev Anand, it seems, was a struggler in Pune, having been given his first break in Prabhat Studios by Babu Rao in 1946. Papaji used to visit Prabhat Studios in Pune as an aspiring writer before he found fame with Raj Kapoor's *Barsaat* in 1949. The tea vendor's kind acts continued to serve the students who would go on to become stars like Dev Anand, Guru Dutt and Ramanand Sagar.

Earlier in Lahore, when Papaji began his journey as a journalist, he joined the Urdu edition of the *Daily Milap* as a copywriter and rose to the position of an editor. Since Urdu was the prevalent language in Lahore, *Daily Milap* was the leading daily of Lahore like *The Times of India* was in Bombay. The newspaper was started by Mahashay Kaushal Chandji on 13 April 1923. Later, he took sanyas and became Anand Swami Saraswati in 1949. Milap's office and printing press was situated at the Mayo Hospital at the end of Nisbet Road in a double-storeyed building, and also at Gawalmandi. Ranbir Singh was the owner and managing editor of the paper, and Papaji worked diligently there.

During the British Raj, listening to the news on radio was a punishable offence. The white media sleuths read each headline in the country to control the press and limit its freedom. During the Second World War, Ramanand would sit late at night and listen to the war news and strategy on his antique radio set. He made detailed notes till the late hours of night. Ramanand had hidden the radio deep inside the office premises so that the patrolling British soldiers would not be able to hear its sound at night. He would slyly slip into the printing press around 4 a.m. in the morning and change the headlines. Since it was a lithograph printing with stone plates, he had to etch and prepare the headlines himself. Early morning, on the front page of the *Daily Milap*, the entire latest strategy of the British and the allies was discussed and revealed, thus exponentially increasing its circulation.

At times *Daily Milap*, through editor Ramanand, would give war strategy advice with the command of a journalist's pen. The British were worried and concerned as to how somebody could predict the exact war strategy of the allies. They started a search operation for the man who knew everything.

After a considerable effort, they finally traced young twenty-six-year-old Ramanand and branded him a spy for Nazi Germany and a paid stooge of Adolf Hitler. He was summoned to the torture room of the British investigators and asked questions like, 'Who do you work for? How do you get such exact information? Admit that you are a spy.' Papaji vehemently refuted each accusation and told them how, at night, he listened to the BBC and other European radio stations and changed the headlines himself since there were no calligraphy staff present in those hours. They refused to believe him since his analysis was accurate and credible. They locked him in jail on remand. This news reached Chandji who was well respected and wielded a lot of political control. On his personal intervention and undertaking, the British released Papaji. My father had, by now, established himself as a strong editor and a prolific writer.

Ramanand Sagar became a renowned name in the literary corridors of Lahore. He mingled with journalists, budding writers and poets, including Manto, Rajinder Singh Bedi and Manohar Singh Sehrai, mostly associated with the film circle of Lahore. Manohar Singh's brother had a plush office on Nisbet Road in Lahore. He was also a film enthusiast, and film journalism was a hobby for him. Fond of a drink or two, he would attend the first shows of every new film.

In his inebriated state of mind, sitting with the audience, he would loudly analyse every scene of the movie and talk loudly to the reel characters. 'Porus! Sikander will cheat you. He will set you free due to your wit and valour.' 'Ravi, your kismet will change.' 'Dilip Kumar, you will be a star.' 'Tani (for Tansen), sing megh malhar.'

Be it Sohrab Modi in *Sikander*, Shobhna Samarth in *Ram Rajya*, Ashok Kumar in *Kismet*, Dilip Kumar in *Jwar Bhata*, K.L. Saigal in *Tansen* or Chandra Mohan in Mehboob Khan's *Roti*, he would have something intelligent to say to the actors about the characters they played, making everyone laugh in the auditorium.

This gave his ego a boost and he became a hero. While walking on the street from the cinema hall to his residence, a drunk Sehrai would talk to a streetlight or a metal pole! After a 'heated' discussion, Sehrai would accuse them of being insensitive, and not appreciating a great journalist like him. On reaching his bungalow, completely sloshed, he would fall flat on his face in the gutter, sinking into a deep sleep. Then, his servants would carry him inside his house while he snored loudly. This was a daily affair. My father was very amused and touched by Sehrai's character and intelligence, and would tell us about him, enjoying every bit of it. The one-act monologue scenes in many of his films were perhaps a tribute to Sehrai.

In all the twists and turns of his life, Papaji had formed a group of aspiring artists. Pashupati Nath Bali, who wrote under the nom de plume Rangeen, was a lyricist-cum-budding writer for whom cinema was the final destination. His association with Ramanand Sagar was for life and all of us addressed him fondly as Rangeen Saheb while Papaji called him just Rangeen.

My father and Rangeen Saheb started a publicity company, together with another literary personality, Chunilal Kavish, or C.L. Kavish. The publicity company catered to Bombay's film production houses coming down to Lahore. They had requested 'journalist' Sehrai if the team could work out of his office. From morning to evening, it was Sehrai's posh office, and from evening to midnight, it was the adda of the three mavericks to meet film producers from Bombay and Calcutta. In a way they conned gullible film producers by changing the nameplate to Cine Publicity and turning the plush office into their place of business and entertainment.

My father, Rangeen Saheb, and C.L. Kavish followed a unique, emotional, human code of conduct in business and work. Every day, one of them would occupy the boss's chair and table. That day, the boss took all final decisions without any questions being asked. That day's earning and cheques received by post or hand delivery belonged to the boss. Every month it depended on their fate as to how much each one would earn to run his home and family.

At times, they would get country liquor and palm it off as a very rare exclusive limited whisky labelled Santara, made from oranges and believed to be procured from the cellars of the ex-Maharaja, Bhupinder Singh of Patiala. The bluff was that the palace insiders would smuggle rare Santara whisky exclusively for them at a premium price which they paid on the sly. The film client would gulp down pegs of orange whisky, feel like royalty and would sign the film advertisement contract papers, not realising that they were tipsy due to the consumption of country liquor.

Rangeen Saheb was part of Sagar Art (1950) right from its inception and was literally the boss (general manager and production-in-charge) till his last breath. For many years, he was the conscience, friend, philosopher, and guide to Papaji and all his decisions, personal and professional. No decision was taken without Rangeen Saheb's consent, approval and participation. Papaji wrote a heart-rending obituary on 10 December 1972 titled 'Mere Humdum Mere Dost' when Rangeen Saheb passed away

After Partition, Rangeen Saheb stayed in Lallubhai Mansion, opposite Chitra Cinema, Dadar, in Bombay, with his second wife and three sons Vijay, Pappu and Ajay. By his first wife, he had two

P.N. Rangeen was the conscience, friend, philosopher and guide of Ramanand Sagar.

Photo collection: Ramanand Sagar Foundation

daughters. The eldest, Guddi, died young and the second, Swarna, got married and settled in Ahmedabad. The entire family stayed in one single room of Lallubhai Mansion chawl which had the likes of film comedian Bhagwan and villain Tiwary living there.

In those days, Lallubhai Mansion was a stopover hub for strugglers dreaming of entering the film industry. During this period, Papaji stayed for a month or two with his family of six children and wife together with Rangeen Saheb's family. In the same room of Lallubhai Mansion chawl which also included the kitchen, fourteen members of the two families slept on the floor huddled together.

Every morning they had to walk to the common corridor of the chawl and relieve themselves on ground level toilets at one end of the building, carrying their own pail of water. When Sagar Art became a major film production house, Ramanand Sagar bought a five-bedroom flat for Rangeen Saheb and family in Vile Parle, a suburb of Bombay.

The movie magnate B.R. Chopra was also a struggling publicity journalist in Lahore during the same period. He published a weekly film journal titled *Cine Herald*, which he nurtured for decades, even after Partition. *Cine Herald* always remained Chopra's first love and weakness as a journalist. In later years, after B.R. Films became a big film production house, *Cine Herald* was still published from Delhi with 'Chita' (Fair) Kapoor as the editor. Chopra bore all its financial expenses and liabilities till the end. There was a constant war between Papaji and Chopra to bag film advertisements or film promotion contracts. They both kept an eagle eye on film production houses and film personalities visiting Lahore. Coincidentally, Chopraji's office was also on Nisbet Road in Lahore and he entertained film producers at the Bristol Hotel opposite his office.

It was a matter of who hit the jackpot and hooked a client. This bond of deep friendship, healthy competition and playful rivalry was a part of their lives and both became super successful. Both the Sagar and Chopra families were like one big family. They would celebrate all important occasions together. Having made deep inroads and friends during the stint as a film publicist in Lahore, Papaji, after

Partition, decided to shift to the Bombay film industry to follow his dreams and aspirations.

The rioting, looting and arson had started in Lahore. Hindus and Muslims were divided. Trusted friends, out of fear, would betray years of loyalty. Each community had defined areas. A person from one community could not walk into the territory of the other out of the fear of being lynched. Tongas with passengers were burnt with petrol doused on them. Fear gripped the city through day and night.

Once, at the peak of the riots, a rumour of a Muslim attack targeting the street courtyard below our mezzanine attic house spread like fire. Within moments, except for silence nothing could be heard. Everyone had vanished behind the safety of their closed doors. The silence was broken by the sound of a lathi over cobbled street stones. It was me, a three-year-old boy with a long solid wooden stick in hand, waving it vigorously and dangerously, valiantly marching towards the open space shouting loudly, 'Where are the enemies? Let them come. I will face them alone and kill them.' Suddenly, from the opposite side, a mob of Muslim youth wielding swords and lathis and with petrol bombs in their hands appeared out of nowhere. The distance between them and me started narrowing.

They were surprised to see a small boy standing alone, trying to fight them. Thinking it was a trick planned by the Hindus, they slowly started forming a circle to surround me. From half-closed slits of the windows in the lane, silent spectators watched the goings-on. My mother ran down the stairs, not caring for her life, darted across the lane, picked me up in her arms and ran back to the safety of her house.

Both the Hindu and Muslim communities felt Lahore would become a part of their country after Partition. Hindus vouched for Lahore to be a part of India and Muslims claimed it would belong to Pakistan. The population of Lahore was perhaps equally divided between Hindus and Muslims.

The English barrister Sir Cyril Radcliffe drew the line that would define the fate of Lahore. The tragedy was that Sir Radcliffe had never visited Lahore.

Many people left Lahore for India with their meagre belongings and sold their assets in desperation. Many of them took the sea route via Karachi to Bombay and Madras. Yet, most of the population was undecided about how to leave their homes and surroundings where they had spent their entire life with family and friends.

Papaji lived through this uncertain period, and what he saw and experienced became the core content of his all-time classic novel, *Aur Insaan Mar Gaya*.

Papaji, being a journalist, had an inkling of the line being envisaged by the British barrister Sir Cyril Radcliffe. The line would leave a trail of blood and instigate one of the worst migrations ever. The line gave away Lahore to Pakistan.

Two or three months before the Partition deadline of 15 August 1947, Papaji, with his family of fourteen members, quietly left Lahore for Srinagar (Kashmir) to the safety of his father's house. On 27 October 1947, he and his family dramatically escaped from an attack on Srinagar airport, landed at Safdarjung Airport, Delhi, in a Dakota DC-3, piloted by none other than the legendary Biju Patnaik. Finally, he and his family were transported by bus to a refugee camp in Birla Mandir in Central Delhi, west of Connaught Place, via Kingsway refugee camp.

Industrialist and philanthropist Baldeo Das Birla and his son Jugal Kishore Birla had built the Birla Mandir which Mahatma Gandhi had inaugurated in 1939 on the promise and condition that it would not only be restricted to Hindus, and people from every caste would be allowed inside.

Safdarjung Airport was established during the British Raj as Willingdon Airfield, named after Lord Willingdon, viceroy of India. It was extensively used during the Second World War and Partition. After Partition, it was renamed Safdarjung Airport after the Safdarjung tomb situated behind it. Lord and Lady Mountbatten took their last flight to England and so did Mohammed Ali Jinnah to Pakistan from Safdarjung Airport.

The memories of Safdarjung Airport and the refugee camp at Birla Mandir remained alive in Papaji's life like most other important incidents.

6

INHERITANCE
(1830–1917)

A painting of the great-grandfather of Ramanand Sagar, Nagar Seth
Lala Shankar Dass (1830–1905) with his personal Shiva Mandir in the
background.

Photo collection: Ramanand Sagar Foundation

In the bustling city of Peshawar, located in the North-West Frontier
Province (now known as Khyber Pakhtunkhwa), Lala Shankar
Dass was born to a wealthy ghee merchant around 1830. He was
the youngest of four brothers, and his father's favourite. The young

boy had just turned fourteen when his father summoned him to his private bedroom. While entering his father's plush chambers, Shankar passed the piercing gaze of his three elder brothers. He was shocked to see his father lying on his deathbed. The dying father slowly managed to slip out a red velvet potli (pouch) and put it in the soft palms of his youngest son. He said to him, 'Hide this when you go out. There are enough diamonds in this potli for you to live a comfortable life. Your greedy brothers will make your life a living hell. They may even try to kill you,' and with those last words, his father gently slipped away.

Shankar walked out of the room, his eyes brimming with tears, when his three brothers confronted him. They put a knife to his neck and demanded, 'What did father give you? Where have you hidden the diamonds?' They beat him up and pinned him down on the tiled floor, kicking him in the stomach. The potli flew out of his hands and a handful of sparkling diamonds lay scattered on the floor. 'You thief! You kafir! Betrayer! How dare you rob our wealth?' The three brothers held Shankar by his collar, dragged him to the door and flung him out of the royal mansion. 'Never come back here, you thug! This is not your home any more. There is no place for cheats like you here,' they roared and shut the iron door in his face.

A desolate Shankar wandered on Peshawar's streets, which were lined with shops of rock salt. The historic city was situated on the salt route to the landlocked Himalayan kingdom extending from the Khyber Pass to Tibet. The road connecting Peshawar to Srinagar for centuries had been named Namak Sadak or Nimak Sadak or Salt Road. By night, still unable to figure out his future, penniless but wearing expensive clothes, Shankar came across a group of equestrians sitting around an outdoor campfire. The friendly Pashtun men welcomed him and gave him some piping hot shorba (soup) and peshteh (mutton ribs) roasted and cooked on fire with mantus (meat dumplings), the common food of the region. The delicious food revived the young boy as he ate heartily. The tribesmen gave him some warm bedding made of yak hair to rest on. But he could hardly sleep on the bare ground as questions about his uncertain future swarmed in his head. With complete surrender and faith in Bhagwan Shiva, he left everything to destiny.

At the crack of dawn, everyone was up and loading their horses with sacks full of rock salt. Shankar was still rubbing his eyes when a tribesman came to him and shouted, 'Oh Lala, you seem to have run away. You are lost! Why don't you join our kafila (herd)? We are going to Srinagar. What is your name?' Drowsily, the young boy replied, 'Shankar Dass', to which the man said, 'Oh, Lala Shankar Dass!' And from that day onwards the name stuck, and he was Lala Shankar Dass till the end of his life.

In those days, salt was one of the main items of trade between Peshawar and Kashmir. Salt was exported to Kashmir and goods like wool, saffron, almonds, walnuts, etc. were imported to Peshawar. The big kafilas comprising over hundred horses loaded with sacks of salt departed via the salt route for Srinagar. They would trade the salt in return for wool, saffron, pashmina shawls and blankets.

The salt trade would continue regularly throughout the year except for a few months when heavy snowfall made the route inaccessible. The kafilas mostly comprised of Pashtun men, some of whom only had one horse, while others had more, depending on the trader. For fear of thugs and dacoits, the kafilas would herd together and move in a single group of a hundred or more horses with a horseman accompanying each pony. The large group would move together from Peshawar to Rawalpindi and then Srinagar via the Kumari Kwala Road. Later, the Dogra king Pratap Singh built a road from Srinagar to Jammu via the Banihal Pass that made it easier for the kafilas to travel via the plain terrain and cross the mighty mountains only on the last leg of their journey.

The Nimak Sadak reconstructed by the Mughals in 1586, was also called Mughal Sadak, and was approximately eighty-four kilometres long. The Mughals used this route from the sixteenth century onwards, right from the times of Babur to the times of Jahangir (who died en route), Shah Jahan and Aurangzeb. It was the shortest route from Lahore to Srinagar.

Lined with goats and nomadic tribes, the route had halting stations known as paraves or sarais. The Persian architect engaged by Shah Jahan to reconstruct the road designed fourteen paraves after every ten to fifteen miles for a halt. Akbar travelled on the road twice while Jahangir passed through the road thirteen times and Shah Jahan and Aurangzeb went across it only once.

Lala Shankar Dass left everything to fate, without any questions asked, and joined the horsemen's caravan. Business acumen ran in his genes. For a few years, rich salt traders employed him as a horseman. After a few trips he saved some money and bought a horse named Hira (jewel) who remained loyal to him till his last breath. Since he had become familiar with the salt route, he began to make multiple trips along the route alone. This way he could move faster and sell on his terms, making more money in the process. At eighteen, he had become a successful salt trader.

Just before the district of Shopian there was a bridge across the Jhelum. Once, on one such solo trip, around the year 1848, Shankar, with a goat hair blanket on his shoulders, which he had bought from his savings, and a cane in his hand, was climbing up the Shopian mountain range. While crossing the bridge, he saw a sadhu walking from the opposite direction of Srinagar. The strange sadhu, while crossing the eighteen-year-old youth, looked at him and said, 'Oye yaar, mere ko loi de do yaar badi thand lag rahi hai.' (Oh friend, give me your shawl, I am feeling very cold.) The sadhu seemed to be testing Shankar.

Without hesitation, Shankar gave his shawl away to the sadhu with folded hands and walked towards the other side of the bridge. They both reached the opposite ends of the bridge without a word. The sadhu turned and asked him his name. He said, 'Mujhe Shankar Dass kehte hain.' (My name is Shankar Dass.)

The sadhu blessed him, saying, 'Go! May Lord Shankar take good care of you.' With that he walked away without looking back.

Shankar was in a daze, trying to make sense of what had just happened, little knowing that this one incident would change the destiny of the Chopra clan for the next four generations, right up to Ramanand Sagar.

While passing through the town of Shopian, an exhausted Shankar, with his loyal companion, the steed Hira, decided to plod on further instead of spending the night in the town like other travellers had been doing for centuries. The fateful incident drew him to another town, Bijbehara, a momentous town for him, from where he would start his new journey to becoming the richest man in Srinagar.

The ancient town of Bijbehara was also known as Vijeshwar, a town dedicated to the god of victory, created by Lord Shiva in the Treta Yug, according to legend. The ancient teerth of Vijeshwar was a historic seat of learning and had the famous temple of Vijeshwar, a site famous in Kashmir even before 500 CE.

After climbing down the mountains of Shopian, one entered the town of Bijbehara. In those days there were no hotels, and only big towns had dharamshalas or sarais. Dharamshalas were charity rest houses where one could spend a night free of charge, whereas one had to pay a nominal rent for a sarai (halting station). Many caravans, traders and travellers rested for the night either in mosques or temples to cut costs.

The night had set in and the mythic town of Lord Shiva, Bijbehara, was visible on the horizon. An exhausted Shankar passed through the town on the banks of the Jhelum. The ancient Vijeshwar Temple was situated in the centre of the town, built on the ruins of the earlier temple by Maharaja Gulab Singh. He unfolded his bedding in the verandah of the temple after tying his horse to a pole and went to sleep. Most of the town's population was Muslim. There were only four or five Hindu families who maintained and looked after the temple. Generally, any temple with 'nath' or 'var' in its name is dedicated to Bhagwan Shiva, such as Pashupatinath or Rameshwaram.

One of the rich Hindu families from the Chowdhary lineage were residents of Bijbehara. They had a big house and were affluent and well-respected. The oldest family member of the clan was a staunch Shiva bhakt. He and his wife visited the Vijeshwar temple regularly, washed the floor and cleaned the compound while offering their prayers to Lord Shiva. They saw a traveller sleeping peacefully on the temple floor. In the morning, they woke him up. A sleepy Shankar slowly opened his eyes to a couple looking at him kindly.

He got up and folded his hands. All three prayed together to Lord Shiva and participated in the aarti. The atmosphere felt spiritually charged as if to indicate the sadhu's prophecy was coming true.

In those days, it was a common tradition to break into a conversation with a visiting traveller and enquire about his family, lineage and requirements like a good host welcoming a guest. In the course of their conversation, the old couple realised that Lala Shankar Dass belonged to the Khatri khandaan of Chopras. He was traditional, cultured and a devout believer of God. He was also a handsome young man of marriageable age belonging to a well-respected, affluent family. They had a daughter for whom they were looking for a suitable boy. In the valley, there were very few kshatriyas, since the majority of the population was either brahmin (pandits) or Muslim. In the entire state of Kashmir or the Srinagar valley, they were perhaps the only Khatri Choudhary khandaan. Due to shortage of kshatriyas in the valley, the couple got proposals mostly from brahmin or Pandit families.

The Choudhary couple took Shankar Dass home. On hearing his complete story, the couple realised that he was not only virtuous and spiritual but also had the rich heritage of his father's reputation. The couple saw a prospective Khatri groom in the young traveller.

They soon decided to marry their only daughter to a traveller they had just met. They proposed marriage to Shankar who immediately agreed. The marriage took place in the mythic town of Bijbehara that changed the course of Shankar's life.

After marriage, Shankar never went back to Peshawar. This was his last trip from Peshawar to Srinagar. The all-seeing sadhu with divine vision had seen this happening and, thus, had showered his blessings on him. On reaching Srinagar, Shankar sold the goods laden on his horse and decided to stay back in Bijbehara, the town that had changed his destiny.

The few Khatris staying in and around Srinagar and Bijbehara were essentially shopkeepers who stocked all kinds of groceries for the locals.

The river Jhelum passing through the middle of Srinagar joined the two parts of the city with the help of nine bridges or kadals. The Chaudharys had a small plot of land in one of the bylanes behind the oldest bridge, Kurdana Kadal. They suggested to Lala Shankar Dass that he open a shop on the plot.

In the old suburbs of Srinagar, it was customary to have one's residence sharing a wall of one's shop. Shankar built a temporary house on the terrace above the shop on the small plot of land. He started selling goods as a general merchant. Soon, he made a handsome profit from his shop. From the money earned, he bought land near the shop about ten to fifteen houses away from his temporary residence. On this land, he constructed a one-and-a-half storey permanent house. The Choudhary couple had another plot in the same area. They also shifted to old Srinagar from their house in Bijbehara to be closer to their daughter.

While narrating this story to me, Papaji mentioned that in his childhood he had seen these three or four houses situated behind the Kurdana Kadal in the suburbs of the old part of Srinagar. Starting from the Choudhary residence in Bijbehara to the first temporary house in Kurdana Kadal in Srinagar, Shankar Dass finally ended up getting the status of a Nagar Seth, the richest man in Srinagar. To further his business, he bought a prime piece of property near the fourth bridge, Zaina Kadal, on the banks of the Jhelum. Little is known of the period of Lala Shankar Dass's rise to the position of the richest man in Srinagar. Born in Peshawar and thrown out of his home when he was just fourteen, Shankar grew in social status and finally shifted his residence and business to the posh locality near Zaina Kadal.

He built a palatial mansion about a hundred yards away from the bridge, just touching the lapping waters of the Jhelum. Tiles for flooring and walls were imported from Samarkhand and Tashkent and the jharokas were embedded with silver and brass metals. The three-storeyed royal mansion had a furnace that kept the entire house warm. Dozens of bathrooms, toilets and hamams lined the basement and half of the ground floor was the zenana (women's quarters) while the other half was the mardana (men's quarters). Every day large groups of people were generously fed and taken care of. There were stables for horses of best breeds and a treasure room full of gold and silver coins.

Lala Shankar Dass also acquired around 500 acres of land below Tangmarg and owned an entire village, Shadipur, on the outskirts of Srinagar. He was conferred with the title of 'Nagar Seth of Srinagar' in the courts of Maharaja Gulab Singh around 1856 and continued to enjoy the title under the patronage of Maharaja Ranbir Singh. He also constructed a trading complex that spread over a large area with shops. The huge maidan must have been 200 x 200 yards. The grand spectacular shopping complex had massive roman pillar-like structures. This circular market was placed in the centre of a large playground. One side of the circle was reserved for the entrance of horses, mules and carriages loaded with goods so that they could unload the wares at the back of the shop without disturbing the customers and traders. Proud of his accomplishment, he named the shopping complex after the reigning king—'Ranbir Ganj'. As per the stories narrated by Papaji, Ranbir Singh was a brave, legendary, warrior king.[2] His Dogra father Maharaj Gulab Singh bought Kashmir from the British but it was the astute statesman Maharaja Ranbir Singh who actually built Kashmir. He not only conquered Ladakh but his army also marched up to Kabul. He encouraged and welcomed Hindu traders, who helped him fill the royal treasuries.

It was Lala Shankar Dass who conceived and constructed Ranbir Ganj. He personally supervised its construction. Later, this unique shopping complex came to be famously known as Maharaj Ganj, which exists even today. Shankar Dass was also the proud owner of 'Shankar Dass and Sons', a row of shops that dealt with import and export. The palatial mansion and the Zaina Kadal were less than half a kilometre away from the famous complex in Ranbir Ganj.

In a letterhead preserved by Chitu, it says that it was in 1867 that Shankar Dass Gangaram Importers & Exporters was established. The

---

2. In his tape recording of 9 September 2004

international business with Barclays of London was routed through the port city of Karachi. There were records of cash transactions right up to Bombay, Calcutta and from Karachi up to Rangoon. There was a metal seal of trust with Lala Shankar Dass's signature that was a guarantee for all business transactions. No one doubted or questioned the credibility of the metal seal imprint, be it on hundis (promissory notes) or hard cash transactions. All accounts were kept in the headquarters at the Maharaj Ganj office.

There are many stories and legends about Lala Shankar Dass. He would leave his mansion mounted on his loyal horse Hira followed by a retinue of servants. The poor and the needy would line up on the half-kilometre stretch from the Zaina Kadal mansion to the massive Maharaj Ganj shopping complex.

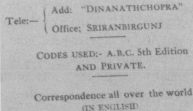

An old letterhead of L. Shankar Dass Ganga Ram.
Photo collection: Ramanand Sagar Foundation

He would then generously throw coins to them in return for their blessings. He was sensitive to the destitute who, out of self-respect, would not line up for the alms and money. So he got small matchbox-sized silver boxes or dibbis made, and filled them with naswar (moist powdered tobacco sniff). Every day there was a friendly gathering of well-wishers, traders, relatives and friends in a darbar-like royal courtroom in his complex. He would summon respectable people of the society who had fallen on hard times. He would keep track of every person in his contact list, their economic conditions and family problems and would tactfully coax them, 'Please have some naswar. Have I displeased you in any way? Saab, this is only naswar. You can't refuse this customary offering.'

He would slowly slip a silver snuffbox into their hands. Hidden inside it would be a gold British pound under the tobacco powder. He would give these dibbis to the genuinely needy people. This way he helped those who did not ask for it without letting others know of their problems.

In that era, it was a tradition to offer naswar to one's guests. This custom had travelled from Iran to Afghanistan to Peshawar to Srinagar. This tradition is still prevalent in Peshawar where Pathans sniff naswar even today.

Another famous legend of the Nagar Seth Lala Shankar Dass was the way kings of Kashmir paid their respects to him. During a court session with Maharaja Pratap Singh, on the entry of Lala Shankar Dass, the Maharaja would raise his right knee in salutation.

Also in times of need, gold coins and money would be stacked in gunny bags and transported to the palace coffers. There was a decoy mud house on the banks of the river touching Shankar Dass and Sons' shops in Maharaj Ganj. Empty boats entered the mud house on the banks of the Jhelum. The inside of the temporary mud house was a solid wall entrance that led to a hidden chamber inside the shopping and office complex. The boats were loaded with the money and treasure in gunny bags and set afloat discreetly into the Jhelum. The gunny bags were camouflaged with freshly-cut crops (dhaan) and piles of rice saplings, grass, flowers and vegetables.

The Jhelum flowed past the Maharaja's palace situated on its banks. There was a moat leading into the palace. Strangers and common people were stopped at the devri (a wooden platform for landing behind the wall of the palace).

Lala Shankar Dass's boats, laden with wealth and gold hidden under rice cuttings, entered the palace through the moat past the devri. To everyone else, this looked like a normal delivery of rice for the royal kitchens, but it was, in fact, money being delivered to the royal coffers.

Lala Shankar Dass served, and was the recipient of the grace of, three kings of Kashmir, Gulab Singh (1846–56), Ranbir Singh (1856–85) and Pratap Singh (1885–1925). Dass had built two separate structures in his royal mansion on the banks of the river Jhelum near Zaina Kadal. The structures faced each other with a courtyard separating them. He was blessed with two sons, Lala Ishwar Das and Lala Ganga Ram. Shankar Dass gave away one section of the palace mansion to his elder son, and the other to his younger son. He stayed in two special rooms inside the part given to his eldest son.

His second son, Lala Ganga Ram, was born around 1856. Lala Shankar Dass breathed his last around 1905. During his last days, he was confined to a bed facing the courtyard. Every day, the loyal horse Hira would park himself in the courtyard, squat in front of the bedroom and look at his master. On the day he died, a sadhu visited the courtyard. He was the same sage Lala Shankar Dass had met on the Shopian bridge. The sadhu looked at Dass and smiled, seeing his success and nobility. Meanwhile, Dass saw the Trikal Darshi sadhu and folded his hands in gratitude. The sadhu, in a clear voice, said, '*O Shankar kahan baitha hain bhai. Jaldhi kar tera samay ho gaya hai!*' (O Shankar, where are you sitting, brother? Your time is up!) Hira also heard the sadhu's divine command. Both Shankar Dass and Hira breathed their last peacefully. Later, the sadhu was nowhere to be seen around the palace.

It was one of the grandest shav yatras (last journeys) witnessed in Srinagar. Lala Shankar Dass's dead body was carried in a decorated horse carriage with thousands of people, Hindus and Muslims, lining the funeral route, throwing flowers, bowing their heads, weeping and paying their last respects. Leading the procession were decorated empty bareback horses without riders and with only an umbrella, together with flower-decked horses and a herd of loyal horses from the stables. Papaji had seen photographs of the funeral procession.

After the death of Lala Shankar Dass, the reins of half the empire came into the hands of his second son, Lala Gangaram. Gangaram did not inherit much of his legendary father's business acumen. His wife Ratan Kaur controlled the entire business, including import-export. However, her biggest grief was that she could not conceive for the first few years of her marriage. It was a popular belief that one would conceive after adopting a child. Gangaram and Ratan adopted Dinanath, who was Ratan's nephew, as their son and legal heir. Ratan's sister was married to Bhagwan Das, a shopkeeper from Katipura Tehsil in Tangmarg. Bhagwan had three sons—Ishwar Das, Dinanath and Amarchand. The three brothers were not well educated because of financial constraints.

Ramanand Sagar's grandfather, Lala Gangaram, who inherited half the empire of Lala Shankar Dass. Lala Gangaram legally adopted Lala Dinanath, the biological father of Ramanand Sagar.

Photo collection: Ramanand Sagar Foundation

Gangaram and Ratan saw an heir in Dinanath who was a god-fearing, simple young boy who could be moulded into the rich and aristocratic ways of the family. After the legal adoption and declaring Dinanath as the legal heir of the vast empire, a year passed by and Ratan gave birth to Baldev. After Ratan's death, Gangaram married again, as was the custom in those days. His second wife Ram Pyaari was from Lahore and it was said that she was very beautiful. Every day she would wear heavy gold jewellery, and using her charm and beauty, betrayed Gangaram and absconded with five kilos of gold.

Dinanath and Baldev grew up to be wealthy and prosperous, but spoilt brats.

In Papaji's words in his taped interview, he said, '*Pitaji aur Chachaji English aadmi the, sirf novelay padhaa karte the library se laake. Novel laana, padhnaa ya shatranj khelna, yehi unka kaam tha. Paise toh khane peene ka zameen aur jaaydad se aata rehtaa tha.*' (My father and uncle would only read novels all the time. Reading and chess were their passions. Their inheritance took care of their needs.)

As time passed, all was lost—the glory, the wealth, the palace, and their royal status. Compared to the palatial mansion in Zaina Kadal, where he grew up, Dinanath finally settled down in Wazir Bagh with his second wife Shanti Devi, also known as Suhagwati, and their family of five sons and one daughter.

It was an upper middle-class suburb of Srinagar a few kilometres away from the city's centre, Lal Chowk. It was a two-storey kothi with three or four rooms and one attic. In Dinanath's early days, the family owned over 500 acres of land above Gulmarg, called Chak Charit Ram, apart from another village, Shadipur on the outskirts of Srinagar. Shadipur was accessible only by a horse carriage, whereas no buggies could go to Chak Charit Ram near Tangmarg. One or two kilometres before the village, the buggy horses would be unsaddled and Lala Dinanath would ride to his estate on those same horses accompanied by a posse of servants on foot.

Papaji remembered accompanying his father to the family estate as a child. The villagers from the entire estate stood in long queues with hands folded in respect. He and his father were received in royal style with fanfare. That was the power and hold of the zamindars of that time. Papaji had a faint memory of visiting the Shadipur village. Living in a feudal setup, as landlords, they always had a trail of servants accompanying them. As time elapsed, the lands remained only in books, with court cases between the families of half-brothers Dinanath and Baldev and the introduction of new laws. All the land had gone to the tenants, tillers and farmers. The family estate was gifted to them during the reign of Maharaja Pratap Singh. The king's ministers in Lala Shankar Dass's retinue marked the estate lands as far as his eyes could see and transferred them to the Chopra family in the land records.

Dinanath refused to exercise his legal right on ownership of the vast estate. He did not even keep fifty acres of land for the benefit of his family that he had through two wives—two sons from his first wife Isha Devi and five sons and one daughter from his second wife, Subhag Rani. Payaji wilfully gave away the massive estate to the tillers, farmers and other workers of the land as Papaji told me later.

I remember the Muthu's advice at Kheer Bhavani temple (Chapter 4) when he explained to Payaji the cause of his misery. Dinanath had decided to give away all his estate to the workers whom he believed were partners in the family's riches. Even the kind-hearted Lala Shankar Dass had changed the sharing ratio between farmers and landlords. In those days, no one was paid a salary, be it the tailor, farmer, domestic help, the barber or even the family priest. Everyone was paid with grains of rice as wages or salary. At the end of the harvest, sacks full of rice were distributed among a hundred people working for the estate. Normally, one-fourth of the entire crop was given to the staff and three-fourths to the zamindar. However, Lala Shankar Dass reversed the ratio—three-fourths of the crop was distributed among the estate staff, tailors, farmers and others while one-fourth of the harvest went to the Chopra clan. The quantity of the harvest and profits earned from them were substantial enough so that even one-fourth of all the produce was not only sufficient for the whole year but also helped amass a lot of wealth. The sacks full of rice were distributed among the entire staff and sent to their homes.

One horse with two gunny bags went to the barber. Five horses with rice bags went to Kashiram and Madh Bhatt. Even the families of the pujari were paid in kind. The rice-filled gunny bags were delivered by Lalaji to workers' homes.

Ramanand Sagar's only biological brother Chitranjan Chopra also faced a turbulent life. Bereft of a mother's love and upbringing, he grew up to be a loner. In Srinagar College, he joined a theatre group as an actor. A Muslim girl who stayed in a house opposite the Zaina Kadal mansion played the female lead. The stage brought them together. They would meet each other on the terrace and soon their friendship turned into love. They decided to get married. The orthodox Muslim community opposed it. She was chased and escaped to Jammu. Chitu followed her out of true love. At that time most of the Muslims in Jammu were being massacred and the community was filled with hatred for the Hindus. Her family was attacked and she hid herself in a Hindu house. The fanatic Muslims closed the gates of the house and thrashed the Hindu family on the terrace. Chitu visited the girl in court and jail. She only asked him one question: 'Why don't you marry me?'

Sheikh Abdullah was a friend of the royal family. He helped to smuggle her out to Lahore. He realised this Hindu-Muslim marriage in a high-profile family might create a political storm and give leverage to Hindus. Chitu finally reached Lahore to meet Papaji for advice and consent. Even though Papaji was stuck in the middle of religious riots, he willingly agreed to their marriage. As soon as they got a whiff of the marriage, the ruthless Muslim henchmen abducted the girl and put her on a train. During the journey she alighted at a station on the pretext of relieving herself, walked up to the bank of the Jhelum, tied her dupatta to a tree and flung herself into the roaring waters of the Jhelum. While boarding the train at Lahore station she had managed to send a telegram to Chitu mentioning that if fate did not allow her to be Chitu's wife she was going to end her life. He never got over the emotional guilt of her death and remained a bachelor throughout his life.

In 1955, he left for London with Papaji's consent by a ship named *Batary*. He settled there and bought a flat at 45, Penywern Road,

Earl's Court in central London. In the private personal concerts at his London flat, legends like Ustad Ghulam Ali and Mehdi Hassan would sing ghazals in abandon, with Dilip Kumar as a regular visitor. Chitu was a great host, a brilliant cook and popular in the creative circles.

Ramanand Sagar's only younger brother Chitu (third from the left, standing) with Ghulam Ali (fourth from the left, standing) and other friends at his central London flat. The photo has been autographed by the legendary Ghulam Ali himself.

Photo collection: Ramanand Sagar Foundation

For the most part of his life he painted, heard soulful music and decorated windows on London's fashionable streets for a living. In the '60s, my father and Chitu opened an office in the name of Jyot Films, London, the overseas distribution wing of Sagar Art. All of Papaji's films were routed through Jyot Films. One of Chitu's many close friends was Shanti Mahendru, sister of the music legend, Madan Mohan, and her daughter, Anju Mahendru. Most of the film industry thought that Anju was secretly married to superstar Rajesh Khanna. Their relationship was beyond platonic. Rajesh Khanna had presented a bungalow to Anju in the Juhu Vile Parle Development

(JVPD) scheme, one of the most expensive and posh residential areas in Mumbai. Many in the film fraternity felt that Rajesh Khanna was a shrewd businessman and would not have gifted her the expensive bungalow just like that. Several people had seen him wait endlessly for hours in his car outside the bungalow. Amit Biswas, son of the veteran music director Anil Biswas, and producer Ashalata Biswas while narrating to me the untold love story, mentioned that he also strongly believed the above.

In the 1980s, Chitu moved from London to Sagar Villa in Juhu, Mumbai. He had great respect for Leelavati since she had brought him up like a son. He addressed her as 'Parjaiji' and would sing 'Lathe di chaddhar rang maiya' to her, a Punjabi folk song both shared as teenagers in Lahore. Chitu occupied the mezzanine floor of Sagar Villa exclusively. The two brothers spent quality time together at Sagar Villa for a decade. Papaji treated Chitu with care and so did the rest of the family. In the last few months of his life, he was bedridden and had lost all control of his faculties. Neelam Sagar selflessly cared for Chitu and would even clean up after him. She would do this not complaining or flinching even once.

The one memorable painting that Chitu conceived from his memory was of Zaina Kadal during the brothers' early days. Papaji cherished these childhood memories of the golden period of his life, the first five years spent with his mother Isha Devi, in his personal Sagar Villa bedroom. Chitu's oil paintings were inspired by the Kashmiri tantrik painter P.L. Santosh's work, and still adorn the walls of Sagar Villa.

Though half-brothers, Baldev Chachaji and Dinanath, who had inherited millions, still lived like blood brothers. The families of the two brothers were in disagreement in matters of inheritance of wealth and land. Even in court, Baldev Chachaji mentioned that all property and wealth belonged to both the brothers. The court case went on for about twenty years. The ending was sad and tragic.

Philosophically, Dinanath's realisation of his sins was divine and justified by fate. Dinanath built a Shiva temple in his Kuti Pura village in the name of his foster father Lala Gangaram and mother

Ratan Deviji and his maternal grandfather, Lala Charath Ramji. The marble stone inlay read, '*Yeh Shiv mandir Dinanath Chopra ne apne Nana Lala Charith Ramji aur apne pujya Mata-Pita Shrimati Ratan Deviji aur Lala Gangaramji Chopra ki yaad mein 1970 mein banaya hai.*' (This Shiva temple has been constructed by Lala Dinanath in the memory of his maternal grandfather, Lala Charith Ramji, and his revered mother and father, Shrimati Ratan Devji and Lala Ganga Ramji in 1970.)

There was no temple in the entire Hindu village of Kuti Pura, from where his biological family hailed. So every year during Navratri, Dinanath would perform the Durga Saptashati Havan to repent for his mistakes.

Lala Dinanath was the adopted son of a rich, loving family but lost everything when he broke the sacred bond of his first wife Isha Devi and her son, Ramanand. To atone for his sin, he burned hundreds of crores of promissory notes and gave away over 500 acres of land to the tillers and struggled for a living himself.

The Muthu's uncanny prediction in the Kheer Bhavani temple had come true. Fate, like a hunter, had killed its prey. Badrinath, one of the third-generation cousins, became a bhagoda (a runaway), leaving a string of bank frauds and robberies behind him.

7

A MOVIE MOGUL IS BORN:
FROM *BARSAAT* TO *ZINDAGI* AND
THE BIRTH OF SAGAR ART
(1947–64)

2 7 October 1947—Papaji and his family of thirteen landed as the first refugees from Kashmir at Safdarjung Airport. Hungry and thirsty for five days, our clothes had become dirty and fear was writ large on our faces. We were shifted to Birla Mandir in government transport buses. Hundreds of us refugees were huddled together, seeking shelter and free food.

Unable to bear the plight of her hungry children, my mother Leelavati quietly removed her gold bangles and handed them to Papaji. Papaji, already known in literary circles in Delhi, went to a writer friend to help him sell the bangles. Since a local was accompanying him, he got good money for the gold.

Half asleep and hungry, the sound of a tonga woke all of us up. Papaji sat in the tonga, in his crumpled clothes, and directed us to get in, saying, 'Let us go for a nice hot meal.'

The tandoor or mud oven was doling out hot rotis to the customers. The aroma of boiling dal and fresh rotis got us all ravenous. As we neared the dhaba, the owner politely told Papaji, 'We do not serve free food to beggars. Please go to a refugee camp where they serve free food to beggars.' Stunned, Papaji quietly walked into the washroom and wept bitterly. Just then, an old Muslim man with a white beard handed a few rupees to Papaji and said, 'Feed your children. They are hungry. I work here as a waiter. The dhaba owner will not give you even one roti for free. Such situations can come in anyone's life. Accept your fate and move on.' He wiped Papaji's tears. Papaji took six one-hundred rupee notes out of his pocket and said, 'I am not a beggar. I have money. I did not ask for free food.' Six hundred rupees in 1947 was a lot of money.

Realising his mistake, the dhaba owner personally made the entire family sit at a large double wooden table with rickety benches. The first batch of hot tandoori rotis and steaming dal started making the rounds. Barely had anyone finished the first morsel when I shouted for one more roti. Everyone stared at me. How could a four-year-old child finish a whole roti at one go? Without any questions, Papaji ordered one more roti. While everyone was focusing only on the life-saving meal, I requested for one more roti and then another, and in no time, I had asked for ten rotis. Mummyji stared at me angrily. With tears rolling down her eyes, she screamed, 'Where have you hidden the rotis? Do you realise the circumstances?' She lifted her hand to slap me, but Papaji stopped her and ordered for another roti. This time they saw me eating my hot roti dipped in steaming dal. I put my hand below the table and sheepishly took out the rotis I had hidden. The entire emotional incident was drowned in the din around and the whole group kept eating roti after roti in silence. As we had not eaten for days, the scene looked like a pack of hungry wolves devouring their meal on a cold winter's day.

Papaji told my mother, 'Our son has lost faith in us as parents who will protect him come what may. We could not give him food for the last three-four days. He was not sure if he would get his next meal. So, he hid those rotis out of fear.' He then reassuringly held my mother's hand.

Papaji was a sensitive man. He could imagine how extreme hunger could haunt a child forever. Till today I have never questioned what comes to my plate or made special food requests. I wipe my plate clean with every meal. My mother had drilled into her six children to never leave even a single morsel on our plate and always thank Annapurna Devi for giving us food and feeding us.

Since Papaji had risen from a reporter to the position of the news editor of *Daily Milap* in Lahore, he went straight to the office of *Milap* in Connaught Place which also served as the residence of the *Milap* family owners after Partition. Ranbir Singh not only welcomed him as a family member but also promised to request his close friend Maulana Azad to help rehabilitate our family. The vacant homes of Muslim families, who had migrated to Pakistan, were lying empty, mostly in the Daryaganj area of Delhi. These houses were allotted to refugees who, while fleeing to India, had abandoned their homes in Pakistan, especially in Lahore.

Maulana Abdul Kalam Azad was a senior Muslim leader of the Indian National Congress, and being a scholar, was appointed as the education minister from 15 August 1947. He was aware of Papaji's literary journey and his rise to prominence as a journalist. To Papaji's surprise, when he met Maulana Azad with Ranbirji, Azad turned out to be an admirer of his work. He not only sanctioned two large houses in Daryaganj but also appointed Papaji as a story/drama writer for All India Radio. Immediately thereafter, Papaji went to the office of the refugee camp at Birla Mandir and showed them a form from the Punjab and Frontier Hindu and Sikh Refugee Committee, Srinagar, requesting for immediate transport for his sixteen family members.

My father decided to stay in the main big house at the dead end of the bylane. The house opened into a foyer which also served as the porch. On the right side of the porch was a room which Papaji allotted to my Nani, Chaiji. This room was adjacent to the room occupied by all of us—Papaji, Mummyji and we five brothers.

The house being a square structure with an open sky-facing courtyard, the other three sides of the quadrangle were allotted to my mamas, mamis and their families. The entry of the house had a double door which could be locked with an iron chain latched to a hook. On the three sides of the courtyard were rooms with long three-sided terraces on the top. The fourth wall was a common wall between the two large houses. Chaiji gave away the adjoining house to her distant relatives from Lahore. The oldest was Hari Mama who, to survive after Partition, bought an axe and became a woodcutter. His two sons, Somnath and Khugoo, worked in book-binding units. The other occupant Jiya Pandit was a purohit who performed rituals and also worked as an electrician to make ends meet. After our escape to Srinagar before Partition, Jiya had stayed put in Chaiji's house in Lahore for three months, trying to protect it. Hence my Nani felt obliged to him.

Name of Refugee	Father's Name	No. of Family members	Destination	If demanding any relief	Remarks
Ramanand Sagar (RAMANAND. SAGAR)	L. Rallya Ram	16 (3 males) (4 females) (9 children)	DELHI	Immediate Transport Facilities.	If obliged for more than a week it may have to ask even for Transport Expenses. 22.x.47.

From THE PUNJAB & FRONTIER HINDU & SIKH REFUGEES COMMITTEE
SRINAGAR

Printed form of The Punjab and Frontier Hindu & Sikh Refugees Committee, Srinagar, filled by Ramanand Sagar, requesting transport for sixteen family members.

Photo collection: Ramanand Sagar Foundation

The area was called Daryaganj—'darya' means river and 'ganj' means a trading market—since at one time the river Yamuna flowed through this locality and there were trading markets lining its banks. Even today major trading markets like the Gala market, named after Premchand Gala, are an integral part of Daryaganj. The famous Golcha Film Theatre is situated in Daryaganj. The former president of Pakistan, General Pervez Musharraf, was also born in Haveli Neharwali in Daryaganj.

It was called Haveli Neharwali because the haveli was located on the banks of a canal or 'nehar'. Haveli Neharwali was about half a kilometre away from the two big houses allotted to my family in Daryaganj.

The story-writing job at All India Radio did not suit Papaji because of bureaucratic interference. He was grateful to Maulana Azad and Ranbirji for their support but his independence as a writer was very important to him. Papaji helped his in-laws' family and our family settle down at 464 Gali Baharwali, Daryaganj, and left for Bombay to try his luck in the film industry there. The next two years were full of struggle and ambition. On the one hand, my mother brought up her five sons with care and love but with no compromise on ethics, education and hard work, and on the other hand, Papaji roamed the backstreets of Chitra Cinema in Dadar, which was a paradise for strugglers, stayed in a one-room rental accommodation at Pereira Mansion on Sitla Devi Temple Road, Mahim, sharing the room with a struggling actor named Dev Anand and an aspiring music director named Madan Mohan. The three shared the rent, and eventually, all three got where they wanted in their respective professions.

Leelavati sent her three older sons to Dayanand Anglo Vedic School (DAV) School on Subhash Marg in Daryaganj. In celebration of India's first Republic Day on 26 January 1950, the school distributed aluminium plates embossed with the national emblem. My mother beamed with joy when her three sons came home, proud of their possessions which were the prized mementos of the family.

Around the same time, Leelavati taught her two youngest children the Hindi alphabet by scribbling with a piece of charcoal on the stone flooring in the courtyard. The three older children going to school were given a 'takhti'—a kind of wooden plank in the shape of a rectangular kite. The takhti was layered with multani mitti (river clay). To write on the takhti, a pen called 'kalam' made from dried reed, chipped and sharpened on one end like a nib was used. The centre of the wooden nib was slightly sliced. This pen was dipped in a pot of black ink and alphabets were written on the takhti. After each session the river mud was washed away. A fresh page was similarly prepared for the next lesson.

In Bombay, the penniless Ramanand would have his meals at Gupta Dhaba which was owned by three brothers, Gurupal Singh, Trilok Singh and Harpal Singh, in the bylanes behind Chitra Cinema. You had to pay only for the chappatis, while the dal was free. If you lingered on for non-vegetarian food, then, at a very nominal rate, Gurupal Singh would give a big plate full of gravy with a tiny mutton piece floating in it. The strugglers would relish mutton and pao (bread loaf), satisfying their craving for a non-vegetarian meal at a low price.

Gupta Dhaba had been leased by the three brothers, who also had a soap factory where they sold washing soap to the strugglers at dirt cheap rates. The only problem was that the five-kilo soap reduced to one kilo within the first few washes itself. Gupta Dhaba was a life-saver for strugglers; it catered to the ambitious dreamers of the film fraternity right up to 1980. Big names who made their mark, and ate their meals there included my father and actors Manoj Kumar, Dharmendra and Rajesh Khanna. However, the Good Samaritan Singh family soon split for practical purposes once their individual families had grown. Trilok opened the famous Great Punjab Hotel on Dadar Main Road where even today, many film industry people enjoy their meals. Harpal opened the Great Punjab Hotel in Bandra while Gurupal, or Kaka as he was fondly called, is eighty years old and now stays at Wadala, behind IMAX Theatre. Of the three brothers, Gurupal catered more to the film industry strugglers. The three brothers, especially Gurupal, still enjoy the karmic returns of their good deeds of feeding people during their times of struggle.

Meanwhile, between Papaji and his two roommates, Dev Anand and Madan Mohan, they had only one pair of decent trousers. Depending on who had a meeting with a film producer, he would wear them while the other two sometimes stayed in the room with towels tied around their waists.

All three of them had a third-class annual railway pass between Borivali and Churchgate. They sometimes travelled together discussing their ambitions and dreams, joking and laughing. If one of them had an appointment either in Roop Tara, Shree Sound or Ranjit Studios in Dadar, he would get off, while the other two continued their commute, idling away the whole day between Churchgate and Borivali.

The third class railway pass of Ramanand Sagar dated 28 October 1948 for Bombay, Baroda and Central India Railway.

Photo collection: Ramanand Sagar Foundation

The Western Line was called Bombay Baroda and Central India Railways (BB&CI Railways) and was constructed in 1864. The central line was earlier called the Great Indian Peninsula or GIP Railways, which opened in 1853. Harbour Line was as it is today, from Victoria Terminus (VT) to Mankhurd. The west coast of Bombay had the cream of the film industry, from top film stars, producers, directors, industrialists to upper-class people, living there. The Harbour Line was for the docks and cantonment defence area constructed by the British in Mankhurd where they stored their artillery and weaponry.

The intelligent British had planned to dock their war and passenger ships called 'East Indian', loaded with gunpowder and explosives, along the east coast on the Thane creek, facing mainland India. The west coast facing the Arabian Sea skirting Africa was not safe from the attack of rival countries like Spain, the Dutch and Portuguese in days past. I presume that the name of Bombay was coined from 'Bon Bay' or 'Good Bay' where warship fleets could be berthed from the safety of storms in the Arabian Sea and the Indian Ocean.

At times Papaji would stay as a paying guest with W.D. Dadlani on the ground floor at Balram Chambers, Dhobi Talao, Bombay, and bank with the Punjab National Bank, Jaico House branch, Bombay, with as low a balance as Rs 91. He would visit the Kashmir Bureau of Information, Advani Chambers, Sir P.M. Road, Fort, Bombay, to update himself with the latest government policies for refugees from Kashmir. He even had an account in the Punjab National Bank, Ilaco House, Bombay, in 1949.

The money that Papaji sent to sustain his large family in Delhi was not enough, and so we all had to do odd jobs. The fruit juice seller on the main road—Netaji Subhash Marg—would send us muskmelon or kharbuja seeds which we then dried on the terrace or courtyard, and for hours, painstakingly peeled the hard shell and separated the soft seeds. A whole day's hard labour would earn us about twenty-five paise.

The other hard task was to make envelopes from raddi or used newspapers and magazines sent to us by different kirana shops lining the streets of Daryaganj. About 1,000 envelopes earned the family approximately 25 paise and involved almost a whole day's work. We children were assigned different jobs from morning to night like getting the flour from the atte ki chakki or flour mill. The flour mill operator very smartly would retain some flour in the cloth funnel at the end of the grinder. Filling buckets and pots of water for the whole day from the community common water pump and milking buffalos in the tabela for our daily milk were a few of the many odd jobs we did, like any other struggling family.

I remember, one day, Hari Mama who had become a woodcutter broke the wooden door separating the two houses with his axe out of sheer frustration. My other uncle, Panju Mama, vegetated. From an expert in the Landa accounting system and handling the entire business transactions of Bhawani Das Di Hatti, he was reduced to doing nothing. His wife, my eldest aunt, known for her beautiful looks, had become a bag of bones.

Once seven-year-old Anand broke his forearm, while playing in Ghodewala Bagh, a park with horse rides for children at the end of Galli Baharwalli. As kids, we believed that the park was haunted by a 'chudail' or a female child-eating monster. We all decided not to utter a word to Mummyji. On seeing the dangling arm broken and hanging from the centre of the forearm, my mother rushed and lifted Anand, carried him on her back and ran the entire two-mile stretch through the narrow lanes of Daryaganj, to the free municipal hospital. No servants or medical facility was affordable. This was the condition of most refugees after Partition.

In Delhi, Mummyji, concerned for her children's health, had got a goat in the house and its milk would be squeezed directly into our mouths. My eldest brother Subhash was almost ten, and the youngest, Moti, three, and we all would roam the narrow lanes absolutely naked with gachi or soft river mud plastered on our bodies, a traditional remedy for good healthy skin. The passers-by would hardly pay us any attention.

In Delhi, Chaiji went into a trance every Thursday. We would pour ice water on her body with buckets because she would scream, 'I am on fire. Pour ice on my head and body.' Some spiritual heat seemed to be spreading through her body. She would often rub her arms and rusted iron needles would come out from the skin. During such bouts of spiritual experiences, she would predict the future and give solutions to problems of neighbours who would visit her out of reverence on Thursdays. People would tell us that someone had done black magic on her. They would say that it was Beriwala Baba of Lahore who possessed her body every Thursday, and spoke in a heavy growling voice through Chaiji. Chaiji was a staunch devotee of Beriwala Baba and used to visit his temple religiously every Thursday in Lahore where my mother's family lived.

Within a year of our escape from Lahore to Delhi as refugees, Chaiji passed away. The same day, I heard the sound of ghungroos (anklets with little bells) tinkling on the terrace. I must have been about five. I was very scared and thought of going to the terrace, but something stopped me. Many years later, Papaji told me that as per 'the other world', when a great soul departs, the musicians and dancers from heaven come down to accompany the soul to a higher plane.

Papaji would meet many successful producers, filmmakers and production houses, but without much result. Eating every day at Gupta Dhaba had made his stomach weak. Some producers who promised to buy his story would steal his script and not pay him any money or give him any credit. One such production house was behind Regal Cinema in Colaba. He never forgot their lollipop technique of exploiting struggling talent. When he became a movie mogul and the two brothers of that production house offered him big money to work for them, he flatly refused. But he always met them and their family with due respect, with no hatred or vengeful feeling. He had told me about the pain he felt when I became very friendly with one of their sons in St Xavier's College where we were classmates.

While struggling to find recognition, Papaji decided to meet his well-wisher, fan, friend, philanthropist and superstar Prithviraj Kapoor. Somewhere behind Khalsa College, the thespian stayed in a two-storey building.

One of the occupants in the same building was the famous actor K.N. Singh who played the role of a villain in films. This was a historic meeting. Prithvirajji treated Papaji like his own son. Aware of his struggle, while seeing him off at the bus stop below the building, the large-hearted Pathan quietly put a 100-rupee note into Papaji's shirt pocket. Papaji returned it with a smile, saying, 'I am fine. I will find someone who respects my talent and pays me for my work.' Prithvirajji looked straight into Papaji's eyes and put the money back into his pocket, saying, 'You are hired. This is an advance for your work. It has nothing to do with any monetary help from a friend as you think.' He then took out a contract that said that Papaji would write a play of his choice for Prithvi Theatres and would deliver it to them when he wanted, with no questions asked, and that he would be paid Rs 500 for each play. He further said, 'You can draw your remuneration of any amount from your contractual dues whenever you want.' A tearful Papaji hugged Prithvirajji and walked away in silence. He then wrote two plays, *Kalaakar* and *Gaura*, for Prithvi Theatres around 1948. While delivering the second act of the second play, Prithvirajji requested Papaji to write a role for a child artiste since he wanted to introduce his second son Shammi Kapoor to theatre. Papaji, despite the obligation he felt towards Prithvirajji, said it would be against his principles, because to him, writing was above any bondage of any kind. Prithvirajji understood his dilemma and the play finally had two credit titles against the writer's name—Ramanand Sagar and Prithviraj Kapoor.

The travelling theatre company Prithvi Theatres was founded by Prithvirajji in 1944 and ran for sixteen years. The thespian was the lead actor in every show being staged all over India. Owing to non-availability of a theatre stage, he would perform his shows at noon at Royal Opera House, Bombay. His legacy was later carried forward by his large family, all of them mega stars, including his sons Raj, Shammi and Shashi Kapoor, grandchildren Randhir, Rishi, Sanjana and Kunal Kapoor and great-grandchildren Karishma, Kareena and Ranbir Kapoor. After every show, Prithvirajji would walk between the aisles of the Opera House theatre with his eyes lowered, asking for alms for the needy refugees. Rich society women would remove their gold bangles and earrings and drop them in his palms. Such was the compassion he felt for his people.

Once he requested his actor-colleague Sajjan to accommodate Papaji in his residence at Theresa Villa, Malad, a north suburb of Bombay. The two-storey old Victorian structure was surrounded by forest-like landscape, with wild stray dogs howling and barking all night. Malad railway station on the BB&CI railway line was about three miles away, connected by a jungle on Marve Road.

Papaji would sit alone all day and late night in the attic on the roof writing intensively to complete his novel *Aur Insaan Mar Gaya* and the script of the film *Barsaat*. Sometimes, during the day, he would visit the office set up by the Indian government for refugees and get a quota of grain and cloth for himself and his brother Chitu as refugees from Pakistan.

The authorities kept records of ration, cloth and grain purchased in the Bombay rationed area in a number of units with coupons issued to refugees. One could buy 'other cloth'; saris or dhotis and 'coating'—ten units for adults and five for children. The ration period came every six months. One unit was either one yard of coarse cloth or half a yard of fine cloth.

Raj Kapoor's first directorial film *Aag* starring Nargis was not very successful at the box office, but at the same time, after the super success of *Andaaz*, the Raj Kapoor–Nargis pair created a stir at the box office. Desperately hunting for a love story where this star pair potential could be optimally and successfully used, Raj asked his father Prithviraj Kapoor for advice. He suggested Papaji's name. Raj drove all the way to Malad to meet Papaji.

At the historic meeting of the two giants in their respective fields, Papaji told him, 'Yes, I have the perfect story for you with all the nine rasas or emotions, but right now, a broken dagger has pierced my heart which I must first pull out. I must first complete my novel *Aur Insaan Mar Gaya* before I can finish writing the ideal love story for you.' The next day, Raj brought Nargis to meet Papaji and they both were in tears, listening to the first narration of *Barsaat*.

Soon after, Papaji finished writing the entire script. In the film *Barsaat*, Raj Kapoor and Premnath have contrasting views on love. What is love, just lust or a selfless emotion? *Barsaat* made a thunderous statement at the box office. While Nargis's love is pure and selfless, Nimmi dies of unrequited love. The film ran for a hundred weeks and joined the ranks of landmark films of 1949 like *Mahal* and *Andaaz*. Papaji had looked at love not as a fairy tale but as an eruption in the dark depths of the human heart. The story of *Barsaat* made the audience think, and not just feel. A month after the release, Papaji became a writer to be reckoned with. The mind-boggling blockbuster's ticket sale of Rs 1.1 crores (adjusted gross Rs 675 crores for our times) led to the setting up of the sprawling R.K. Studios in 1950. The legendary RK banner logo designed by master artist S.M. Pandit was from an iconic scene in *Barsaat*.

Papaji was paid Rs 7,000 for the story of *Barsaat*. It was the first big cheque of his life. On the day the story of *Barsaat* was sold to Raj Kapoor, my mother went into labour in Delhi in the Daryaganj house. In the government-allotted refugee house she delivered a baby girl. It was as if Goddess Lakshmi had come to Ramanand Sagar's house. After five sons, finally a girl was born, who was named Sarita.

After the birth of Sarita, everything Papaji touched turned to gold. Right up to her marriage, Papaji gave his life's biggest hit films from *Barsaat, Insaaniyat, Paigham, Ghunghat, Zindagi* to *Arzoo, Ankhen* and *Geet*. He temporarily shifted his wife and six children from Delhi to the Malad house in Bombay till the time he made arrangements for an alternate accommodation. From the little money earned as the writer of *Barsaat*, Papaji bought his first home, a 648-square-foot flat in Bhatia Building, Mahim. The chawl-like flat had three rooms of 10 feet by 10 feet in one line on the left side next to a long passage of three feet from the entry door. Behind the passage was a kitchen and on the right side of the passage was a lavatory of 4 feet by 4 feet and a bathing area of the same size. Above the bathroom and lavatory was a small attic.

There were three buildings, one behind the other, and the complex was called Bhatia Building, Brothers Cooperative Housing Society. Bhatia was a builder and encouraged the idea of flats and co-operative housing societies in Bombay. Each block, A, B and C, had around twenty-five to thirty-five flats each. We stayed in Flat no. 24 in C block on the second floor overlooking an empty ground where the Hinduja Hospital stands today. The three single-lined rooms had a very narrow common hanging ledge balcony of three feet. Papaji paid Rs 7,000 for the flat situated at Pittalwadi, Mahim. Now that he had a legal residential address, the first thing my father did was to make ration cards for himself, his wife and six children and his younger brother Chitu, together with our first domestic help, a brahmin, Devilal Shri Krishan. The ration cards were issued by the government of Bombay in June 1950.

The best part of our childhood and adulthood was during our struggle and success period of the twenty-odd years we lived in the 648-square-foot flat among hundred-odd families, mostly refugees from Pakistan. Actor Raj Mehra lived on the third floor.

Comedian-villain actor Radha Kishen and struggling hero Prabhu Dayal lived on the ground floor. In later years the handsome tall well-built Prabhu Dayal married the then reigning heroine Nalini Jaywant. He would flash his Impala Sedan given to him by Nalini Jaywant to all the middle-income group residents. He carried a round tin box of 555 brand cigarettes, flaunting his new social status.

Financiers were queuing up for Papaji to produce and direct a film for his own company. One night, he dreamt of a logo showing a conch shell placed in a lotus floating on the seven seas. He interpreted the image as an announcement of art in the seven seas around the globe. The lotus was the symbol of beauty. The seven seas connect all the countries, religions and cultures of the world. The next day he made a very rough sketch of the logo he had dreamt of, and showed it to me.

And Sagar Art Corporation took birth. After many years of success and a string of hit films, one day I realised the shankh or conch in the logo was a 'Lakshmi' shankh—a Dakshinavarti Shankh with a rare reverse–turning spiral which twists rightwards. The Lakshmi conch occurs only once in 100,000 conches. In 1964, Papaji and I, while visiting the famous Ajanta Caves, saw the same conch painted on the ceiling of a cave. In 1970, we saw the same conch carved in marble outside the Somnath Temple in Gujarat.

Setting up his company in 1950 under the banner Sagar Art Corporation, he bought a biscuit-yellow chocolate-brown Studebaker car. Papaji launched his first film, *Mehmaan*, as writer-producer-director, starring Premnath, Nimmi, Sajjan and Purnima. The film was released in 1953 but was a big flop at the box office. This put the entire family on the backfoot again.

The Sagar Art logo, which stayed for seventy years, was conceived by Ramanand Sagar in a dream in 1950.

Photo collection: Ramanand Sagar Foundation

Balraj Sahni, Anwar Hussain, Ramanand Sagar and others at the premiere of *Bazooband* held at the Royal Opera House.

Photo collection: Ramanand Sagar Foundation

Ramanand Sagar's first film *Mehmaan* and second film *Bazooband*
did very badly at the box office.

Photo collection: Ramanand Sagar Foundation

He sold his Studebaker car and bought a Baby Hindustan. With whatever meagre means and contacts he had, and with help of his friends Ashalata and Anil Biswas, he managed to make a small budget film *Bazooband* with Balraj Sahni, Sulochana, Roop Mala and Om Prakash. Again, the film was a disaster. On the first day of its release at Royal Opera House, my father very proudly took me along to see his labour of love.

We landed in our Baby Hindustan for the noon show and kept waiting at the ticket counter for the audience to arrive. But not a single person came and not a single ticket was sold.

During the making of *Mehmaan*, Papaji was driving his Studebaker car to an outdoor locale in Mahabaleshwar/Panchgani. Also seated in the car were Anil Biswas and Prakash Kohli, the younger brother of the music director, Madan Mohan, who was a promising cinematographer of the time. Papaji recollected how the steering wheel had got jammed for no logical reason as if it was fated to happen. The sturdy Studebaker car swerved to the left, broke the parapet of a small culvert on a dry stream and fell head-on fifteen feet or so on the rocky bed of the dried streamlet. The villagers rushed in, broke the windshield glass and rescued the three of them without a scratch. It reminded Papaji of Tantrik Nityanand's prophecy in 1941 (Chapter 3), giving a detailed visual account of this accident when Papaji could not afford even a bicycle! Cinematographer Kohli had just returned from England, having been trained in the Technicolour Laboratory. *Mehmaan* was his first assignment. Halfway through the making of Papaji's maiden film production he was shot in the chest by an unstable boy near Ratlam. Kohli was the lone passenger in the four-berth first class compartment of Frontier Mail.

On reaching Bombay Central they found his dead body in a pool of blood. There were rumours in the film fraternity that while returning from a marriage from Delhi he was shot to rob the jewellery he was carrying. Train robbers were trailing him from Delhi and since they could not find the right moment to murder him, the information and contract killing was allegedly passed on to the next territory of the Ratlam gang at a price, and they were successful.

The cameraman of *Mehman*, Ramanand Sagar's first film in Sagar Art, was cinematographer Prakash Kohli, the brother of music director Madan Mohan.

Photo collection: Ramanand Sagar Foundation

The partner in Ramanand Sagar's initial productions *Bazooband*, *Badi Bahoo*, etc. was music legend Anil Biswas, husband of Ashalata Biswas.

Photo collection: Ramanand Sagar Foundation

It seemed that the thugs even had their plans in place. The three other berths in the compartment were cancelled at the last moment to target a lone passenger. Papaji was shattered by the loss of a brilliant cameraman for his first venture.

He once told me about memorable incident that took place on the sets of *Mehmaan*. Pandit J.C. Bhakri, Papaji's childhood friend from Lahore, was now handling the production of Sagar Art. A huge statue of Bhagwan Shiva was erected in Famous Studios on the shores of Prabhadevi beach. A song '... *khol de pujari dwar khol de* ...' was being filmed. Papaji, a devout Shiva devotee, realised that there was something missing in the idol, maybe because there was no garland around his neck. It was an early morning 7 a.m. shift. Panditji was assigned the task of getting a garland. The unit waited till late evening and packed up at sunset but there was no sign of the garland.

Late in the evening, Panditji ran to the empty sets with a beautiful garland. In order to save some money, instead of buying the garland at the local Prabhadevi market, he had gone all the way to the wholesale Crawford Market to buy it. Papaji laughed at Panditji's ignorance, as to save a few rupees they had incurred the losses of missing a whole day's shoot. Whether it was *Mehmaan* or *Bazooband*, Papaji's ethics were ever intact. Just imagine losing thousands of rupees to express his bhakti for Shiva Bhagwan with a fresh flower garland. Also, deep down in his soul, he was attracted by the Ramayana. After seeing the mesmerising power of Prithviraj Kapoor and Shobana Samarth's *Ram Rajya* on the cinema audience, he chose to join films to complete his mission and writing. Even in *Bazooband* in 1954 he picturised a song on actress Sulochana with the lyrics of Prem Dhawan '... *bina dosh Sita mata ko diya Ram ne ghar se nikal* ...' (she was not at fault, yet Ram turned mother Sita out of the house) which would form the basis of *Luv Kush* or *Uttar Ramayan*, his TV show in 1987 on Doordarshan.

During the struggle after the failure of *Bazooband*, Mummyji went into a total tight fist mode. Our shirts were stitched at home. A daily wage tailor Bachubhai was hired who had to stitch a minimum of five shirts a day and would be paid Rs 5 as his labour charge. A full thaan or fabric roll was bought from the Kohinoor Mill retail wholesale shop at Shivaji Park.

Once the collar of the shirt became threadbare due to heavy sweating, the paan-chewing Bachubhai would reverse the collar of the shirt for one more use. Except for bidis and many cups of tea, Bachubhai had no other needs. In later years we bought our shirts from the 'Seconds' shop of Liberty shirts on Reay Road at 30 per cent of the cost. A little button defect or a wrong stitch did not matter. The idea was to save every penny. In our spare time we would also weave plastic baskets, do zari embroidery, work on lathe machines and just to make an extra rupee, sell brass powder fallen from the lathe machine and buy cheap carbon iron rods from the Darukhana shipbreaking yard across the shores of Victoria Terminus.

Outside our school, during 'khadi kamaaye', which is putting up a stall to earn some money, I would sell ice-fruit sticks and get five annas for every rupee's sale. This helped me to buy dog-eared second-hand books from my rich classmates at Don Bosco at 25 per cent of the original cost. I would then bind the books on a wooden binding stand, get them cut at a printing press, and sell the brand-new-looking books at 75 per cent to middle-income students. I would use the profit to fund my studies and books. A little extra money was also made by selling old newspapers. I still see the ice-fruit manufacturing unit below the bridge of King Circle station and admire young boys working there to make a dignified living.

Despite the cash crunch, Papaji always strove to give us the joys of a joint family. He would pack us off in the Baby Hindustan for a picnic at National Park in Borivali, now called Sanjay Gandhi National Park (SGNP). We had no cricket bats or badminton rackets to play with, but my parents would lay down a cloth-woven mat and a scrumptious home meal would be served. Those were our first picnics.

Another year, Papaji took the whole family by the toy train to Matheran. He made a deal with a Gujarati lodge-owner for Rs 100 a night for unlimited meals for the entire family. We were heavy eaters and finished the food within minutes.

The next morning the shrewd Gujarati owner returned the money to Papaji and requested him to find another accommodation. He also very sarcastically told my father to treat the meal we had the night before as complimentary for 'your six lovely children'. All the six children exchanged looks and giggled. There was a sigh of relief on the owner's face when we left his lodge.

After the super success of *Barsaat*, Papaji wrote the screenplay and dialogues of *Jaan Pehchan* in 1951 with the same box office hit pair of Raj Kapoor–Nargis, directed by cinematographer–director Fali Mistry. He followed it up with the screenplay of the 1952 hit film *Sangdil*, starring Dilip Kumar and Madhubala. It was an adaptation of Charlotte Bronte's classic *Jane Eyre*. And so, he came into contact with director R.C. Talwar. Papaji wrote two more films with Talwar as director, the 1954 film *Ilzam* starring Meena Kumari and Kishore Kumar with music by Madan Mohan and the 1955 film *Rukhsana* with the same star cast. In 1952 he wrote the story of *Poonam* starring Ashok Kumar and Kamini Kaushal, directed by M. Sadiq with music by Shankar Jaikishen for producer P.N. Arora. The same year he wrote *Shin Shinaki Boobla Boo*, directed by P.L. Santoshi with music by C. Ramchandra.

In 1953, he wrote *Shagufa* directed by H.S. Rawail, starring Premnath and Nimmi, and in 1951, *Badi Bahu*, produced by Ashalata Biswas, with music by Anil Biswas had won Papaji the Mussoorie Film Festival Award for Best Story. The one-and-a-half feet trophy had the four lions of the Ashoka Pillar and was a proud display in the 10 x 10 feet drawing room of the family. He worked day and night to re-establish himself in the industry, especially after the failure of *Mehmaan* and *Bazooband*.

Fate and experience had yet to teach him that directing or writing for a film is different from writing a book. To translate the word into a visual for the medium of cinema was always going to be difficult. What reads well on paper need not lend itself to the medium of cinema is what he had yet to understand.

When *Bazooband* failed, Papaji received an IT notice for the non-payment of dues of Rs 975. To recover the amount, they would

Ramanand Sagar won the Best Story award for *Badi Bahu* at the Mussoorie Film Festival. Ashalata Biswas and Ramanand Sagar holding the trophy of the Ashoka Pillar with four lions for Best Story at the Mussoorie Film Festival and a poster of the movie.

Photo collection: Ramanand Sagar Foundation.

Poster of *Badi Bahu* sourced from the internet.

After the failure of *Mehmaan* and *Bazooband,* Ramanand Sagar wrote multiple films, including *Jaan Pehchaan, Sangdil, Ilzam, Rukhsana, Poonam, Shin Shinaki Bublaa Boo, Shagufa,* etc., and re-established himself in the industry that does not forgive failures.

(Images sourced from the internet)

The faded IT notice of auction of his meagre furniture for recovery of Rs 975 which were his income tax dues for 1950–51.

Photo collection: Ramanand Sagar Foundation

publicly auction the furniture of two single sofas and one double sofa rented for Rs 100 per year from Mistry and Company, Charni Road. The next day the court executors were expected around 10 a.m. in the morning. But a miracle happened and spared Papaji of the shame and loss of reputation which I will talk about later in the chapter.

The failure of *Bazooband* brought the family on the road. All six children had to make a weekly budget of expenses which would then be approved by Papaji. My mother fixed a wholesale rate with a hair cutting saloon next to City Light cinema hall. Every month, we five brothers would stare at the glamorous chart of haircuts displayed in the saloon window. We would point at the window for a 'hero cut' but on reaching home and after a bath, would realise it was the same 'katora cut', month after month. The katora cut was something like a crew cut, as if someone had placed an inverted bowl at the centre of our heads and cut the hair around it mercilessly! After many years we found out that Mummyji would pay the saloon just one rupee for five haircuts once a month!

At times, she would lay newspapers in the narrow long corridor for two or three of us to relieve ourselves at the same time since the one latrine and one bathroom were occupied by older siblings, all getting ready to go to school. So usually it was Moti and Sarita, the two youngest who would sit facing opposite directions with their backs touching each other.

His professional struggles notwithstanding, Papaji was always aware of our academic progress. He would be very happy to find out that Subhash stood third in his class. Little did he know that there were only three students in Class VII of Belvedere School. The manager of the yet-to-open Mahatma Gandhi Memorial Municipal swimming pool gave Papaji a good deal on a lifetime membership for all his six children. We learned swimming there with friends from Bhatia Building and Don Bosco, including Avinash Sarang who later became famous by swimming across the English Channel.

My brother Anand and I would beat Avinash in swimming competitions from the beach outside the pool to Mount Mary Church in Bandra across Mahim Bay. Early mornings we would run from where Hinduja Hospital is right now, up to Worli Fort, and back before going to school, walking a further four miles to King Circle. Subhash and Shanti were admitted to Belvedere School (next to the Scottish orphanage) in Mahim run by a strict South African white family and then did their Punjab Matric in a shed-like shady institute run by a sardar named Gyaniji.

The kind of education they got in Lahore and then in a non-professional institute took a heavy toll on their future life. They worked as car mechanics at Nikhil Garage, opposite Lucky Restaurant, Bandra, under an expert named Sunder. They later opened a lathe workshop on Reay Road and sold automobile spare parts under the name 'Sagar and Sons'. At Belvedere School, Subhash was in charge of drama and Shanti would insist on a major acting role in his plays. Once, Subhash cleverly gave Shanti the role of a corpse lying on the cremation ground while the whole drama was staged around the dead body.

Mummyji was very strict in monitoring the movies her sons could see. Shanti and Subhash would buy two tickets for two consecutive days for the same evening show. One brother saw the first half of the movie the first day and came home, the second brother saw the second half. The second day they would reverse the viewing pattern. This way they escaped being caught missing from home for a long time and watch a movie in spite of neighbours complaining to Mummyji that they saw her sons at the nearby Shree Cinema theatre.

Once they bought a second-hand car from Chor Bazaar seeing only one side of the car, not realising the other side was totally burnt. They moved around from Bhatia Building in Mahim to the Reay Road workshop on a small Yamaha scooter. Anand and I would walk every day from Mahim to King Circle, maybe four miles or so every day to and from Don Bosco High School for over eight years. To save coal, Mummyji would make extra rotis on the sigdi or charcoal stove the night before while cooking dinner.

For our school lunch she would put some white homemade butter on the rotis with a pinch of salt and wrap them in a newspaper. The burning hot coals after the night's cooking were reused in a coal iron to press our school uniforms till the red burnt coal turned into grey ash. The rich children at Don Bosco had maids and lunch tables in the school corridor, laid with napkins, spoons and forks. Anand and I would walk across the huge Don Bosco ground and eat our salted rotis under the coconut trees.

At times we peeled matar ka chilka or pea pod skins to make a vegetable called 'kater' for zero wastage. In winter we dried cauliflower strung with thread for round-the-year summer consumption. Since cauliflower in winter was cheaper than in summer, this novel idea saved a few pennies. Even the waste stem of cauliflower was cooked. Anand and I would win free scout camps by our sheer diligence which was appreciated by our godfather, Macfarren, a Scottish missionary, a guru to us both. He instilled in us discipline, the pleasure of hiking and the joys of being near mountains and rivers. I will always be indebted to him for shaping my character. We won many prestigious awards for the school in sports and scouting. Academically we topped our class and won many diplomas and prizes. The youngest, Moti, was educated at St Joseph's in Wadala and my sister Sarita in the all girls' convent, St Joseph's, in Bandra. The fees were reasonable to the extent that even a lower middle-class person could afford them. The missionary education never ever made us feel poor or inferior to any other rich student. I went to St Xavier's College in Dhobitalao and then to the FTII in Pune. Despite the hardships, the education of the last four children of Ramanand Sagar and Leelavati got a sound foundation.

Prithviraj Kapoor was a genuine humanitarian. He convinced the government in Delhi to free the dreaded dacoit Jagga. Jagga daku had been sentenced to life imprisonment and Prithvirajji requested for him to be rehabilitated back into mainstream society. Realisation had transformed Jagga into a poet and singer. He was so dreaded in Punjab that mothers would make their children drink milk and put them to sleep saying 'Jagga daku aayega'. Prithvirajji had read Jagga's poetry, visited him in jail and heard him singing, playing his ektara. He requested Papaji to invite Jagga to his Bhatia Building flat. We were very excited. The house was filled with admirers and curious

neighbours and friends. As a courtesy, our help Deviram asked
Jagga what he would have. 'Milk,' he replied. Deviram immediately
brought a small Bombay-style cup of milk for the mighty Jagga.
There was suddenly an eerie silence in the air. Jagga took the guest
tray and drank all the twenty to thirty cups of milk followed by
drinking from the entire jug of milk meant for the fifty to hundred
guests. It was a sight to see. Everyone was stunned as Jagga broke
into a bhangra dance. Everyone joined him, forgetting that he was a
dreaded daku. Prithvirajji was very happy and embraced Papaji for
giving Jagga a chance to be accepted in society.

Once Papaji's first film hero Sajjan and music director Anil
Biswas convinced Papaji's actors Raj Mehra and Radha Krishen
staying in Bhatia Building to have a men's day in the tiny flat. All the
wives were put into one room. The men attacked the kitchen, boiling
potatoes, cutting coriander and kneading besan to make bondas
(something like a batata/potato vada). At the end, the wives were
laughing and the big boys crying as the entire cooking session was a
total disaster.

After *Mehmaan* flopped, Papaji owed around Rs 12,000 to its
leading man Sajjan. So when *Ghunghat* succeeded in 1961, he drove
to Sajjan's house and handed him an envelope with Rs 12,000 in it.
Sajjan's eyes were filled with tears as it was his daughter's marriage
and his economic condition had worsened to the extent that it
was difficult to meet the marriage expenses. His son had settled in
America and did not treat his father well. There was a big crack in
their relationship.

Papaji ensured that he never owed money to anyone. If he was
not in a condition to pay up immediately, he would honestly tell
the creditor that he would pay his dues someday. Even with his
film distributors, he compensated their losses with M.G. (Minimum
Guarantee) in his future productions. I have seen Papaji live by his
principle till his end. One day, sometime in the mid-1950s, during his
struggle period, Papaji came home, tired by his search for work. My
mother told him that a gentleman had come to meet him saying that
he was a friend. Papaji thought he must be important because the

neighbours surrounded him. Mummyji had not seen his face. Papaji found out that it was Dev Anand who had come to visit him in his humble flat. Dev Anand had become a big star by then and had a massive fan following.

Dev Anand never forgot his friendship with Papaji, their struggle period together and cherished it even after forty years. Once I met him at the Taj Mahal Hotel. During the making of *Hum Tere Ashiq Hain*, my first directorial venture, I had approached Dev saab for the role of Professor Higgins in *My Fair Lady*, with Hema Malini and Jeetendra. He looked at me and curtly replied, 'I fit into the lover Jeetendra's role and not old Professor Higgins.' *Hum Tere Ashiq Hain* was inspired by Bernard Shaw's *Pygmalion* and to suit the Indian audience I had to have a younger lover in the romantic lead role. Dr Shriram Lagoo finally did the role of Higgins.

Growing up in the 648-square-foot flat in Bhatia Building was an experience of life which I will always cherish. We had to go to City Light municipal vegetable market and buy vegetables at as cheap rates as possible, get free bunches of coriander, whole green chillies, lemons, curry leaves, etc. Also, at times we would accompany Mummyji to Dadar West wholesale municipal market next to Kohinoor Cinema to buy a gunny bag full of potatoes and onions. Even flowers for functions were bought early in the morning at 5 a.m. outside Dadar station wholesale footpath markets. During the Maharashtra-Gujarat riots in the 1960s, we brothers as teenagers, out of curiosity, would go out on the road and run back with gun-wielding police chasing us.

Papaji had formed a close bond with Ashalata and Anil Biswas. They had become family. Anilji would encourage weekly gatherings of intellectuals from the film industry on Sundays at his second-floor residence on Vincent Road. The double-lane road which caters to Mumbai traffic even after 100 years was built by the British as a sample road between Dadar T.T. and King's Circle. The whole building was owned by the Biswas family. Pradeep, being their eldest son, the building was named 'Asha Pradeep'. The creative, well-read group had to write something every week which had to be non-filmy. At the end of the stimulating intellectual session, Pandit Chandrasekhar Pandey, a Ramayana scholar and exponent, would read a part of the Ramayana followed by an analytical discussion. Those who attended these educational sessions included Hindi scholar Pandit Narendra Sharma, Hindi professor Ramlal Shukla, filmmakers like Mahesh Kaul and Phani Majumdar, lyricist Majrooh Sultanpuri, singer Talat Mahmood and writers like C.L. Kavish, Vishnu Mehrotra and P.N. Rangeen. At the end of the session, the entire Ramayana mandali (group) would sing the famous Ram bhajan, *'Sri Ram Chandra Kripalu bhajaman haran bhav bhay darunam ...'*

These regular Sunday Ramayana sessions were the foundation of Papaji's serialised blockbuster *Ramayan* for TV after thirty to thirty-five years.

Ashalata, by birth, was a Kutchi from the Bhagat community who later converted to the Arya Samaj. She came from a poor family and joined films to help run her family. She worked as a leading lady in multiple films in the 1930s and '40s and finally went into production in the '50s after marrying Anilji. One of her close friends and confidante was actress Shobana Samarth, who played Sita in the film *Ram Rajya*. Ashalata's eldest son, Pradeep, was a pilot in the Indian Air Force and died young in a plane crash. Returning from Jodhpur to Begumpet Airport, Hyderabad, his Dakota crash-landed on the airfield. Pradeep used to help us pluck jamuns on Mahabaleshwar Road standing on the roof of the Studebaker car. Ashalata's second son, talented Utpal Biswas, popularly known as Munna, became a music director and died tragically after a fall from the staircase of a bungalow in Lonavala. The youngest son Amit joined the merchant navy and became a shipping magnate. His passion for photography connected him to me deeply. Their only daughter Shikha married an Air Force pilot and did a lot of selfless service as a nurse. The Biswas and Sagar family siblings bonded well, growing up together.

Ashalata produced both of Papaji's initial films *Mehmaan* and *Bazooband*. Her company was named Variety Productions. Even after two flops, Papaji's spirit was alive. During this testing period he was introduced to Kandivali Swamiji who worshipped Kale

Hanumanji. Swamiji was a stout man with medium height, always in a white dhoti kurta and a Maharashtrian type of turban. There are many legends and miracles around Swamiji.

In September 1954 when Papaji's furniture of two single sofas and one two-seater sofa set was to be auctioned publicly in the compound of Bhatia Building following an income tax notice, Papaji was very calm and woke up in the morning as usual and had his cup of tea in his 10 x 10 bedroom. He had not told anyone about the auction. I was sitting on the floor next to him when the doorbell rang. He thought it was the court receivers who had come to make arrangements for the auction. I do not know why, but I insisted on opening the door. There was a well-dressed gentleman at the door. He then took out ten one-hundred-rupee notes, placed them in my palm and walked away hurriedly saying that he had borrowed it from Papaji. He didn't even mention his name before rushing out. In a daze, I handed the money to Papaji. He just smiled and looked at Maa Durga's photo in his room and folded his hands. When the court receivers arrived, he handed them the exact amount to be recovered by the auction and they turned back without a question.

Next week Papaji went to Kandivali Swamiji, who smiled and gave him a folded paper slip which read, 'Sagar, such a day will never come again in your life.' Swamiji knew about the entire IT incident. He became a part of the family and attended all functions such as the marriages of Papaji's six children, including my sister Sarita's marriage in Delhi.

I have personally seen and felt that Swamiji had mastered some 'siddhis' or spiritual magical powers. There are eight classical siddhis like 'Anima' which is reducing the size of your body like Hanumanji did to enter Lanka or to enter the mouth of Surasa the demoness; 'Mahima' which is expanding your body to a large size, again like Hanumanji did many times in the Ramayana, e.g., before jumping across from the shores of Rameshwaram to Lanka or 'Prapti', the ability to be at two places at the same time like Maha Avtaar Babaji was in Kolkata walking on the streets with Yoganand. There are siddhis to vanish, or become small, become very heavy or be at two places at the same time. Hanumanji and Ganeshji have the ability to transfer siddhis to a sadhak. The *Hanuman Chalisa* says, 'Ashta Siddhi Nav Nidhi ke Daata'. Ganeshji's two wives are named Riddhi and Siddhi. There is the 'karn prast' siddhi where paranormal forces appear and tell the sadhak or attainer, 'You have a ten-rupee note in your pocket.' An astrologer or a sadhu, when he meets you, to win your confidence, mentions the ten-rupee note in your pocket. Actually, it's the paranormal force that has conveyed this to him because he has attained karn prast siddhi. I have seen Swamiji walking on the road and just disappearing into thin air. This happened once when after Subhash's wedding, Swamiji left Sagar Villa to walk towards Laxmikant-Pyarelal's house in Juhu. I was behind him and suddenly I just could not see him anywhere.

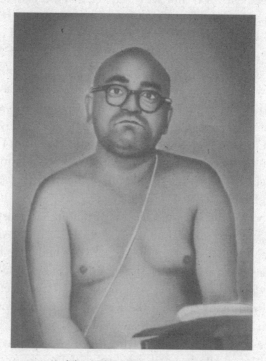

Kashikar Maharaj (Kandivali Swamiji)
Photo collection: Ramanand Sagar Foundation

Later, some of his devotees told me that at the same time he was counselling troubled souls in the premises of the Kale Hanumanji Temple in Kandivali. Till today I often go and sit in front of Kandivali Swamiji's statue behind the mandir to pay my obeisance.

Papaji was a firm believer in the blessings of saints and siddha purushas. During the family's dark uncertain days, he would make genuine efforts to seek their blessings. Once, sometime in 1954, he took all of us to Shirdi to pay homage to Sai Baba, whose life-like statue had recently been installed. By this time, Papaji had bought a second-hand Dodge, a strong sturdy car. We stayed the night in the chawl-like dharamshala which had common public washrooms in the compound of the temple. It took us almost a whole day's journey via Nagar to reach Baba's shrine. In the morning we had Baba's darshan and his life-like statue looked wonderful and blissful. The neem tree was there, so also was Dwarkamai.

Every year, for over fifty years, Papaji and the whole family would visit the holy shrine to seek Baba's blessings. Even when Shanti's daughter Geeta was hospitalised in Pune with little chance of survival, Papaji, at midnight, sent me to Shirdi to get the miraculous holy ash or bhasma, from Baba's samadhi. I arrived in the early hours and Geeta soon recovered from a coma she had slipped into, the minute we put a little ash into her mouth.

In the early '50s, Papaji visited a saint, Nityanandji, in Ganeshpuri. Devotees called him Bhagwan Nityanand. Papaji himself drove the car via Bhiwandi onto a dusty bullock cart road to Ganeshpuri. Bhagwan Nityanandji was lying naked on a cot. The soles of his feet were white. Many devotees were seated all around him offering fruits and garlands.

Nityanandji appeared to be in a different state of consciousness. My eldest brother Subhash, without any instructions, went straight ahead and touched the feet of Nityanandji. He woke up from his 'neend mudra' (trance-like state) and stared angrily at Subhash. He shooed him away and Subhash was very frightened, not realising what had happened. Later, Papaji told us that such a siddha purusha does not want anyone, let alone a devotee, to touch their feet, since the power of the golden aura around their body is diluted.

Once Papaji's ex-assistant Bolten Nagi had eaten a live bat flying around his room out of sheer hunger during his days of struggle. Without any warning, he held Nityanandji's feet and begged him to cure him of a dreaded disease he had caught by eating a bat. Nityanandji scolded him, got angry, shouted at him and even threw stones at him. But miraculously, Nagi got cured just by Nityanandji's touch. Nityanandji became our family's ishta guru. Right up to 1961, we had our guru's grace on us.

Nityanand means 'always in bliss'. Before the age of twenty, Nityanandji became a wandering yogi. He gained a reputation for performing miracles. His devotees have seen him pay his workers daily wages for making an ashram in Kerala by diving into a crocodile-infested pool and producing a handful of money. By 1923, he had wandered to the Tansa Valley in Maharashtra. In 1936, he took shelter in a hut outside the Shiva temple in Ganeshpuri. As his devotees increased, the hut expanded into an ashram. Workers were paid wages by Nityanandji by pointing at rocks where their money was either miraculously found or miraculously kept. He had the power to transmit spiritual energy or shaktipat to his ardent devotees by just keeping his hand over their heads. Muktanand of Ganeshpuri was the chosen one on whom Nityanandji showered his kindness.

It is believed that Muktanand used to drink the water flowing from Bhagwan Nityanand's bath. Later many film stars like Vinod Khanna and foreigners from around the globe became Muktanand's disciples. He would give them an experience of kundalini awakening at a cost. He wrote the book *Chitshakti Vilas,* one of the best books I have read on consciousness. Once, late at night, Papaji had to rush to Ganeshpuri with Dr Hemant Kumar to nurse Muktanandji back from a heart attack he had. Papaji was surprised and shocked seeing all the rich carpets and expensive items in Muktanand's private chamber.

After the darshan of Bhagwan Nityanand in Ganeshpuri, prayers and a visit to the temple of Vajreshwari, which was just one kilometre away, always followed. A bath in the hot springs of Vajreshwari was a must, with a packed lunch under a chaddar-covered pandal at a nominal rent. In *Navanath Kathasar* it is mentioned that Machindranath served Vajreshwari Yogini Devi for a month by giving her a hot water bath daily, brought forth by himself. The ancient hot springs of Vajreshwari are a testimony to that. There are around twenty-one hot springs within a five-kilometre radius of the temple. The prominent water springs are named after Surya, Chandra, Agni, Vayu, Ram, Sita, Lakshman, and so on. Many have been cured of their skin diseases, polio and physical disabilities after taking a bath in the hot spring water of these kunds.

Bhagwan Nityanandji spent most of his time in the Vajreshwari temple. He also renovated the temple of Gorakhnath–Machindranath, whom he admired as his guru. Today the Nath Mandir right opposite the Vajreshwari temple holds the 'padukas' (footprints on stone) of Bhagwan Nityanand. The temple's main inner sanctum has the saffron murti (idol) of Maa Yogini Vajreshwari, on her left is Goddess Renuka (Parshuram's mother) and on her right is Goddess Kalika (the village goddess). The samadhi of the seventeenth century Giri Gosavi saint Godhadebuwa is on top of the Gautam hill, behind Mandargiri hill rock where the temple is located. The temple is taken care of by the Shree Vajreshwari Yogini Devi Public Trust, and members of the Giri Gosavi sect are its trustees.

Over the last seventy years Maa Vajreshwari has been our ishta devi. For all my new ventures and on birthdays I make it a point to get the blessings of Maa. There is a mystic and spiritual charge in and around the temple. Saints and siddha purushas like Nityanandji, his disciple Muktanand and presently Satyanand, all of them stayed in and around this Shakti Peeth. At present the temple is managed by Anita Gosavi, a direct descendant of Ramchandragiri Gosavi belonging to the Gosavi sect. I have personally witnessed many possessed souls being brought to the temple. Vajreshwari Temple was rebuilt by Chimaji Appa, a sardar of the Peshwas in 1739. It is regarded as one of the Shakti Peeths in India. The town of Vajreshwari, seventy-five kilometres away from Mumbai, was called Vadvali in the Puranas and was visited by Bhagwan Shri Ram and Parshuram. The hills in the area are a residence of volcanic ash where

Parshuram performed a yagya. Shree Vajreshwari, an incarnation of Maa Parvati, is located on the Mandargiri hill rock. The legend says that Indra and Devas went to Maa Parvati, requesting her to slay the demon Kalikala. The goddess suggested that they wage a war and said that she would come to their rescue at the right time. In the battle, Kalikala swallowed or broke all the weapons thrown at him. Finally, Indra hurled his vajra at the demon, which Kalikala broke into pieces. From the broken vajra emerged the goddess and slayed the demon. The gods sang her praises as Vajreshwari and built her temple. Lord Ram requested the goddess to stay in the region of Vedvali and be known as Vajreshwari, the goddess of Vajra or thunderbolt.

In the next few years, Papaji worked day and night to get his foothold back in the film fraternity as a writer who delivered meaningful content with commercial success. He wrote dialogues for the hit film *Rajkumar* starring Shammi Kapoor, Sadhana, Prithviraj Kapoor and Pran, directed by K. Shankar. During the making of *Rajkumar* he came in touch with Sadhana whom he cast after a few years in *Arzoo*. In 1959 he wrote *Didi* for producer Sadashiv J. Row Kavi, starring Sunil Dutt and Feroz Khan. Again, he chose Feroz Khan in 1965 for *Arzoo*. During this period of struggle, Papaji worked tirelessly on a script about Ashoka the Great. Since Sohrab Modi was a star for costume dramas, he sold the script to him. He was so fascinated with the subject and the research that had gone into the script that was so original that he could not resist buying it from Minerva Movietone, Sohrab Modi's production house, despite the tight monetary crunch. Papaji even met Pandit Jawaharlal Nehru in Delhi to discuss the finer details of Ashoka's era. Panditji informed him how women in that period wore high-heeled sandals as mentioned in the research of historians Lal and Panicker. Papaji was very impressed by the fact that Panditji, who, despite being the prime minister of India, took out some time and gave invaluable inputs on Ashoka. During the time when he was in a very poor economic condition, Papaji received an invitation from the government of India's education ministry headed by his well-wisher Abul Kalam Azad. The invite was to go on an all-India tour.

It was a month-long, all-expenses-paid tour with a group of progressive writers handpicked by Azad and sponsored by the government of India. It was indeed a commendable progressive scheme to uplift and project the general public. At night he told all of us and his associate Rangeen saheb about the invitation. We persuaded him to go. He was concerned about us and wondered who would take our responsibility. Rangeen saheb and Papaji at times indulged in the ouija board, summoning 'spirits'. They would sit across a table with the English alphabet (in capitals) written on a sheet of paper. One side had two words, 'Yes' and 'No'. Numbers from one to ten were also written boldly in one line on the sheet. A small half-inch candle was placed on a metal coin and lit in the centre and then covered with a metal lid to put the candle out, inviting a spirit roaming in and around the area. Both of them would put their index and middle fingers on both sides of the metal lid. A question was asked and the lid would move to the alphabets to form a word or to 1234 to indicate a date or answer yes or no or they would have to work out a code to get the answer. I would sit on the floor, watching this supernatural play of spirits. Papaji asked the spirit if he should go on the tour. And the spirit said 'Yes'. He asked who would take care of his family in his absence. But the only answer he got was 'Go'. Convinced that he was destined to go on the tour, he packed his bags.

We children broke our piggy banks and collected a few coins. My mother managed to collect a hundred rupees or so, hidden in her jars or below a pile of old clothes in the cupboard. Papaji very reluctantly left for this destiny-changing journey. The last halt was Madras, now called Chennai. The entire intellectual writers' group got out with their baggage to be escorted to some government accommodation in the city with a few visits and lectures at institutions on the agenda. A short man, wearing a spotless white dhoti, was moving all around the platform asking who among them was Ramanand Sagar. He told my father humbly, 'I have come to receive you on behalf of Gemini Studios.' Papaji immediately recognised him and was shocked to see that the head honcho of Gemini Studios, S.S. Vasan, had personally come to meet him.

Telegram from Gemini dated 20 October 1955 requesting Ramanand Sagar to rejoin Gemini Studios.

Photo collection: Ramanand Sagar Foundation

Gemini Pictures was the top production house of the Indian film industry with superhit films like *Chandralekha*, a milestone in Indian cinema. S.S. Vasan, known as the Cecil B. Demille of India by film historian Randor Guy, had been closely following Papaji's literary and film-writing graph. He wanted to infuse fresh talent to expand the institution beyond Gemini Studios.

The rest is history. Papaji's first film with Gemini Productions was *Insaniyat*. He convinced Vasan to bounce back with a mega starcast film. Papaji, having worked with all the top stars, brought actors he had earlier worked with, including Dilip Kumar, Dev Anand and Bina Rai, together. Vasan punctuated the mega star cast with 'Zippy', a cinema-trained chimpanzee from Hollywood. *Insaniyat* made the Gemini flag flutter. The Gemini Twins bugle blew pan India and S.S. Vasan, opened distribution offices across India in all major film circuits, including Kastur Building at Nariman Point, Bombay. One success followed another. On 20 October 1955, Papaji received a telegram from Vasan requesting him to come back to Madras to rejoin Gemini Studios. This was right after the success of *Insaniyat* which was released sometime in 1954.

Papaji wrote *Paigham* (1959) starring Dilip Kumar, Raj Kumar and Vyjayanthimala. *Raj Tilak* (1958), starring Gemini Ganeshan, Vyjayanthimala and Padmini, had screenplay and dialogue by Papaji, who also wrote and directed *Ghunghat*, followed by *Zindagi*. All films were blockbusters in a row. The Gemini conglomerate became a formidable entity in the film business with their studios, film laboratories and distribution offices. Ramanand Sagar became a big name again and a star who had made it on his own talent and strength.

Papaji often told me that his only guru, who taught him film craft, editing and the skills and intricacies of mass media communication,

Rajendra Kumar, Ramanand Sagar and Dilip Kumar at the premiere of *Zindagi*.

Photo collection: Ramanand Sagar Foundation

was Vasan. He used to call him 'Boss'. Vasan tapped the intellectual writer in Papaji and opened his boundless creativity to the masses, to all age groups and religions. Vasan used to host test marketing shows of his films before release. The sample targets were women, school and college children, lawyers, doctors and people from middle class and upper class income groups. He gave all of them a gift and the thrill of seeing Gemini movies before release and a questionnaire to fill in, talking about the best or worst scene of the film, what made them laugh or cry, and so on. After the show, Vasan would sit in his office alone and analyse the answers. He would then re-edit the film and at times ruthlessly delete a whole scene! It was under Vasan that Papaji grew to be a master filmmaker who could later garner a viewership of 650 million for his TV serial *Ramayan*.

Born in 1904, Vasan started as a journalist and writer. During his early struggling days, he wrote light pornographic masala novels, at times one novel a day, to earn his daily wage. Such novels were popular and sold at railway stations. He graduated to start a Tamil magazine *Ananda Vikatan* and slowly rose to become a business tycoon. Vasan's mother was his north pole star or dhruv tara who gives direction to sailors lost in the ocean.

Papaji often used to tell me a story, not known to many, of Vasan saheb's rise to fame and wealth. Vasan was fond of horse racing and at times would bet on horses that were underdogs. His study of equestrian history and genetics was admirable. He came across a horse named Gemini who he felt had great potential but had never won a race. He made a deal with the owner and started training the horse secretly at night. When the day of the kill came, he got Gemini into the race with maximum odds. Vasan sold his mother's jewellery, borrowed money from his friends, collected as much money as he could and put it all on Gemini, and Gemini won, to everyone's shock! Vasan became rich overnight and with the money he won, he bought Gemini Studios. Padma Bhushan Vasan went on to become a member of parliament in 1964.

Once it was Papaji's birthday and the children decided to give him a surprise. We had one common cupboard for five brothers where

A young Ramanand Sagar in the mid-1930s

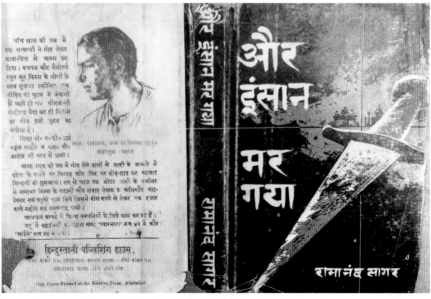

An early cover of the novel, *Aur Insaan Mar Gaya*

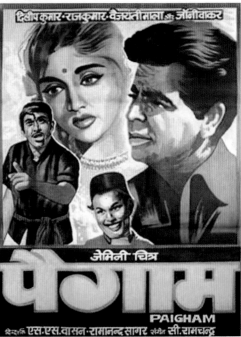

Posters of *Zindagi* (1964) and *Paigham* (1959), both extremely successful Gemini productions

Stills from *Charas*, a movie which was shot extensively in Malta.

Another still from *Charas*

Ramanand Sagar and the Kashmiri leader, Sheikh Abdullah

Stills from the shooting of *Ramayan*

Another still from the shooting of *Ramayan*

This iconic photograph of Arun Govil as Ram and Deepika Chikhalia as Sita was perhaps the most enduring image of the show, *Ramayan*.

TV spell cast by a Hindu myth

A bride was late for her wedding in the Satara district of Maharashtra. She explained she had been watching *Ramayan* on television.

Two new ministers were late for their swearing-in ceremony at the President's palace. It was suggested that they had also been watching *Ramayan*.

Hundreds of thousands of people all over India — including my Hindi teacher, for example — will not make an appointment for 9.30 on a Sunday morning for fear of missing an episode of the television serial with a special appeal.

When a group of people in Bangalore found that they had to miss an episode, they demanded that the episode be repeated immediately, and threatened mass demonstrations if it did not appear.

Ramayan is India's most successful television serial, watched weekly by an estimated 40 million. The advertising revenue it generates amounts to about 10 million rupees (£450,000), 10 per cent of the monthly income of Doordarshan, the state-run television network.

But the story of *Ramayan* is as well known as a Bible story would be in the West. It contains no surprises, and is agonisingly slow to unfold.

It tells one of the best loved legends of the Hindu religion; Rama, an incarnation of the god Vishnu, born the eldest son of the King of Ayodhya, is banished to the forests for 14 years at the urging of his stepmother. He is accompanied by his brother, Laxman, and wife, Sita. She is kidnapped by Ravanna, the wicked King of Lanka, and eventually rescued by Rama with the help of Hanuman, the monkey-god.

Rama's high moral principles lead him to put Sita aside, even though he knows she remained faithful to him during her imprisonment. She is driven to suicide, but her funeral pyre does not burn her and so she is proved publicly to be innocent. Rama and Sita return in triumph to Ayodhya to take possession of his inheritance.

Not much there to transfix a nation, you might have thought, especially since the heavy gilded costumes appropriate to gods and demons lend a certain formality to the proceedings, and the tale is told only slowly: one recent episode was devoted almost entirely to a debate between Rama and the sea god about whether parting the waves, Moses-like, to cross to Lanka would not be contrary to the nature of the sea.

But transfixed the nation is, and more, for the viewers often become worshippers, draping the television set in cloth and setting out joss-sticks and candles before it like an altar while the programme is on. Arun Govil and Dipika Chikhlia, who play Rama and Sita, are greeted with religious reverence in public as devotees scramble to touch their feet.

Some object to state television in an avowedly secular society devoting so much effort to a strictly Hindu religious story, and feminists object to the evident subjugation of Sita to her husband.

But the Broadcasting Ministry has allowed an extension of the number of episodes, and imitators of the serial's success are said to be planning the serialization of another Hindu epic, the *Mahabharata* — the history of Krishna, another incarnation of Vishnu.

The serial's producer, Mr Ramanand Sagar, seems to have been infected with the grandeur of his project. "This achievement has been bestowed on me by God," he has said. "It is not a human achievement...I don't take criticism seriously."

Michael Hamlyn

THE TIMES - LONDON
MONDAY 22 FEB. 1988
PAGE 8

The *Ramayan* phenomenon received worldwide attention as this February 1988 article from *The Times* (London) illustrates.

Ramanand Sagar receiving the Padma Shri from President K.R. Narayanan in 2000

This Ramayan stamp was released by the Department of Posts and Telegraph in 2017

everything from our love letters to our underwear, school uniforms, books, etc., were stacked, on one shelf each. Someone brought out an apple he had hidden, one made a birthday card, another wrote a poem. The treasure trove was in place but the problem was the money required for the ticket and the journey from Bombay to Madras. The neighbourhood kids pooled in, and with the money the five brothers had put in, there were just sufficient funds collected for the two-day journey. Mummyji was told that Anand was going to a five-day scout camp. In the train to Madras, Anand shivered with cold, and the family sitting next to him gave him a bedsheet and some food to eat, thinking he had run away from home.

Anand went straight to the sets of *Paigham* with actor Pran about to give a shot. A single lone voice 'Happy Birthday to you Papa' echoed on the floor. The bag of goodies, poems and cards was opened in front of the stunned unit. Everyone was misty-eyed. Pran saab picked up Anand and started clapping, followed by unit members joining in. Papaji was deeply touched and moved by his children's love. Anand was given a royal treat and stay.

During Papaji's stint in Gemini, all of us would visit him in Madras. The family would board a third-class unreserved compartment. The boys would jump through the windows at the beginning of the platform itself as the train rolled into the station and occupy one upper and one lower birth lying across the wooden seats. My mother would make besan ladoos and methi parathas for us for the two-day journey.

Once, after the first day of the journey, our train halted for over three hours in the midst of nowhere. It would not move because of some technical hitch. Following other stranded passengers, we managed to walk to a small hamlet where we could buy some cheap idlis to fill our growling stomachs. On reaching Madras, we were not recognisable because of our black faces, due to the coal and smoke of the steam engine.

In the same ghastly condition, Papaji drove us straight to the Dasaprakash lunch home for an unlimited meal. We had our first full South Indian meal, with multiple rice items and sambhar, rasam and curd topped with pure ghee helpings. Papaji was given an old-style huge bungalow in T. Nagar all to himself where he stayed alone with caretakers, a cook and servants. We had never seen or stayed in such a huge house. We went mad running up and down and all around. Summer holiday fun had just begun.

We boys would wander on the streets of T. Nagar wearing the same gaudy red shirts and yellow pants since our mother, to cut costs, would buy the same cloth from wholesale markets and make clothes for us. On one of our trips to Madras, Papaji planned to take the family for a budget spiritual holiday. We travelled by train to Tanjore, Pakshi Tirath, Rameshwaram, Dhanushkodi and finally to Meenakshi Temple at Madurai. It was the last day, and the train was to leave before midnight. Papaji searched his pockets and realised he had no money left to feed his six hungry children. We were all huddled in a group, sitting silently on the long stone stairway in the temple premises. No one spoke a word, but Mummyji and Papaji knew their children were starving after a hectic day. Papaji looked at Maa Meenakshi pleading for some divine intervention. Suddenly, a Namboodiri priest from Kerala rushed towards us with banana leaves filled with prasad that had rice, dal, vadas and sweets, among other things. He told Papaji that the prasad was for him and his family. Papaji smiled at Maa's kripa.

During his days at Gemini Studios, Papaji once came across a Tamil brahmin named Subbu in Madras. Subbu suggested that Papaji go to Madurai and Tanjore temple towns and meet the Nadi Shastra exponents and the astrology pandit. Nadi astrology believed that past, present and future lives of all humans were written by Rishi Agasthya in the ancient Tamil script. The Nadi palm leaves are searched by the thumb impression, right for men and left for women.

This act is like a password, like in computers, to open the 'transmigration of souls' file and all births of the individual. Papaji may have been born 300 times in 30,000 years. Nadi astrology is like a mirror of your karmas or deeds in your previous births. As it is, my father always believed in astrology and met the best astrologers all his life. While in Madurai, the Nadi astrology palm leaves of Papaji's

Ramanand Sagar and wife Leelavati performing the first Durga Saptashati havan in 1954 in their small flat in Bhatia Building, Mahim.

Photo collection: Ramanand Sagar Foundation

present life were found. The advice given by Agasthya Rishi was to perform a Durga Saptashati havan every ashtami. A havan is a Hindu ritual of offering grains and ghee while reciting mantras to Agni Dev, thereby creating a spiritual positive energy and aura all around.

The word 'havan' comes from the Sanskrit root word 'hu', meaning 'to offer'. Havan is also called yagya and is a Vedic ritual where you sit around a fire and make offerings with the chanting of mantras to please the Gods to get blessings for certain objectives. Durga Saptashati is a collection of 700 shlokas or verses in praise of Maa Durga. Papaji was in a fix as to how to perform this ritual in the right Vedic way. He went back to Madras and started inquiring about a shastri who was well-versed in Nadi astrology and Vedic rituals. Before entering or leaving Madras, Papaji would never miss going to Kapaleeshwarar Temple in Mylapore, Madras. Only once, after shooting, he rushed to the airport, but the flight had already departed. Papaji left the lounge and proceeded to the parking lot, praying to Kapaleeshwarar. Soon after, there was an announcement that the Bombay flight was coming back due to a technical snag. The flight took off again with Papaji on board. This was his spiritual bond with his Maa Kapaleeshwarar.

A few days later, he came across a Nadi scholar, who advised him to put the holy kalash or pot on an Indrayani Yantra drawing filled with coloured rice and recite the Indrayani mantra twice between each shloka of 700 shlokas of Durga Saptashati. Hence it meant a total of 2,100 mantras during the entire havan, offering ghee after every three mantras and a fruit or a different offering at the end of every chapter (thirteen chapters). Having understood the ritual, the difficult task was to find a brahmin to do the havan. Papaji's search took him to the narrow busy lanes of Kalbadevi in Bombay where thirty-five people live and survive on one square foot of floor space.

Under the wooden staircase of a heritage brick and wood Mangalore-tiled building he came face to face with a tantric pandit named Chandrashekhar. On inquiry he confirmed he was a specialist in this ritual and would be privileged to bow before Maa Durga. So, the first havan on Ashtami of Navratri in 1954, when he was with Gemini, was performed by Papaji in our house at Mahim.

It is said there are approximately 70 million mantras which are melodic mathematically structured meters resonant with numerous qualities. The word mantra can be broken down into two parts: 'man' which means mind and 'tra' which means transport or vehicle. Mantra is a Sanskrit word meaning sacred message which connects with the divine within ourselves. The vibrational power of each specific mantra is the power of the deity that presides over it. The Kapaleeshwarar Temple had kapal (skull) worshippers as devotees in a bygone era. As per legend, Shiva Bhagwan cut off the kapal of Brahma for lying about finding the end of the pillar of fire created by Shiva. Hence Brahma built this temple with the slain kapal as the shivling. Also, Shiva Bhagwan's consort Maa Parvati became a peahen to please her god, Shiva. After the birth of their son Kartikeya whose mount is a peacock, she gave him a spear to vanquish the demons. In the Kapaleeshwarar Temple Parvati is worshipped as the Karpagambal goddess of the wish-yielding tree.

The most memorable period of the family had started. Year after year, the Durga Saptishati havan was performed. It was the biggest spiritual and social event of the family. Friends and residents from all the three buildings visited us to become part of this yearly ritual. Chandrashekhar Swamy was a very hard taskmaster and a perfectionist. He would put us kids and the women in the family in charge of little tasks for over a week. Buying marigold flowers from the wholesale market in Dadar, stringing them in multiple different size garlands for the gods, collecting five different kinds of mud, water from seven rivers and the sea, and eleven different kinds of leaves; we gathered all of this. The toughest job was to make chandan (sandalwood) paste from a solid sandalwood block by rubbing it for hours and days on a flat surface until there was no wood block, only paste. Many miracles happened to true devotees who stayed the whole night, putting offerings in the fire of the havan kund made of bricks and cow dung.

Mrs Raj Mehra had not had a baby for twenty years. Opposite her flat was a Sindhi hotelier family in a two-room, 350 square feet flat. One room was occupied by five brothers and their wives. They had bedsheet partitions to keep their privacy at night. One room was occupied by the head of the family and over eight children of the five brothers. One of the teenage brothers was named Hemu. He fell very sick and was shifted to the nearby National Hospital. Moments before his death he fervently requested and pleaded to call Mrs Mehra to see him. Holding her hand, he said, 'I am coming to your house,' and died. Within a month she was pregnant. It was a miracle!

Mrs Mehra was an ardent devotee and would participate in the havan with great fervour. It seemed like Maa Durga had blessed her and our other neighbours like the Nanda and Bhakri families.

Papaji and Mummyji religiously performed the havan from 1954 to 2004. In 2004 Papaji made seven havan kunds, one for himself and his wife, and one each for his six children's families. In 2005, my father passed away. After Papaji's demise, Maa Durga's blessings fell into my kitty to continue the havan since my elder brothers couldn't do it for health reasons. Our family has followed the ritual right up to 2018 and hopefully the next generation will continue with the yearly ritual.

We brothers had a strong bond and so many childhood memories. We would pool in twenty-five paise each, every week, and from the kitty of one rupee and twenty-five paise, we would buy one Kwality vanilla ice cream stick. The one who won the lucky draw licked and ate the ice cream while the other four watched him, waiting for their turn in the next four weeks to come. We played games like vanjwati, kitti kitti, one leg langdi taang and badminton with two rackets among fifteen kids on the terrace. We flew kites, stole manja (thread coated with glass), broke glass window panes to make our own glass thread, had gang fights with rivals from other buildings over manja, but all in good fun! We pinched rasgullas from street vendors and burnt Diwali cracker rockets in a bottle kept on wooden planks, which at times flew into different flats creating havoc. The cops would come looking for the naughty culprits and we would pretend to sleep on the burning terrace.

Our childhood was full of joys and pranks. We carried rented cycles on our shoulders to the terrace of the three-storeyed building and the bet was to pedal a minimum of a hundred rounds of the huge terrace; and on holidays or Holi, cycle from Mahim to Chembur to buy the cheapest water balloons. The Diwali sparklers had to be aimed at the top of the coconut tree crown. A mob of twenty rowdy boys would jump up and down right above the flat of character artiste Raj Mehra to not let his unwell wife sleep because she wanted only her little son to play on the common terrace!

During the making of Ghunghat in 1959-60, Papaji faced an uphill task. He approached Meena Kumari with whom he had worked earlier. She was thrilled hearing the script in her make-up room in Filmistan Studios, Goregaon. She told him tearfully, 'This is an ideal role for me. I want to and would love to do this film. But, you know, my fate and decisions are not controlled by me...' Papaji immediately understood that a puppet's strings are always held by someone else, and walked out. While going out, he passed by three to four bodyguards who were not only listening to the actress' conversation with Papaji but were also restricting entries and exits from her make-up room!

Finally, Papaji managed to get Bina Rai, a superstar once who he had closely worked with, but who had totally faded by then. Bharat Bhushan and Pradeep Kumar were the male leads. The only fresh and upcoming star was Asha Parekh. Music by Ravi was another saleable credit. The release was fixed at Royal Opera House, the top movie theatre of that period. The frontal view of the theatre was reserved for multiple banners extending from Hughes Road to Lamington Road. These banners meant prime exposure for a film and its box office potential. Papaji drove down to the magnificent theatre on the release day to realise there was only one banner on display!

Someone from the Gemini organisation had sabotaged the fate of the film. Their distribution offices in every city were instructed not to spend a single rupee more than required for a minimum release. But then history was made as *Ghunghat* turned out to be one of the biggest black and white box office hits ever. Bina Rai won the coveted Filmfare Award for Best Actress. Papaji became the undisputed movie mogul. From the money earned from *Ghunghat*, he bought an old bungalow on Linking Road towards Santacruz for a lakh-and-a-half rupees. He tried his best to vacate the Jain tenant residing there earlier.

Finally, after waiting for five years, he sold it off to a builder and bought a small one-acre farm on the Bombay-Pune Highway between Panvel and Khopoli for Rs. 5,000 only. As time passed and with the success of *Zindagi, Arzoo* and *Ankhen*, Papaji slowly expanded the mango orchard farm to over forty acres. Every year he would celebrate his birthday on the farm as a staff picnic. The entire Sagar Art staff would drink, eat, play cricket and make merry. That day was everyone's day. Everyone was an equal on that day. The most-awaited part of the day was the prize distribution ceremony where everyone got a gift or a prize, from a refrigerator to a steel almirah to an electrical oven. Anand and I would manipulate the lucky draw to ensure that the biggest and most expensive gifts went to the lowest salaried staff. Of course, Papaji was part of our plan.

During the making of *Paigham*, its stalwart lead stars always wanted to hog the limelight. There were ego clashes a number of times. Papaji had worked with Dilip Kumar on a number of films from *Sangdil* to *Insaniyat*. They had mutual respect for each other's art. It was known that if you had Dilip Kumar in the lead and Ramanand Sagar as the dialogue writer, no way would Dilip saab give a shot if the lines were changed or fiddled with, until Papaji was called on the set, even if it meant cancelling the shoot for a day or a week.

Their combination was lethal. Raaj Kumar was aware of that. One day on the sets in Gemini Studios, in a highly dramatic scene of a clash of ideological difference between two brothers, Raaj Kumar said, 'Jaani, this scene's lines do not do justice to my fiery character; please bring in more drama than the soft-spoken brother of mine, Dilip Kumar ...' There was dead silence. No one had ever spoken to Papaji in such a commanding tone. He and Dilip Kumar looked at each other. Papaji called his first assistant and said loud enough so that everyone could hear, 'Please tell Raaj that the character is more important than the actor. I cannot change the lines even if I want to, as the philosophy behind the ideological clash between the two brothers will be diluted. The actor will overtake the content ...' and he went and sat on the director's chair. It was dark all around and no one spoke or even whispered. Time kept ticking, both the actors sitting on their chairs in deep silence. Hours passed and slowly Raaj Kumar rose and walked up to Papaji and said, '*Kya shot hai, jaani?*' The shooting resumed in a tension-filled atmosphere. Papaji went on to win the Filmfare Award for Best Dialogue while Dilip Kumar and Raaj Kumar never worked together again till Subhash Ghai brought them together years later in *Saudagar*.

Arvind Kejriwal, in his swearing-in-speech ceremony as chief minister of Delhi, quoted C. Ramachandra's song '*Insaan ka insaan se ho bhaichara ... yehi paigham hamara ...*' Iconic films like *Paigham* are not easy to remake as there are multiple factors that have made them iconic, as in this case the combination of Dilip Kumar and Raaj Kumar, with the dialogues of Ramanand Sagar. The making of

Zindagi during Papaji's stint with Gemini Studios was his crowning glory. He had secretly signed Rajendra Kumar, so that no rival could get a whiff of the casting coup.

Papaji booked the entire presidential suite of the Taj Mahal Hotel in Bombay. Superstar Rajendra Kumar was sent word and the deal was locked, signed and sealed in the presidential suite. The entire film industry woke up to the biggest movie announcement of its time. I remember my brothers and I had gone to the presidential suite, jumped all around and ordered the choicest ice creams.

During this period, Papaji was not only associated with Gemini Studios but also wrote for other filmmakers. His star was on the ascent as he had come a long way from his Prithvi Theatre days. From *Barsaat* to *Zindagi* and *Ghunghat*, his career had seen ups and downs but Papaji had risen above circumstances and marched ahead every single time. He had truly become the 'movie mogul' of that era!

8

PAPAJI'S RISE AND RISE:
FROM *ARZOO* TO *RAMAYAN*
MOVIE MOGUL TO TV CZAR
(1964–87)

In 1965, Papaji wrote, produced and directed *Arzoo* under his own banner of Sagar Art and created box office history. It was his company's first comeback film; superhit *Arzoo* took him to international shores including Berlin, Moscow, Sydney and Tashkent. From 1961 to 1970, Papaji was the writer, producer and director for six silver jubilee mega hits in a row—*Ghunghat, Zindagi, Arzoo, Ankhen, Geet* and *Lalkar*—a unique unparalleled record on the Indian screen.

I have always felt that *Arzoo* is Papaji's best work. Though he told me that it was inspired by *An Affair to Remember*, I think *Arzoo* starts where *An Affair to Remember* ends. During the outdoor shooting of *Arzoo*, Papaji had bought tons of artificial red poppy flowers and laid them on the banks of the Dal Lake. This was the site of his most remembered and perhaps best silent love scene, where Rajendra Kumar and Sadhana are walking together with only their thoughts speaking to each other. '... where does this road go, Usha? ... you are thinking of this road; I am thinking where the road of life will lead us ...' goes one memorable dialogue. Ghulam Mohammed

Sadiq, the then chief minister of Jammu and Kashmir, on a visit to the location asked Papaji how he managed to find the poppy flowers at that time of the season. Papaji just smiled.

Hasrat Jaipuri, the lyricist, was specially flown to Srinagar to visit all the locations that Papaji had chosen for filming a poignant sad song at the separation of the selfless lovers. The song was 'Bedardi Balma Tujhko'. Looking at the silent lake reflecting the pure love of Sarju and Usha, Jaipuri was inspired to write '... *iss jheel ka khamosh darpan tujhko yaad karta hai* ...' The real life-like visuals woven with the lyrics made the song a superhit, and the audience felt for Usha's fate. I have yet to come across a film director who has conceived and written lyrics matching the locations.

Papaji wanted to get the exact red-brown autumn colour of the crumbled chinar or maple leaves, which he had seen during his time in Srinagar. He would receive daily phone-call updates from the tourism department describing the autumn state of the maple trees. Sadhana had kept her bags packed and the unit shot off to

The white dress designed by Oscar-winning Bhanu Athaiya worn by Sadhana for *Arzoo*.

Photo Collection: Ramanand Sagar Foundation

the autumn-brown valley of Srinagar within hours of the tourism minister's telephonic confirmation about the required colour of the chinar. That was the kind of dedication the actors had. A super busy star like Sadhana flew to Srinagar within hours of the call for the shoot since that particular hue of sad autumn was going to last only a week or so, before winter set in. The pristine white salwar kameez designed by Bhanu Athaiya, the Oscar-winning dress designer, did the rest.

How the evergreen song was recorded within hours is also very interesting. Papaji was shooting in Raj Kamal Studios in Parel. Music director duo Shankar and Jaikishan had assembled a hundred-piece orchestra for some other song they were scheduled to record, which got cancelled. Jaikishan rushed to Papaji and told him that the best-ever hundred-piece orchestra was ready, along with playback legend Lata didi (Lata Mangeshkar) and sound-recording wizard Mangesh Desai, with his high-end technical recording studio—so why not record the song he had in mind! Papaji was caught unawares, but he didn't want to let go of the opportunity. The problem was that the tune had not been finalised or even rehearsed. Jaikishan pulled in a square wooden stool and started drumming on it with his fingers, humming and composing the tune. Slowly, the sound stage echoed with his voice in kali panch pitch and the song was born. The alaap before the song was one of Lata didi's best. For over half a century, the lyrics and the song topped the music charts. Even today, many music critics believe it to be Lata didi's best song.

While filming another intense love song, '... *Aji rooth kar ab kahan jaiyega* ...' where the two lovers lock eyes, a funny incident took place. The unit had three or four shikaras running alongside the shikara being filmed. On the shikara with the filming unit was Mr Shivdasani, Sadhana's father. In his enthusiasm to see his charming daughter, he kept moving back and forth, and ended up falling in the cold waters of the Dal Lake. The shoot came to a halt, but much to everyone's relief, he was immediately pulled out of the icy water.

Most critics felt that Sadhana never looked more beautiful than she did in *Arzoo*. Her costumes became a national craze among teenagers. Sadhana was an excellent cook and would rustle up delicious biryani for the entire unit. Being a still photographer and painter myself, I think the heroines who looked most beautiful on the silver screen are Sadhana, Madhubala, Hema Malini, Simi Garewal, Perizaad Zorabian and Ingrid Bergman (*Casablanca*).

Ramanand Sagar filmed *Arzoo*'s famous shikara love scene and the song 'Aji rooth kar ab kahan jaiyega … Jahan jaiyega hamein paiyega …' on the picturesque backwaters of the Dal Lake. Ramanand Sagar brought Kashmir to the audience in a way rarely seen before. Even today, Kashmir Tourism uses photos and clips filmed for *Arzoo* in their brochures.

Photo collection: Ramanand Sagar Foundation

With *Arzoo*, Ramanand Sagar brought Kashmir to the audience. People had never seen something so beautiful before. Till date, Kashmir Tourism uses the pictures of Kashmir filmed as part of the movie's publicity material.

All the money earned from the premiere of *Arzoo*—organised by Vanita Samaj in Shivaji Park—was donated for the welfare of ship-building painters, especially those who contracted tuberculosis from inhaling paint fumes. Some of the money earned was used to make a badminton court in the premises of Vanita Samaj. After the success of *Arzoo*, guru S.S. Vasan called up Papaji, saying that he wanted to produce a Tamil remake of the film. 'Can I have the rights? What will it cost me?' he asked. An emotional Papaji replied, 'Boss, it is all yours ... never ever talk of money ... I can never ever repay you for the Saraswati kripa you have bestowed on me. I am sending you the print by the next flight.'

A week later, the boss rang up again. 'Sagar, I cannot make this film. It is not possible to capture what you have done. I cried (while) watching it and realised it is not possible for anyone to make *Arzoo* again.' After seeing the film, especially the climax, Vasan saheb had realised this could only be done by someone mad about cinema. Papaji had portrayed the visuals of heavy snow all around to project the tragic irony of ski champion Sarju (Rajendra Kumar) limping with an amputated leg, refusing to recognise his true love, Usha, who had been desperately looking for him. Sarju walks away with a walking stick, saying, '... *aapko dhoka hua hai! Main toh bachpan se hi apaheej hoon* ...' (You are mistaken. I have been a cripple since childhood.)

The whole unit and the stars were kept on red alert, waiting for snowfall at Kufri in Shimla. The two busiest superstars of their time rescheduled their shooting dates and rushed overnight to Kufri to make Papaji's vision of the heartbreaking climax come alive. The crippled ski champion lies to his lover because he truly loves her; he doesn't want to ruin her life, and makes the sacrifice of leaving her. 'Sacrifice' is one of the nine rasas or emotions in Bharat Muni's *Natyashastra*. Sarju wants to sacrifice his love at the altar of duty.

Ramanand Sagar waited for the snowfall in Kufri, above Shimla. Super-busy stars Rajendra Kumar and Sadhana rescheduled their dates and reached Kufri overnight to film Ramanand Sagar's vision of the boundless snow and the tragic irony of a ski champion who, now a cripple, refuses to recognise his true love.

Photo collection: Ramanand Sagar Foundation

For four days, no unit member dared to leave their hotel room. It snowed incessantly with howling winds and blizzards. After seven days of testing, when it still kept snowing, Papaji told both Rajendra Kumar and Sadhana, 'I am grateful and touched by your passion, but we have to be practical. Here are your tickets. You can leave, but such snow landscapes happen rarely, and this sequence may not only be memorable but also perhaps be the best scene of the film.' The next morning had Mediterranean blue skies, with white fluffy snow. The skies opened up, and Papaji and his crew shot the beautiful unforgettable climax. *Arzoo* was nominated for many Filmfare Awards for acting and technical finesse, perhaps for more than six awards in various categories, but got none, for some reason.

But on international shores, it won the Best Story Award at the Tashkent Film Festival, was screened at the Berlin Film Festival, and was the official Indian entry at the Film Festival in Moscow as well as in Sydney. The film was bought by the USSR and dubbed and released all over the Soviet Union, with a massive 2,500 prints. In India, it won twenty-five awards, had the box office rocking, with sixteen silver jubilees and all-time box office records at forty-two stations. During its screening at the Berlin Film Festival, Papaji met Satyajit Ray, who had won a Silver Bear for his classic *Charulata*. Ray asked Papaji about me and what I was doing. Papaji told him that I was a fourth assistant to cinematographer G. Singh. Ray retorted, 'If you do not give him a film with credits of a cinematographer, I will come to Bombay and take him with me to Calcutta.' Ray had seen my student film *Rose Bud* and had highly appreciated it publicly in the FTII (Film & Television Institute of India) auditorium, especially the handheld camerawork of chasing a rabbit and a child. He was serious in his proposition. Papaji came back from Berlin, drove straight to Pune, saw my gold medal-winning diploma film *One Plus One* and—in the next issue of the trade weekly, *Screen*—announced my name as the cinematographer of *Lalkar*. Navin Nischal, the leading man of *One Plus One*, was chosen to be the hero of Mohan Sehgal's *Sawan Bhado*. Rehana Sultana, the heroine of *One Plus One*, won the National Award for Best Actress in 1970 for her role in *Dastak*.

All the money earned from *Ghunghat* and *Zindagi* went into the making of *Arzoo*, but it was still not sufficient, so Seth Kapurchand of Roxy Cinema, Lamington Road, agreed to finance the entire film.

In India, *Arzoo* won over twenty-five awards, scoring sixteen silver jubilees and fourteen station box office records.

Photo collection: Ramanand Sagar Foundation

That's why the world rights of *Arzoo* were with Kapurchand and Company. At the time of the release of *Arzoo*, Kapurchand owned not only the iconic Roxy Cinema but also (as someone told me) half the buildings that lined the Queen's Necklace at Marine Lines, Bombay. Even today, three buildings stand there—'Kapur Mahal', 'Keval Mahal' and 'Zaveri Mahal'.

Papaji would tell us the success story of the super-rich Seth Kapurchand, but the veracity of that incredible story and Kapurchand's kismet (destiny) cannot be confirmed. He had left home when he was

За мир, социальный прогресс
и свободу народов!

Диплом

Фильму

« Любовь в Кашмире »

(Индия)

За участие в кинофестивале

Arzoo won the Best Story Award at the Tashkent Film Festival, was the official Indian entry at the Sydney and Moscow Film Festivals, was screened at the Berlin Film Festival, and Sovexport released *Arzoo* with 2,500 prints.
Photo collection: Ramanand Sagar Foundation

still a boy, with just a four-anna coin in his pocket, accompanied by a loyal servant of his father—perhaps a khazanchi or treasurer in the courts of Bijapur. Seth Kapurchand stayed in Kalbadevi Temple, surviving on the prasad given by the devotees. A month or two later, he got a job as a shopkeeper with a rich wholesale cloth merchant in Kalbadevi.

Unknown to Kapurchand, the partners of the shop had an internal dispute. One of the aggrieved partners made a plan to ransack the entire shop to recover his dues. One night, sleeping on the backroom floor of the shop, Kapurchand heard some robbers counting the bales of cloth, worth a fortune, as if the entire goods were being illegally distributed. Hearing them talk, the teenager realised it was one of the partners. He decided to get in on the loot. There was nothing

За мир, социальный прогресс
и свободу народов!

Диплом

Рамананд Сагар

(Индия)

За участие в кинофестивале

Ramanand Sagar received the Best Script Award for *Arzoo* from the Writers Union of Soviet Republic.

Photo collection: Ramanand Sagar Foundation

wrong, he thought. With his loyal servant, Kapurchand barged in and demanded a share of the loot or else, he threatened, he would call the cops. They reached an understanding. The robbers took one bale and the young boy took another, with the value of the cloth left to one's luck. With the money earned from selling the cloth, Kapurchand opened a small film distribution office and landed at the biggest film company, 'Bombay Talkies', to buy the worldwide rights for their about-to-be-released film, *Kismet*, starring Ashok Kumar. Though the actual price of the film was around Rs 80,000, seeing the small boy and his enthusiasm, they quoted a price of Rs 1.20 crores. The loyal servant realised Kapurchand was being cheated and decided to leave. But Kapurchand took out his cheque book and wrote a single cheque for the entire final agreed amount. The rest is history. The first blockbuster of India, *Kismet*, earned much more than a crore of

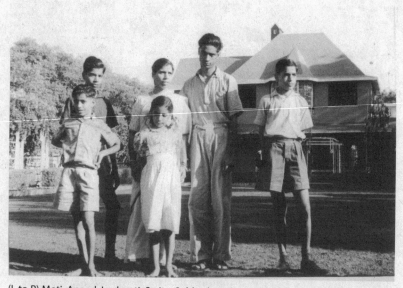

(L to R) Moti, Anand, Leelavati, Sarita, Subhash and me. Seth Kapurchand's bungalow in Pune in the background.

Photo collection: Ramanand Sagar Foundation

rupees, equivalent to over seven hundred crores in today's times. It ran at the Roxy Cinema, Calcutta, continuously for over three years.

Roxy Cinema in Calcutta was a theatre for the entertainment of the British soldiers during the Second World War. No exhibitor was ready to release *Kismet*, keeping in mind the exorbitant price Kapurchand had paid for the distribution rights. The exhibitors thought the film would doom their theatres. Not finding any exhibitor to release his ostensibly foolishly bought film, Seth Kapurchand purchased the Calcutta Roxy theatre from the British. He took one more risk and released *Kismet* in a single screen in Calcutta, in his own Roxy Cinema, which still had a theatrical stage before the viewing screen. The success of *Kismet* changed his destiny.

Once, Papaji took us to Pune to stay at Sethji's bungalow. We were shocked to see him sitting on the footpath outside, with a weighing scale, selling grapes picked from his farm behind the bungalow. Perhaps this is what made him 'Seth' Kapurchand. At night at the dining table, we could not believe when the butler cut out only two slices of the alphonso mango and threw away the guthli (kernel). For us, wasting any part of the expensive mango was sacrilege!

Papaji shot *Arzoo*, *Ankhen* and *Geet* in the Kardar Complex. B.R. Chopra's *Dharmputra* and *Waqt* were also shot in the same complex. His younger brother Yash Chopra was groomed and learned film craft techniques in Kardar Studio. Those days, there were whispers about Yash Chopra wanting to marry his *Waqt* leading lady, Sadhana. Many hit films of L.V. Prasad and G.P. Sippy were also shot here. Kardar Studio was very lucky for all of us.

There are many interesting anecdotes related to our time at Kardar. Sudhendu Roy was the art director of most films shot in Kardar. He had a great sense of camera lenses, perspective and compositions. He would also design his sets in such a way that they were always camera-friendly. The entire Dal Lake in the film *Arzoo* seen behind Sadhana's house was painted on the huge backdrop all around the studio floor but kept slightly out of focus, or hazy. This made it look realistic.

Roy's backdrop painter, Yusufbhai, was a genius. Illiterate, paan-chewing Yusuf bhai, in dirty white pyjamas and shirts not washed in weeks, would use brooms and sticks instead of paint brushes, to paint the forty feet high and 200 feet in circumference backdrop. He would spray colour on the canvas cloth using a long rubber pipe, pumping with a cycle pump the liquid colour from a tin bucket. At times he would throw colours using a household broom to paint the sky or water. Up close, all the visuals looked smudgy, but on screen one could not make out that the backdrop of the Dal Lake behind Sadhana and Nazir Hussain's house in the film was actually the floor of the Kardar Studio. Yusufbhai's great camera sense was also seen with the backdrop of the Dal Lake for Nandu's (Mehmood's) houseboat interiors. Producers and directors would not leave him even for a day. He slept, ate and freshened up in the studio compound, mostly on the floor itself. One huge massive background painting of 8,000 square feet would take him a week or so to finish.

One day, Yusufbhai walked into the cabin Anand and I shared. He put his hand in the pockets of his pyjamas and took out wads of 100-rupee notes. He threw them into the air and kept doing so repeatedly. Then he yelled and laughed hysterically, shouting, 'What should I do with all this money? I cannot go home ... I do not meet my family! What is the use of this money if I cannot enjoy peace, happiness and good health?' This incident made me really sad. I realised that in show business, you get fame and money but no peace and happiness. Yusufbhai was a legend in his field, as was his mentor Sudhendu Roy. Once I mentioned to Dada that we were tight on budget and could not afford a set depicting a cave. Dada requested me to get a pile of old newspapers and created a killer set with just the paper pulp and brown paint. What an innovative and accommodating art director Dada was, compared to the present crop of art directors who spend extravagantly on film and TV show sets.

Furniture from Sharaf Ali's shop was Sudhenda's favourite. Sharaf Ali Furniture Company, established in 1936, was the most

This statue of Krishna came into Ramanand Sagar's life in 1968, during the making of *Ankhen* and stayed lifelong with him. It was an inspiration for the TV serial *Shri Krishna* in 1993.

Photo collection: Ramanand Sagar Foundation

sought-after supplier to the post-Independence film industry. A spiritual incident connects Papaji with Sharaf Ali for the filming of the song *'Meri sunle araj banwari ... tere dwar khadi dukhyari'* written by Sahir Ludhianvi, sung by Lata Mangeshkar with music by Ravi. Sudhenda hired a marble statue of Shri Krishna from Sharaf Ali. When he entered the film set, Papaji felt a spiritual connect with the idol. After the shoot, he told Sharaf Ali to name his price, as he did not want the idol to be returned. Later, Papaji got a Radha made by the master moulder Phadke of Natraj Studios, since he could not see Krishna without Radha. Every day, Papaji religiously prayed at the feet of Radha-Krishna in his office at Natraj Studios. The smile of Radha Rani captured by the master craftsman Phadke was mystically alive. Her eyes looked into your soul. Even today the two statues, with Papaji's energy, adorn a prime place at the entrance of my office, Sagar World Multimedia. Shri Krishna had entered Papaji's life in 1968, leading him to make the TV show *Shri Krishna* in 1993, which topped television rating charts for over 120 weeks.

At the time *Arzoo* was being filmed, the present top art director Sharmishta Roy was very young and was being trained by her father Sudhen-da. Papaji and Sudhen-da worked together on hit films like *Arzoo, Ankhen, Geet, Lalkar* and *Hamrahi*.

I used to take a local train and travel third class from Matunga Road station to Marine Lines and then walk to St Xavier's College. Film producer A.R. Kardar's beautiful daughter Rukhsana would arrive in her limousine. B.R. Chopra's son, Ravi, and daughter, Shashi, were my seniors. Actor Kishore Sahu's daughter, Naina, Feroz Khan's brother, Sameer and Balraj Sahni's daughter, Shabnam, were also studying there. Papaji had his office Sagar Art Corporation in Kardar Studios owned by A.R. Kardar. B.R. Films, G.P. Sippy and L.V. Prasad were also tenants of Kardar saheb. Ramesh Prasad, Ramesh Sippy, Ravi Chopra (Kuki) and Narinder Bedi (son of the author Rajinder Singh Bedi) all grew up together in Kardar, playing underarm cricket during lunch breaks. Kardar Studio was a training ground for all of us, where we learned filmmaking. After the success of *Arzoo*, Papaji decided to make a spy drama, *Ankhen*. In search of a newcomer, Papaji and I went to Kohinoor Cinema in Dadar to watch *Shola Aur Shabnam*, starring a tough-looking newcomer named Dharmendra. Papaji liked his big sturdy hands and thought how perfect they would look holding a pistol! Papaji immediately signed him for *Ankhen*. *Phool Aur Pathar* starring Dharmendra, who was rumoured to have a romantic thing going with its leading lady Meena Kumari, was released earlier. The superhit and box office success of *Phool Aur Pathar* forced Papaji to change the scale of his small-budget spy thriller. Finally, *Ankhen* was shot around the world—from Iran to Hong Kong and Japan. It is the biggest money-spinner of the Sagar Group to date. Dharmendra became a superstar.

Ramanand Sagar, in search of a leading man for his patriotic spy thriller, saw newcomer Dharmendra in *Shola Aur Shabnam* and was impressed by his huge hands. Dharmendra was soon signed on as the leading man for one of his most memorable and successful box office films, *Ankhen*.

Photo collection: Ramanand Sagar Foundation

In *Ankhen*, Ramanand Sagar conceived an unusual sequence, whereby Dharmendra is imprisoned in a cage, with a tiger guarding the cage. To film the sequence, a special cage was made for cinematographer G. Singh.

Photo collection: Ramanand Sagar Foundation

While shooting *Ankhen*, Papaji conceived a very unusual sequence of leading man Dharmendra imprisoned in a cage guarded by a tiger on the loose outside the iron bars. The dramatic sequence full of suspense culminates in a hand-to-hand fight between the tiger and the hero, at the end of which the 'He-Man' Dharmendra tricks it and escapes. The production team found a tigress called Uma Devi. Her trainer gave off a pungent body odour, which desisted Uma Devi from coming near him. A special cage was made for cameraman G. Singh, to film the sequence in safe conditions.

Only after the camera unit was fitted into the iron-barred cage would Uma Devi be brought on to the set—hanging upside down, tied to a solid wooden pole shouldered by four people, just as a marriage 'doli' is carried. Many years later, some unit members were told that one of the carriers of the 'doli' was the Indian guru, cult leader and philanthropist Satya Sai Baba of Puttaparthi. I don't know if this is true, but there was a rumour for sure.

One day during the shooting, Uma Devi came running, jumped over the camera cage and just vanished into thin air. There was a big hue and cry. Unit members present on the huge thirty-by-sixty-feet floor climbed up the footboards for set lighting, hanging twenty feet above the ground. There was panic all around. The main studio compound gate was immediately shut to prevent the tigress from running off to the main road leading to the King Edward Memorial (KEM) Hospital. After hours of search and confusion, Uma Devi was found snoring behind the canvas backdrop of the floor, sleeping peacefully. Apparently, Yusufbhai had painted a jungle on the studio floor backdrop and it looked so real that Uma Devi believed it was a real jungle and went and hid behind it, frightened of the humans and the studio lights around.

While shooting in Japan, we stayed in Hotel New Japan. I was twenty-three and was in charge of all the passports, travellers' cheques, permissions, etc., which were in a briefcase with me. Returning from Osaka in a bullet train—my first time and a once-in-a-lifetime experience—we reached our hotel, quickly freshened up and left for a Japanese dance opera. On return, Papaji asked me for the invaluable briefcase. My face turned red as I had left it in the bullet train some five to six hours back! Everyone was shocked. After a brief meeting and consultations with senior unit members, Papaji and I went down to the hotel reception to figure out what could now be done. The man behind the counter smiled calmly and asked us to go to the lost-and-found department at Tokyo Central. We could not believe it when we saw the suitcase in a row of over hundred briefcases neatly lined on the shelves in the lost-and-found room.

And though the briefcase wasn't locked, everything in it was totally intact. The attendant just let us take it without any questions asked, simply because we claimed that it was ours. I have never seen a more honest people than the Japanese. Papaji had hired an A/C luxury bus to take us all around Japan—the hot springs of Hakone, the Buddhist temple in the city of Kamakura, which housed the forty-three-feet high bronze Buddha statue; and Kyoto's Red Temple, the head shrine of God Inari (god of rice), the patron deity of businesses practising Shintoism, the traditional religion of Japan.

The government of Japan had given us a tourist guide and interpreter to facilitate our shooting schedule. The entire unit travelled by the same bus, including the leading pair—Dharmendra and Mala Sinha—and family. The Japanese guide was silent the entire time, not speaking to anyone and relaxing, with minimum communication. While shooting in the Red Temple of Kyoto Shrine, Papaji told Dharam and Mala of the mischievous suspense-filled love scene where they just had to look at each other. As soon as Dharam drank the holy water with a wooden ladle, a high priest charged towards us, pointed a finger at Dharam and placed the ladle back, with respect, into the holy water well. Our hitherto non-communicative guide opened his eyes, came out of the bus, took a kung fu pose as seen in Bruce Lee films, ran and jumped six feet in the air, and drop-kicked the angry priest on the ground! All were stunned. He firmly said something to the head priest in the local language and asked us to resume shooting. He was like a leopard in disguise. Later, we learnt that he was a black belt commando guide specially designated

Ramanand Sagar shot *Ankhen* in locations from Japan to Iran. In Japan, he shot inside Kyoto's Red Temple, the head shrine of God Inari, and also filmed Japan's famous tourist attraction, the forty-three-feet bronze statue of Buddha at Kamakura.

Photo collection: Ramanand Sagar Foundation

for our protection. No one dared disobey his command—he had kicked the head priest for merely pointing a finger at the guests of their country.

One night, Dharam, Shanti and I decided to go pubbing. We arrived at a nightclub. Dharam found a very chic Japanese babe in a green outfit at the bar and invited her to join us for a drink. She sat at our table. While Dharmendra could not take his eyes off her, she kept ordering drink after drink for all of us. Our hard drinks were coloured, her drink was transparent. After a few pegs we were all drunk, but she was on her feet—alert. We later realised she was drinking water in the guise of vodka. We were told that it was a regular practice at these nightclubs.

The pretty ladies were on the bar's payroll. They had to cater to multiple clients and ensure the clients ran up a huge bill. We left the bar all smiles and with no money, hailed a taxi and showed him the matchbox with our hotel address. The taxi driver murmured something and sped away. Dharam, with his liberal Punjabi vocabulary, broke the silence of the midnight Tokyo streets. It was a laugh riot. We had no idea what to do in such a situation—deserted streets, no money and in a half-drunk stupor. Suddenly, we heard the sound of an engine behind us and saw the headlights of two cars approaching us. We thanked our stars—our cabbie had taken the trouble to look for a taxi to take us to our hotel, which was outside his jurisdiction. In Japan, since cabbies speak only in the local language, every hotel has matchboxes with printed maps and addresses for the tourists' convenience. Imagine the Good Samaritan Japanese cabbie, finding a cab at 3 a.m. to help three unknown tourists whom he could have fleeced and taken advantage of!

The next day 'Garam Dharam' went to the massage parlour in the hotel lobby. For company and bill payment, he requested Rangeen saheb, who handled production, to accompany him. Lying in his birthday suit he saw a young pretty girl come in and start massaging Rangeen saheb. Excited, Dharam waited anxiously to see who would turn up for him, when in walked a middle-aged, strong-fisted masseuse. She put her hands under the sheets and started pounding Dharam's body like a sumo wrestler. She was tough even for Dharam, the muscle man. He kept winking at Rangeen saheb and whispering in Punjabi to exchange the masseuse, but Rangeen saheb refused, saying 'to each according to his kismet'. The unit members went into peals of laughter when Rangeen saheb later narrated the incident over Japanese sake (rice whisky) at night.

Shaw Brothers Ltd., Robinson Road, Singapore, were the Southeast Asia Distributors of *Ankhen*. Papaji had formed a personal friendship with Run Run Shaw based in Hong Kong during his stint at Gemini Studios. Once a journalist had asked why he was called Run Run Shaw and he had replied, 'Because I run very fast.' The Shaw Brothers had a sprawling business spread all over Hong Kong with over hundred Chinese film productions to their credit. Run Run Shaw's younger brother, based in Singapore, invited the entire unit for drinks and dinner at his palatial mansion. After a whole day's shooting in the Thai Dancers statue garden in Singapore, the unit got ready for the big evening. Ramy, Run Run's younger brother, had called for special cooks from Shanghai to play host to the top filmmaker from India. The entire unit seated on a single long dining table was served by butlers and uniformed waiters. But after tasting the first morsel of the food served, everyone looked at each other with disappointment. The food was unpalatable, bland and insipid. Every dish was raw—mutton, fish, prawns and vegetables. Dance master Satyanarayan became our saviour for the day as he had carried a bottle of lime pickles from India. At night, the unit feasted on bread, pickle and their 'Patiala' pegs. When Run Run Shaw came to Bombay with his wife, Papaji held a grand reception for him.

Having finished shooting in Japan, the entire entourage moved to Iran where the overseas distributors of *Ankhen* had their business and offices. It was mutually decided earlier that on landing in Tehran, the distributor would fund the overseas expenses out of his overseas distribution rights dues. The next day the entire unit was crestfallen. It seemed something was not right. The story going around was that the office of the distributor had refused to pay unless Papaji signed an additional contract with more clauses. It was a pure backhand bullying tactic. It seems Papaji refused, flew to London, arranged for funds to get the unit and production free of all expenses for them to leave for India after the short shooting stint in Iran. He did not react or utter a single word to the wealthy distributor brothers, who had made a fortune with box office hits like *Arzoo* and *Sangam*. Papaji gracefully retained and valued his friendship with the family till the end, visiting their London office and eating home-cooked meals by a Sindhi cook in their London house.

Papaji had a philosophy—everyone's decision is based on the code of ethics that one believes in. In those days, it was common for film distributors to find a moment of weakness or circumstance to squeeze a better deal.

In the *Ankhen* song *'Tujhko rakhe Ram, tujhko Allah rakhe ... de data ke naam tujhko Allah rakhe ...'* actors Mehmood and Dhumal

Ramanand Sagar filmed the famous *'Tujhko rakhe Ram ... tujhko Allah rakhe ...'* on the streets of Tehran (Iran).

Photo collection: Ramanand Sagar Foundation

were dressed as fakirs who live solely on alms. After sunset, someone would lay a carpet in the middle of the Star Hotel in Tehran where the unit was staying. After a while, a few unit members chanting mantras and folding their hands would guide the two fake fakirs on to the carpet. One unit member would pretend to go to the fakirs for their blessings, and in turn, the two actors would touch his head with peacock feathers and bless him. The act was to put a $1 or $5 or $10 bill in front of the fakir, fold hands, touch his feet and leave. This was followed by a few more unit members doing the same thing. The word was spread among the guests of the Star Hotel that they were holy, spiritually elevated men who could cure all their life's problems. Many a foreigner would follow suit and drop a green dollar bill in payment for the fake blessings. At the end of the day nothing less than a few hundred dollars would be collected, which would then be equally distributed among all the 'thugs' who participated in the 'holy' drama.

Working with a multi-talented artiste like Mehmood also had its share of drama. While shooting the climax of *Ankhen* at Roop Tara Studios in Dadar, the entire staff was on red alert for the twenty-four-hour day-and-night shoot, since the release date had been committed. Actors, technicians and unit members ate and slept in the studio premises—except for the captain Ramanand Sagar who kept awake all night and all day, taking only cat naps on the director's canvas chair. After arranging the shot at midnight, Papaji would order his assistant to fetch Mehmood. One day, Mehmood bhaijaan left the shoot late at night, without informing Papaji. On hearing he had left, after waiting for over twelve hours as per the roll call time, Papaji drafted a legal notice mentioning the humiliation and mental torture Mehmood had caused to his fellow actors and the unit. As soon as Mehmood received the telegram, he was on the sets, at the feet of the maker. After that, in spite of superhits like *Arzoo* and *Ankhen*, with Mehmood in a major role, Papaji never cast him again in any of his movies.

Such incidents happened not only with actors but also with technicians. While shooting the superhit song '*Milti hai zindagi mein mohabbat kabhi kabhi*' at the hot springs of Hakone, there was a clash between Papaji and the cameraman. It was the last day of the shoot. Time was running out. Mala Sinha—dressed in a Japanese kimono, holding an umbrella—was singing lyricist Sahir saheb's lines. But the rain would not stop. The atmosphere was heavenly and would have only added meaning to the beautiful lyrics. G. Singh, the cameraman, refused to take the shot, pleading bad light and that a bad shot would ruin his reputation. Papaji tried to put some sense into him asking him to at least take the shot, since it wouldn't be

While filming the song '*Milti hain zindagi mein mohabbat kabhi kabhi ...*' for *Ankhen* in the Japanese hill station Hakone, the weather got bad and cameraman G. Singh refused to shoot in the bad light so as to not tarnish his reputation. Being the last day, and as is the director's right, Ramanand Sagar forced G. Singh to film the song. The song won G. Singh the Filmfare Award.

possible to come back to Japan and it was the last day of the shoot. If the shot was not good, Papaji assured Singh, they could reshoot it in Bombay. But G. Singh was adamant. A frustrated Papaji came to me. I was in the second year of the cinematography course at the FTII. I told him, 'This will be an award-winning shot for any cameraman. Such divine light with multi hues and tones—nature only opens up sometimes.' G. Singh won the Filmfare Award for best cinematography for *Ankhen* and Ramanand Sagar for direction, but the latter never hired G. Singh for any of his future films. He firmly believed that it is the director's duty to be more responsible for a fellow technician's work, but a technician cannot refuse the captain of the ship. Filmmaking is a director's medium.

Ramanand Sagar won two Filmfare Awards—Best Dialogue in 1960 for *Paigham* and Best Director in 1969 for *Ankhen*.

Photo Collection: Ramanand Sagar Foundation

As for *Arzoo*, there were multiple nominations for *Ankhen* too, but it got only two Filmfare Awards. The industry gossip was that the jury refused to budge for these two prestigious awards even if over six awards were given to a much lesser-deserving film, perhaps due to financial equations. *Ankhen* was Papaji's biggest box office grosser, with a diamond jubilee run (seventy-five weeks) at Society

Cinema, Ludhiana. It smashed box office records at over forty-eight stations with silver jubilee runs at twelve stations and hundred days at twenty-five stations. It bagged more than fifteen awards on the home turf, including the UP Film Journalist Association Award for best colour film, best actress and best supporting actor. It was also screened at the Indian Film Festival in Moscow.

During the premiere of *Ankhen* at Ludhiana, Dharmendra's fans went berserk. They wanted to catch a glimpse of their Punjab-da-Jat and son of Ludhiana. One of the fans, not being able to see him through the tinted glasses of the limousine, picked up a stone and smashed the windscreen for a better view of his idol seated on the front seat. Dharmendra very coolly brushed off the glass pieces, came out and hugged the over-enthusiastic fan. The fan, a stout Punjabi, was in tears and begged forgiveness saying that he could not help it and did it out of love.

The lettering for the poster of *Ankhen* was inspired by the lettering of Dunhill cigarettes.
Photo collection: Ramanand Sagar Foundation

The lettering of *Ankhen* was inspired from the lettering of Dunhill cigarettes. The 'k' and 'h' straight lines divided the layout in three parts, making it creative and projecting its spy thriller angle. The ingenuous letterings were designed by Papaji's favourite publicity designer, Diwakar Karkare of Studio Diwakar. Diwakar was a talented creative designer who had graduated from the J.J. School of Arts in Bombay and was a genius at creative designing. The biggest production houses and even stars made a beeline to his humble one-room studio in Shivaji Park. Diwakar's speciality was painting with a palette knife or overpainting with a knife. Green was his favourite colour. He believed that in the seven colours of the rainbow, the first three colours violet, indigo and blue represent water whereas the last three yellow, orange and red represent fire—and when water and fire combine, they give birth to life which is the colour green (since all foliage is largely green).

After *Ankhen*, Ramanand Sagar had begun shooting for his next film *Geet* in Kardar Studio. But there were problems brewing between Mr Varma, who owned the land, and Mr A.R. Kardar, who had perhaps leased it. One day, court receivers walked in to seal the studio floors, as rumoured, due to non-payment of dues to Mr Varma.

The light boys put the seal of recovery only on the very low-value base stands that hold the lights and not on the multiple 2K, 5K and 10K lights of huge value. It seemed Mr Kardar had cleverly won over the confidence of the workers. At night, on the sly, all the studio lights were cleverly removed from their base stands without disturbing the court auction seal and transported in a truck outside the studio compound. Ironically, they all lost their jobs and the studio was shut permanently. The light boys were perhaps not even compensated for their good deed. All the big filmmaking institutions under one roof—Sagar Art, B.R. Films, L.V. Prasad Films, G.P. Sippy Films and Pramod Chakravorty Films—had to pack up and vacate the Kardar Studio set up in the early 1940s, technically one of the best studios, fitted with the best equipment and with air-conditioned make-up rooms.

Kamal Amrohi owned an abandoned studio on the Andheri Kurla road, perhaps called Mahal Studios, which now belonged to Shyam Sunder Seksaria of Navrang Film Processing Laboratory. Five top producers including Papaji, Shakti Samanta, Pramod Chakravorty, F.C. Mehra and Atmaram (Guru Dutt's brother) shifted to this ill-kept studio full of cobwebs, with three shooting floors. They revamped it into the posh Natraj Studios.

Having shifted from Kardar Studio to Natraj in Andheri East, there was no road to cross over from west to east, except for crossing the railway track at Andheri station. Hence, we would drive under the Khar subway, cross over to the east side and take a muddy village road right up to Andheri, which joined the Andheri Kurla road, to enter Natraj Studios.

During the making of *Arzoo*, Anand joined Sagar Art in 1964 as production-in-charge and assistant to Sudhendu Roy. I joined in 1966–67 as a still photographer for *Ankhen* and fourth assistant to cameraman G. Singh. After *Ankhen*, I was promoted to the post of assistant cameraman in *Geet*, under the award-winning cinematographer K. Vaikunth. During the same period, on 5 June 1970, we shifted from the 648-square-foot flat in Mahim, to the 10,000-square-foot Sagar Villa. The two-storey large bungalow in JVPD, Juhu, Vile Parle, could house our large family, including future daughters-in-law and grandchildren.

During *Ankhen*, Dharmendra's father, Kewal Kishen Singh, bought a plot in JVPD, Juhu, and built a bungalow for the Deol family. Since it was not safe staying alone, he requested Papaji to also buy a plot next door so that there could be one more Punjabi family in the neighbourhood. Papaji bought the plot in 1968 for only one lakh and thirty thousand rupees. It took more than two years to build Sagar Villa. At that time in 1968 most of JVPD, comprising fourteen societies, was still a khadi (creek). Sea water would flood in at high tide, hence there were not many buyers. The plots were very cheap—one lakh for a thousand square feet plot was the going rate. Three or four years later, Papaji bought the adjoining plot of Sagar Bhavan for just two and a half lakh rupees. Slowly JVPD started attracting Bombay's elite.

Over the next four to five years, the rich and powerful were all making a beeline to JVPD's societies—be it actors, industrialists or businessmen. Today, most of the top stars and industrialists stay in this posh locality spread over one square kilometre of Mumbai, like

Shatrughan Sinha, Amitabh Bachchan, Hema Malini, Ajay Devgn, Dilip Sanghvi of Sun Pharma, Mohanbhai Patel of Patel Extrusion and Anand Pandit of Lotus Builders. On the nearby Ruia Road at Silver Beach, the Hindujas and Godrejs have built their bungalows.

The asking price of a plot in JVPD today has no figure; it is priceless. One very interesting incident occurred after Papaji bought the second Sagar Bhavan plot. A Malayalee gentleman had built a hut on the plot and occupied it. It was not easy to vacate him. One day, the municipal van arrived and demolished the illegal structure. Before all the people could gather, Papaji hired over five hundred junior artists to act like goons. Within an hour there was total tension as hordes of Malayalees and their goons walked in with their coconut-shaving sickles, threatening to kill whoever had wrecked the illegal hutment. The junior artists, not to back down, spread the word in the crowd that no one should dare touch Ramanand Sagar or his family, or else they would be finished. The goons realised that they were outnumbered, and retreated peacefully. There was total loot all around; at times truckloads of iron rods, cement bags, bricks, etc., were openly robbed from the plots under construction. At night, Papaji would chase away robbers and petty thieves with his two Doberman dogs, Raja and Rani. Initially, the family was huddled into just four rooms on a single floor. One for Papaji and Mummyji, one each for the two married sons and one common room for the three bachelor sons and other family members.

Sagar Villa was heaven on earth. There were three to four lunch and dinner shifts on Sundays. There was an army of domestic helps from cooks to drivers to watchmen and gardeners. Once Shri Ram Bora, the then president of Indian Motion Pictures Producers Association, mentioned in his speech that Ramanand Sagar and family stayed in a chawl with over thirty-five occupants under one structure. The full family ate together. The kitchen was never shut due to the steady stream of VIPs, friends, intellectuals, writers, musicians etc., wining and dining throughout the year. From Ustad Alla Rakha Khan, Mehdi Hassan, Shakila Bano Bhopali, Arshi Hyderabadi to Maharashtra's chief ministers, presidents of India or Sheikh Abdullah himself, everyone had graced our home. The coming decades for the Sagar family in Sagar Villa was the golden period as a joint happy family lived under one roof, with Mummyji and Papaji.

I personally feel all this grihasthi sukh (family happiness) was due to the birth of a cow at the main entrance gate of Sagar Villa. A month or two after settling down, one early morning the watchman came running up to Mummyji to tell her that a pregnant cow had delivered a calf right at the bungalow's gate. The whole family ran down to witness the divine act. They fed the cow and calf with jaggery and chana, cleaned and washed the weak mother and child. I feel that it was Gau Mata Kamdhenu—the wish-fulfilling cow— who had come to Sagar Villa to grant all of Papaji's wishes, which culminated in the making of the blockbuster *Ramayan* for television.

Meanwhile, after the success of *Ankhen* in 1968, Papaji had started work on his next film, *Geet*, a musical romance set in the Himalayas. He specially flew to Manali (Kullu) nestled in the Himalayas to write the story of *Geet*. The hero of the film, Sarju, played by superstar Rajendra Kumar, was supposed to be a simpleton and a wild singer residing in the remote hills of Manali. Papaji wanted to give an authentic local flavour to his film, through costumes, rituals, mannerisms, language and social behaviour in the hidden valley. Sarju, while playing on his flute, sings to the mountains, streams and clouds in search of his unknown lover whom he has never seen, and feels that his songs will bring her to him. The title song '... *mere mitva, mere meet re, aaja tujhko pukare mere geet re* ...' reflected the theme of the romantic musical.

There were no flights to Kullu, and the roads in some parts were blocked by landslides and not motorable. So Papaji requested his pilot friend, Sardarji Baguna, to fly him to this scarcely-visited valley in his private piper plane. While flying into the tricky valley, Baguna showed Papaji the Sutlej river, saying, 'We have to follow the road on the left of the river bank until we reach a dead end of a cliff-like mountain. I will fly straight into the cliff, and we will suddenly see on the left an opening of the illusionary Kullu valley.' After the frightening experience, they finally landed on the rather small airfield of Bhuntar a few kilometres away from Kullu. The next three to four hours by jeep from Kullu to Manali was stomach-churning. Papaji was put up in the most esteemed guesthouse, Sunshine Orchards, run by one Mr Sharma, wedded to a Banon girl Shakuntala. Below the Sunshine Orchards resided middle-aged Col. Richard Banon from the Banon family. He owned a two-acre plot with a wooden bungalow built on it. It was the rarest piece of property in the entire Manali valley surrounded by snow peaks and pine slopes, with a panoramic 360-degree view. Papaji would sit the whole day in this heritage property and write continuously—scenes, dialogues and at times even the opening line of a song for *Geet*.

Manali was exposed to the outside world by Irishman, Captain A.T. Banon of the Royal Munster Fusiliers in 1870. He married a local girl and built the iconic Sunshine Orchards. The half-built roads were constructed after the British left India. Initially, the apples from Manali valley were carried to the plains by labourers or coolies.

Back in Bombay, Papaji narrated the story of *Geet* to the family, with dialogues and the opening lines of the superhit song '*Aaja tujhko pukare mere geet re* ...' He got so involved in the narration that he wept after every emotional sequence as if he was himself experiencing the pain and longing for the unknown lover. We kept staring at him as tears rolled down his eyes.

The day of shooting arrived. Since there were no flights to Manali, Papaji chartered a private Dakota with a Dutch pilot, who would fly us in and out of Delhi to Kullu. The whole excited unit ran up and down the aisle, not believing the entire plane was theirs. Actors Rajendra Kumar, Mala Sinha with her daughter and father, Papaji with his three sons, including me, were all smiles as we took off from Delhi's Palam Airport. The fun had begun, and the atmosphere was charged. The pilot soon announced that we would be touching down at Bhuntar in about twenty minutes. But minutes ticked by, and even after ninety minutes, we had not landed. Everyone was restless. Looking out of the window, it felt that the white mountain slopes were so close we could almost scrape the snow off. People were getting anxious. Suddenly, the pilot's voice echoed on the speakers, 'We are lost!'

There was pin-drop silence. Papaji rushed to the cockpit. The experienced Dutch pilot's face was pale. He had flown to the valley a few years ago and, as per his latest map, was following the road running parallel to the Sutlej. Unknown to him, a new road had been constructed now on the right bank of the river. Hence when he had reached the dead end of the cliff-like mountain, instead of turning left in the opening of the illusionary valley, he steered his plane right into the interlocking valleys of the Himalayan range—a sure death trap, with no chance of escape. There was total panic, with Mala Sinha screaming, 'I will die with my entire family!' and Rajendra Kumar whispering, 'I will die alone without my family.' Some members like Tun Tun and Keshto Mukherjee became uncontrollable, not ready to accept the situation of certain death. Nazir Hussain was in stoic silence. Some of the youngsters were laughing and joking, not having realised the gravity of the situation. The plane was just managing to steer left and right, avoiding a crash into the snow-covered mountain slopes, which were just a few feet away from our windows. As a director, Papaji was always scouting locations, so he had a fantastic memory. He asked the pilot to show him the flight route on the map.

Having flown earlier in the private piper plane with Sardar Baguna, who had pointed the left road and the cliff end of the illusionary valley, within seconds Papaji realised where the pilot had taken a wrong turn, due to the new road on the right bank of the Sutlej. He asked the Dutch pilot to retrace his flight route to that point. The reluctant pilot refused to turn left, since all he could see was the cliff's dead end. But Papaji forced him to turn; the pilot could not believe it when he saw the hidden entry at the opening between the cliffs into the sunlit beautiful green valley of Kullu. Just as we neared the airstrip, the engine started to chug. The petrol was depleted since we had been airborne for more than two hours. The experienced pilot glided the plane without fuel onto the airstrip. The doors were unlocked, and with smiles on our faces, we walked towards the exit. It was nothing short of a miracle. It had been a lifetime's experience as the clock kept ticking between life and death. Papaji's quick decision had saved the lives of the unit members.

The crowds surged up the staircase; there were hundreds of fans, well-wishers, locals and officials on the Bhuntar airstrip who picked us up on their shoulders and in their arms. On reaching the terminal, we saw thousands of people surging all over the building, compound walls and roads. The entire Kullu population was there to greet and welcome us. It was an emotional reunion between Papaji and my eldest brother, Subhash, who had not left the air traffic control tower even for a minute, praying to the local deity, Devi Maa Hidimba, for our safety. A week earlier, Papaji had sent Subhash to do a recce and organise things for the production. Subhash had not given up hope despite the odds. The Bhuntar air traffic control tower had already announced the aircraft 'missing'. The Kullu air traffic control tower had declared the plane lost and possibly crashed; the Chandigarh air traffic control tower had announced the plane as missing; and the local well-wishers told Subhash there was no way the plane could survive in the snow-clad Himalayas for two hours. Preparations were on to send a special mountaineering search team to spot the wreckage and dead bodies. The radio stations were announcing the deaths of superstars Rajendra Kumar and Mala Sinha, and Ramanand Sagar and his three sons. The evening papers all over the country, too, announced the crash and the death of the Sagar family, the stars and the entire unit of twenty members.

The month-long shooting was as per Papaji's dreams—nature, locales, actors and their performances—as everyone had opened up to the passion of the maker. I was second assistant to cinematographer K. Vaikunth. I had taken a portable processing kit with me, and at night I would develop a small negative portion of test footage to the relief and joy of the director and the cameraman. Papaji would beam proudly, seeing his son bringing technical innovation in the traditional set-up of a shoot. During shoots, one had to wait for the film processing lab to greenlight the shooting. Great footage would often be lost due to some technical error or wrong exposure.

One day, due to an overcast sky and rain, Papaji decided not to shoot. Early morning, I left with Shakuntala Sharma, alias Shakuntala

Banon, to visit an astrologer in Kullu town, some forty kilometres from Manali. Papaji, being very fond of meeting astrologers, instructed me to send the jeep back if I found the astrologer good. In a small room plastered with cow dung, a very strange-looking man with extra large outer ears sat on his gaddi (seat). Shakuntala kept asking him questions about the future of her son, Prithviraj. The big-eared astrologer kept looking at me and noted down something in his pad. After some time, he asked me who I was and if I wished to know about any aspect of my life. I politely thanked him. He smiled and started reading the notes on his pad. 'Does your name start with P ... your mother's name with L and your father's name with R?' I was shocked out of my wits.

He seemed to be a trikal darshi (three-dimensional visionary) blessed with spiritual power. Remembering Papaji's instructions, I told the strange-looking astrologer that I was going out and would soon return. He looked at me with a smile and said, 'No need to go, he will be here soon.' I could not understand what he meant. I rushed outside to tell the jeep driver to go and fetch Papaji when I saw Papaji walking through the rickety lane of the old hill town towards me. 'Since you did not send the jeep, I decided to come immediately myself,' he said. The amazing astrologer and Papaji spent a fair amount of time together, smiling and nodding at each other.

Despite the gruelling shooting schedules, Papaji would always be the first to rise, as early as five in the morning, and the last to sleep—making merry with the tired unit over drinks and food. Moti would dress up as a sexy woman and perform a cabaret dance, with the unit members whistling. No actor was ever late for a shoot, even in the toughest of locales, or threw any tantrums. Papaji would be the first to reach the summit of the snow mountain while we were still panting to reach the top. He had inexhaustible energy. He had timed the shooting schedule with apple trees full of white apple blossoms, and you could see their beauty in the reel. Kaviraj Indivar did not change a word of the opening of the title song that Papaji had written while conceiving the film, '*Mere mitwa mere meet re, aaja tujhko pukare mere geet re ...*' Papaji had correctly judged that the song

Ramanand Sagar visualised white apple blossoms to film the super hit song 'Aaja tujhko pukare mere geet re ...' The shooting schedule was chalked out accordingly. *Geet,* a musical love story between a stage actress and a wild mountain singer in search of his dream girl, who becomes a big star, required unusual costumes and settings, from Manali to Natraj Studios.

Photo collection: Ramanand Sagar Foundation

would set the box office on fire. While editing, he used the song four to five times in different situations, despite the young creative team being vehemently against it. Papaji was sure, perhaps possessed, but his judgement proved right.

It was soon time to leave the divine mystic valley of Manali. As I was trying to board the chartered Dakota with metal boxes of exposed negatives, the Dutch pilot stopped me at the gate and said, 'Either your negative boxes or you—only one can go. We are already overweight, and I cannot take a risk.' There was no question of delaying the negatives being airlifted to Bombay for processing at Film Centre Laboratory. Naturally, I was offloaded.

Papaji was sitting in a jeep parked on the tarmac, with the Punjab distributor R.R. Nanda ready to drive down to Hoshiarpur near Jalandhar to see the *Bhrigu Samhita*. I shouted from the top of the stairways, asking if I could join in. Soon we were speeding through the mountains, on our way to Hoshiarpur. Bhrigu Rishi, one of the seven mansik putras (born from the mind) of Brahma, wrote the *Bhrigu Samhita*. He concentrated on a few interesting souls, predicted their life journey graphs and provided advice and ways to overcome obstacles. Film distributor Gulshan Rai, associated with Yash Raj films, including *Deewar* and *Trishul*, was a firm believer of the *Bhrigu Samhita* and visited Hoshiarpur regularly. He religiously followed spiritual remedies and had a long and successful career. Papaji knew that only a few horoscopes with life-destiny graph details were preserved in Hoshiarpur with Pandit Des Raj Sharma's family.

On reaching Hoshiarpur, we began a search for Papaji's kundali (astrological birth chart) from a pile of papers scattered all over the room. Within minutes, Papaji found a kundali that matched his exact birth chart. Once the papers outlining his life's graph and journey were found, Pandit Des Raj Sharmaji read it out, 'Today one soul has come to me whose name is Ramanand Sagar. He is accompanied by his business partner Rewati Raman Nanda and his son Prem Sagar … *vaayu marg se mrityu likhi hui thi* (he was destined to die through air route), but due to his good karmic actions in this birth, he has been saved) ... he is in a profession of "parde pe chhaya" (images on a screen) ...' Maharishi Bhrigu had also predicted the making of the *Ramayan*, by saying that in his seventies, Papaji would do something that would spiritually awaken mankind.

Maharishi Bhrigu was a compiler of predictive astrology, and has authored *Bhrigu Samhita*, a classic in astrology. He decided to write the book by collecting interesting birth charts. He wrote full life predictions and compiled them as *Bhrigu Samhita*—perhaps five thousand years ago. The massive database—charts of people—were lost during various invasions of India. The great great-grandmother of Pandit Janardhan Devi Sharma was a Sanskrit scholar. Around 1923, she found *Bhrigu Samhita* completely by accident, in the paper used for wrapping something she had bought in the market. Realising what an astrological classic she had in her possession, she traced the source to a junk dealer. She bought all that was left to preserve the treasure of such a remarkable, intriguing system of knowledge.

Geet turned out to be a superhit, as predicted by Maharishi Brighu. It had ten silver jubilee runs, eleven hundred-day runs and fifty-two all-time theatre records to its credit. One of the major reasons for its success was the flute played by the village simpleton singer Rajendra Kumar. The lilting heart-touching music of the flute was the hero of the story. It was a tough search to find a flautist who could carry the entire film on his own. Papaji finally decided to collaborate with Hariprasad Chaurasia, one of the senior musicians then in the orchestra of Kalyanji-Anandji. The multiple shades, moods and nuances of the flute had the nation glued to the screen in the theatres, gave them a feel of honest true love and made them cry at the tragedy of that love. The music of *Geet* made Pandit Hariprasad Chaurasia what he is today—one of the most respected music maestros. After the success of *Geet*, thousands of flutes were exported to Morocco (North Africa) by the film distributor Chandi Ramani. Papaji was given a royal reception on his visit to Morocco. His Majesty, King Hassan II, deeply appreciated the Indian musical instrument at a special screening. The flute tunes of *Geet* were

The flute was the highlight and star of *Geet*. The magical spellbinding flute played by Rajendra Kumar on the screen was actually played by Pandit Hariprasad Chaurasia. The flute played a very significant role in the well-planned, innovative publicity campaign for the film.

Photo collection: Ramanand Sagar Foundation

similar to a five-hundred-year-old rim-blown flute's made from a reed, called nai (nay/ney) in the Arab world. A special, well-planned publicity campaign was organised in and around the flute. For the first time in the history of the Indian Railways, 10,000 square feet of space was booked on all major stations' hoarding sites, including Lucknow, Delhi, Bhopal, Bombay and Calcutta. It was a massive, very successful campaign spread over six months of display on hundreds of huge hoardings, showing Rajendra Kumar playing a flute. The designs were changed every month from only a flute and the lettering 'G-E-E-T' on the entire hoarding to a silhouette playing a flute, followed by a profile playing a flute and, finally, a full-colour poster of Rajendra Kumar with his flute. This innovative campaign gave *Geet* its initial audience and then the film's music, content, writing and acting completed the super success story of Papaji's musical hit.

Ramanand Sagar tried never to repeat his stories, as a creative challenge. Every film was a new subject. The seed of *Ghunghat* was from Rabindranath Tagore's story *Naukadubi*. All else in the film was Papaji's forte—evoking deep emotions and portraying the ideal Hindu woman. The base of *Zindagi* was the Ramayana, when circumstances make Vyjayanthimala spend a night in Raaj Kumar's house. The clash between father Prithviraj Kapoor, a judge, and son Rajendra Kumar, a lawyer, was original and innovative. *Arzoo* began where the Cary Grant–Deborah Kerr film *An Affair to Remember* ended. *Ankhen* was a romantic, patriotic spy thriller with Netaji Subhas Chandra Bose's Indian National Army as the background. *Geet* was a musical love story between a flute-playing simpleton in search of his unknown lover and an actress who not only recognises his unbelievable talent but falls in love with him.

Papaji's next film, *Lalkar*, was going to be a war drama set against the backdrop of the Second World War and the Japanese-occupied Northeast India. *Lalkar* was also my first film as a director of photography. I had specially designed bounce light banks that gave a very credible touch of the north light prevalent in Nagaland. Dharmendra was very concerned and sensitive about his appearance and look, handled by a first-time twenty-seven-year-old cinematographer. On some pretext or the other, he would manage to see the rushes every day in the Natraj Studios' dubbing mini theatre. After the initial reservations, we became the best of friends—even sharing our smuggled whisky during late-night shoots, hidden under the camera patlas (wooden square tables used for placing the huge Mitchell N.C. movie camera). *Lalkar* got me over fifteen awards all over India.

Papaji created a coup of sorts by bringing in a multi-star cast comprising actors like Dharmendra, Dara Singh, Dev Kumar and Ramesh Deo, who played army men on a mission, while Rajendra Kumar, Sujit Kumar and others played the Air Force daredevils. While filming a swamp sequence in the Assam forests created indoors, Dara Singh strangled with his bare hands a ten-foot-long python that had wrapped around his neck, forming a constriction coil.

Dharmendra's role as a major in the Indian Army who sacrifices his life on realising the meaning of true love was much appreciated. While filming a love sequence with Dharmendra in the hills of Assam, an arrow shot by a Naga princess pierced my cheek, barely missing the camera and the huge wooden silver foil reflectors.

There were a few pitfalls during the outdoor shooting in Manali too. On the last day of the shoot, Papaji decided to take the actors down a deep gorge near Solang valley for some glamour shots of guerrilla commandos. He organised a wireless walkie-talkie to communicate with the actors and the camera crew. It took Dharmendra, Dev Kumar and others half a day through the rough terrain to reach the bottom of the gorge. The camera was readied, and the assistant was asked to load the magazine. After a long wait, when the frightened assistant came and whispered something into my ears, my face went white. Mustering courage, I told Papaji that we had forgotten to get the raw stock. He looked at me, smiled and shouted to the half-dead actors through the walkie-talkie, 'Pack up! Today is picnic day.' Biryani, beer and laughter followed—but Papaji was cool and calm. Nothing could shake him. This was the stuff the man was made of. His crew and technicians were his life. He knew over the years the humiliation and lack of appreciation they go through and was super conscious of this fact.

I remember, during the indoor shooting schedules at Natraj Studios, a long table was laid in the studio compound for lunch and dinner. The entire unit, including the light boys, technicians, actors, Papaji with his children, guests and distributors all ate the same food sitting on wooden benches. During extended shoots, no one complained about lunch break or demanded food on sets. Papaji would sometimes forget that a hundred-odd unit members were working on an empty stomach—at times from 9 a.m. to 4 p.m.

And then there would be a feast of chicken dishes and dessert. Right from the spot boys, everyone admired and saluted their boss's honesty, integrity and work ethics. The unit members and studio staff blindly followed and trusted Papaji's vision. This also applied to filmmakers like Guru Dutt who pawned his wife Geeta Dutt's jewellery to pay the daily wages of his workers.

Originally, *Lalkar* was based on the battle of Asal Uttar during the Indo-Pak War of 1965. Param Vir Chakra awardee Abdul Hamid destroyed seven Pakistani tanks, including the impenetrable Patton tanks, to the credit of the Indian Army. It was a graveyard of tanks. Papaji went to the battlefield at the Khem Karan sector and sat on the nozzle of the abandoned tanks. Prime Minister Lal Bahadur Shastri readily agreed to give all assistance. The signing and declaration of the peace agreement at Tashkent between Pakistani President General Ayub Khan and Indian Prime Minister Lal Bahadur Shastri in a way derailed the entire project. Dharmendra was to play the role of Commander Abdul Hamid. A rumour was circulating that the Pakistani cook had poisoned the Indian prime minister, who died the day after signing the peace agreement.

Natraj Studios

There were five partners in Natraj Studios Pvt. Ltd, namely Shakti Samanta, F. C. Mehra, Pramod Chakravorty, Atmaram and Ramanand Sagar. With an equal one-fifth share, all the five partners shifted their offices to the two-and-a-half acre plot. From day one, it was a hit studio with major films shot there, including Papaji's hit films, *Geet*, *Lalkar*, *Charas* and *Bhagwat*. Similarly, Shakti Samanta's *Aradhana* and *Kati Patang* were shot in the same premises as well as the films of the other partners. It was a hub of filmmaking activity, shooting, dubbing, recording, theatre and all the paraphernalia required in an 'A' grade film studio. All the top actors from Amitabh Bachchan to Rajesh Khanna and Dharmendra, from Hema Malini to Rekha were in and around the studio—shooting, dubbing or seeing the rushes.

Papaji had a cabin in the centre block. The spiritual coincidence was that it was surrounded by five peepal trees, not very obvious to anyone. I realised the significance of this unseen panchvati (garden of five trees), where an electronic-age rishi—Papaji—was doing his tapasya, learning mass media and communication, leading him to make *Ramayan*. After that, the Natraj complex went into redevelopment. Papaji's table was right in the middle of the panchvati. His private air-conditioned office was surrounded by five peepal trees. The electronic-age rishi would do his research in the air-conditioned room instead of a cave or a jungle. It is believed Maa Lakshmi resides in the peepal tree. Hanumanji used to sit on a peepal tree and witness Sita Mata's hardships in Ashok Vatika. In the Brahma Puran, it is said Vishnu was born under a peepal tree. Bhagwan Krishna in the Bhagavad Gita declares, 'Of all the trees, I am the peepal tree.' Devotee of Ram, Ramanand Sagar, born to rewrite the Ramayana in the electronic media, completed his mission under the five peepal trees acting as a canopy for his cabin in Natraj Studios.

Lalkar was a silver jubilee hit and changed the concept of multi-starrers, bringing in a new trend. A special Dakota aeroplane with sofas and bed was sent to Bombay to pick up the stars and take them around different Air Force bases—including Halwara, twenty kilometres from Ludhiana—to entertain squadrons, pilots, crew, Air Force personnel and their families. The final stop was at Lucknow, where a Sagar Night and Jashn-e-Sagar were the highlights. Coincidentally, not only was *Lalkar* my first film but I also got married five days before the release of the film—on Sunday, 21 May.

After the week of marriage celebrations was over, from Monday onwards, the new bride saw one brother after another disappearing on the sly and not coming back home for two or more nights. She feared that she had married into a weird filmy family, not realising the day-and-night job involved in the making of prints, checking them and despatching them all over India. I met my wife directly after four days in the special presidential Dakota aeroplane. On the morning of the 25th, the just-married couple flew to Delhi, Halwara and then on to Srinagar. On landing at Srinagar airport, I realised Papaji had booked a full houseboat for us. The houseboat had red curtains with a poppy flower design. The next day, after multiple functions in Lucknow, he gave me two tickets for Kathmandu (Nepal) with prepaid stay at Hotel Soaltee Oberoi for my honeymoon.

After we shifted to Natraj Studios, the government of Maharashtra decided to make a 'film city' in Goregaon. Chief Minister Vasantrao Naik, together with Papaji, scouted for a suitable location, riding a helicopter on the edge of the Sanjay Gandhi National Park. Ramanand Sagar, as a successful creative filmmaker, had made an impact on the government. He was offered one share of the Film City, which took off and has still not been surrendered as per further government notification. Once the project took off and became a success, the entire film industry was instructed to surrender their shares. The government turned a blind eye to their contribution.

During the Natraj Studios period, Anand and I would sit day and night in the tiny editing and film-processing rooms of Navrang Cine Lab. The living conditions were pitiable whether it was the bathrooms, floorings or the staircase. At times, a tireless Ramanand Sagar would edit day and night without a break. He would take his cat naps on the rickety chair, and we would stretch ourselves on the bare cement floors, at times for the whole night.

Once, leaving the edit, Papaji and I sat in the white Chevy to come home half asleep at 4 a.m. in the morning. Unknown to us, riots had erupted in Bombay. Navrang Lab on Tulsi Pipe Road towards Mahalaxmi, being a workers' area, was affected the most. Suddenly, Papaji's faithful driver, John, brought the car to a screeching halt. Right in front was a fierce-looking rioter with a huge stone in his hands. Before we could realise it, he hurled the stone at us. Papaji and I were covered with broken glass from head to toe. A brave John drove through like a Rambo and took us home. The family was shocked and went into panic mode, cleaning every inch of our bodies.

Superhit *Charas* was made when the Dharmendra–Hema Malini romance was at its peak. The sale campaign slogan was 'the hottest romance of the year'. *Charas* was shot all over Europe, including Italy, Venice, France and the Swiss Alps, with the Mediterranean island of Malta as the drug mafia base. Dharam, Hema and Papaji stayed at the Hilton, whereas the entire unit with the stunt team from the UK stayed in a villa, with a swimming pool and one of the best bars I had ever seen.

The owner of the resort, John, had won many gold medals for his cocktail innovations. He could make a cocktail bearing the colour of your choice. Whether one wanted apple green, brinjal purple, carrot red or pumpkin yellow—he would do it. For the whole month of the shoot the bar was kept open round the clock, and the key was given to us. We only had to note the drinks consumed. We all learned our invaluable bar lessons and wine fundamentals from John.

The total filming unit from Bombay comprised only six members, with no production manager, make-up or dress man, or light boys. Anand and I combed the wigs needed and ironed the clothes till late at night. The actors did their own make-up. A green MG sports car was purchased for stunt shooting. Rented Mercedes-Benz cars were used for the trolley and follow-up shots. Silver foils pasted on plywood were used as light reflectors. The entire Arriflex II CBV camera was dismantled and carried in coat pockets of our blazers. At night, we boys would roam around the discos of Hilton, the bars of Mdina and Valletta. Every day, Dharmendra's secretary, Dinanath, would see to it that Hema's father Mr Chakravarty was kept busy for the whole day, at times, the whole night. He would convince Mr Chakravarty to visit the sister islands of Gozo and the casinos and ensure that he missed the last boat back, compelling him to stay the night at Gozo island.

For the song '*Aaja teri yaad aaee*', Papaji wanted to film two versions: one real and one dream sequence. I flew to Paris, bought some very expensive special prism, glued them on a four-and-a-half-inch ultraviolet filter and made a special lens on location. It was the same idea designed by the American photojournalist David Douglas Duncan conceived in his 1972 book *Prismatics*. Papaji used the fragmented and detailed dream prism shots to indicate the end of the film. The new technique was much discussed among cinematographers.

While shooting in Les Deblacaire, a remote French village in the Alps, the seeds for the making of the *Ramayan* were sown. Having watched for the first time a colour TV sitting in a French bar, Papaji decided to shift to TV with a trilogy of *Ramayan, Shri Krishna* and *Maa Durga*—Ram being the twelve sampoorna kala avatar, Krishna with sixteen kalas and Maa Durga, sampoorna shakti. He realised that with a medium like TV, his creative liberty would not have to be governed by the sale of tickets.

TV viewing is free. If you like the content you continue to watch it, otherwise you switch the channel. For films, you have to specially go to a theatre, sit for a few hours in a totally dark room, whereas television can be viewed from the comfort of your own drawing room. The option of video cassettes is also available to view the story at your convenience whenever you desire. We were all shocked by his firm decision to move to TV, but his futuristic thinking and judgement way back in 1975–76 rings true even now.

While shooting the climax of *Charas*, a huge villain's den was constructed in the Natraj Studios' waterproofed floor. One lakh fifty thousand gallons of water were pumped in to create the filmy Mediterranean. The shooting set depicted the interior of a cave with a wooden bridge situated in a remote Mediterranean island, with the sea going into a natural cave—a grotto. Drugs laden in boats were transported and stored in this villain's headquarters, carved out of the walls of the grotto, including bridges, offices, bedrooms, tunnels and passages.

It was a month-long gruelling shoot, with the involvement of the entire star cast. After a week's shoot, I was taking a shot in the temporary construction lift connecting the boat landing platform in

Charas was shot extensively on the island nation of Malta in the Mediterranean, known for its medieval look, archipelago, labyrinthine narrow lanes, churches and lagoons—a perfect backdrop for the drug lord villain's hideouts, including the natural grotto. Forty years later, the same locations of the capital city of Valetta, the medieval 'Silent City' Mdina, Grotto island at Gozo and the Blue Lagoon at Comino have been used in TV shows such as *Game of Thrones* and movies like *Thugs of Hindostan, Troy* and *The Count of Monte Cristo.*

Photo Collection: Ramanand Sagar Foundation

the water of the 'Mediterranean' to the bridge above, identifying the hidden villain's den. From about forty feet, the trolley slipped from the wire operating the lift hoist. Five bodies lay on the bare floor— dead! The stunt master Mansoor Bhai leapt on to a hanging light rope like Tarzan and swung himself down to reach the still bodies.

The first thing Papaji asked was whether they were still breathing. There was total chaos. Hema transported an unconscious me to the Nanavati Hospital in her limousine, resting my bleeding head in her lap.

Two people had died on the spot from the impact of the fall. One of them was my friend, income tax inspector Bhide, who had come to meet me. The other person was a camera attendant. My assistant Billy, today's star cinematographer Binod Pradhan, being super lightweight, was still conscious. He got up and saw the other four lying unconscious and just fainted. My assistant Gopal was hospitalised for over a year, plastered from head to toe, with Mummyji religiously sending him home-cooked food daily to his hospital bed. The whole industry was aghast. There were thousands of well-wishers crowding Nanavati Hospital, praying night after night for our survival. With sixteen fractured bones, I stayed put in the hospital for less than a month. Not able to bear the tragedy, Papaji and Mummyji would quietly go outside my room to cry silently. My wife, Neelam, too couldn't control her emotions seeing me in that condition. They would give each other solace. It was a miracle that I lived. Many VIPs including N.T. Rama Rao, the legendary leading man of Telugu cinema and a prominent politician, specially flew to Bombay to see me recouping.

The biggest problem was that if this shoot was not completed, the movie would have been delayed by a year, trying to get combination dates for all the stars together for a one-month schedule. It could be a financial disaster for Sagar Art. I will always be grateful to my true friend K.K. Mahajan (KK) who came and took over the film at such a crucial time. All he said was, 'The show must go on.' From the very next day itself, he single-handedly helmed the camera and the director's baton to continue the shoot. Papaji joined him in a day or two, always grateful to KK, who had been my senior at the FTII. We had a lot of fun together, participating in inter-department cricket matches, and so on. At the time of the *Charas* tragedy, KK was at the peak of his career doing two shifts daily. Imagine leaving his personal schedule to stand like a rock with Ramanand Sagar for a whole month!

In life, it is difficult to find a true friend like KK. *Charas* was a superhit, completing a diamond jubilee, a seventy-five-week run at one single theatre, Society, in Ludhiana. The film achieved all time box office records at over seventy-five theatres in over forty cities and celebrated hundred days at more than thirty stations. It won many awards all over India.

Charas tested Ramanand Sagar's trust and faith and iron will right up to the day of its release. One day, he received a letter from the anti-narcotic cell of the government that they would like to view the contents of the film due to its explosive title, *Charas*. Then came a circular from the censor board, restricting the length of the fight sequences and number of fistfight blows so as to restrict the influence and impact of violence in cinema.

Papaji complied with all government directives and the country was flooded with release publicity material, including hoardings displaying a bare-chested Dharmendra pointing a gun with his outstretched arm. Immediately, another notice came for the entire film industry, putting a ban on the display of guns in film publicity. The lame excuse was to curb violence among the youth. At night, with my outdoor publicity workers, I went all around Bombay with a wooden ladder and colour cans, painting the gun on the publicity posters with black paint.

Before *Charas* could hit the silver screen, the multi-starrer *Sholay* was released in the theatres, creating a box office sensation. Villain Amjad Khan was the hero pitted against three superstars Dharmendra, Amitabh Bachchan and Sanjeev Kumar. The distributors of *Charas* went crazy with Amjad Khan in the star cast against Dharmendra and Hema Malini. The film became hot property in the film distributor circuit. Papaji had to redo the script and make Amjad Khan the main villain in the Europe drug peddler's operation. *Charas* was Amjad Khan's first signed film as he was chosen by Ramanand Sagar in a contest by Wadala Junior Chamber of Commerce to introduce new talent in cinema.

After the release of *Sholay*, the various bans, restrictions and objections against *Charas* acquired some meaning as they seemed to be motivated with an agenda. It seemed that someone in Delhi at a very high position had a percentage share in the box office returns of the superhit film *Sholay*. The anti-narcotic cell could not find any reason to either get the title 'Charas' changed or to ban the film. All kinds of publicity visuals like the gun were effaced, deleted or removed. The stunts and fights were re-edited and shortened as per censor board circulars and directions.

Keeping the gravity of the situation in mind, Papaji flew to Delhi and held a special screening of *Charas* for V.C. Shukla, the then information and broadcasting minister. A week before the release of the film, Papaji received a phone call from the ministry that the minister would be flying to Bombay on Thursday, a day before the Friday release, to review the film. Some industry insiders swore that they had heard that the minister would ban the film a day before its release.

On Thursday morning, 27 May 1976, a day before the release, the heavens came to Papaji's rescue and it started pouring from very early in the morning. It poured incessantly for hours with winds and cyclonic conditions. Geographically, it could have been the Atlantic hurricane named Belle which formed on 20 May 1976. Subtropical storms hit the Indian shores on the fateful day of 27 May 1976. All flights from Delhi to Mumbai were cancelled.

V.C. Shukla then had to fly directly to Geneva from Delhi, where he was committed to attend an international convention. On 28 May 1976, *Charas* was released to full houses with stupendous success. Papaji smiled at the divine intervention which was nothing short of a miracle. After all, it was just May-end, and it had rained!

Apart from the interesting twists and turns before the release and super success of *Charas*, there are many interesting anecdotes and incidents involving artists, politicians and actors, and some of my spiritual experiences with Papaji.

Before the film's release, Hema Malini's mother Jaya Chakravarty presented Papaji a 3D gold-plated photo of Tirupati Balaji. The miracle of the release of *Charas* against all odds and its super success could be because of Balaji's blessings on him.

One day a fan came to Natraj Studios while we were shifting from Kardar Studios and presented Papaji a laminated colour photograph of the Siddhivinayak idol. Our production company had a very

After the release of *Sholay*, produced by G.P. Sippy, all sorts of restrictions, objections and hurdles were put up by the Narcotics Cell (Delhi) and the Censor Board (Bombay) to not only stall the release of Ramanand Sagar's *Charas* but to actually ban its theatrical release. Photo above shows information and broadcasting minister V.C. Shukla at a special screening of *Charas* in Delhi.

Photo collection: Ramanand Sagar Foundation

successful stint in Natraj Studios with some hit films, and maybe, it had something to do with the blessings of Siddhivinayak. All of us learned our film craft in Natraj Studios and finally Natraj Studios was rebuilt into Natraj Rustom, a modern corporate complex with a steel and glass building, giving economic stability to the Sagar siblings. The Siddhivinayak photo gifted by that fan always adorned the walls of Papaji's office.

After the success of *Geet*, Ramanand Sagar had bought the heritage bungalow of Col. Richard Banon in Manali where he had written the story of *Geet*. With the legendary success of *Ramayan*, the bungalow at Manali was converted into a forty-eight-room hotel called Sagar Tourist Resort, situated on the most prime location in entire Manali with a 360-degree view of pine tree slopes and snow mountains. Papaji hired a luxury bus and packed the whole extended clan, including the first family from Bombay, his married daughter, her in-laws' family from Delhi and also the Chopra family from Kashmir for the opening of the Sagar Tourist Resort in Manali—his first major expanded business venture.

After bypassing Chandigarh, since it was getting late, he decided to take a shortcut through the thick jungles to reach Kullu. In the middle of the dense jungle inhabited by ferocious animals, the luxury bus halted while ascending a steep mountain bend. The half-full petrol tank would not supply fuel to the engine due to the forty-five-degree slope. Imagine his entire family with women and babies stranded on the dangerous jungle road. For more than an hour, no vehicle passed by. The night was setting in. There was tension all around. I saw Papaji quietly going towards the roadside jungle, finding a quiet spot and sincerely praying for some divine intervention. Within minutes, we heard the roar of an engine and saw two headlights coming towards us. It was a truck with two handsome men, who were nothing short of angels for us. They stopped their truck, asked no questions, got down with a petrol jerry can, filled up the half-empty tank of our bus, sat in their truck and drove away. It looked like the gods had come down to our rescue.

Papaji was bewildered and folded his hands in prayer and thanked Durga Maa, his ishta devi for the timely help. I have seen and experienced such happenings time and again. I remember, in the early '50s, some unknown devotee had sent him Maa Ambe's framed photo to which he prayed till his last breath.

The vice president of India, Bhairon Singh Shekhawat, had a special bond with Ramanand Sagar. During the outdoor shooting of *Baghavat*, Shekhawatji offered a whole fort in and around Jaipur for Papaji to buy and convert into a hotel and also shoot his costume drama, a period film. From a helicopter in mid-air organised by Shekhawatji for a recce of locations to boosting tourism in Rajasthan with Papaji performing the aarti of Shila Devi, the famous idol of Durga in Amer Fort, all this happened during our Natraj Studios days. On my humble request, Shekhawatji agreed to launch our TV serial *Prithviraj Chauhan* for Star TV in Delhi, and visited the family at Sagar Villa for dinner during its filming. Sagar Villa often had VIP visitors. The ex-president of India, Giani Zail Singh, spent a night in Papaji's personal library discussing politics and the Ramayana for hours. Maharashtra chief ministers like Y.B. Chavan and Sushil Kumar Shinde attended family and personal functions in the Sagar Villa. All of them had very personal friendly relationships with my father. One evening, there were three chief ministers in the expansive lawns of Sagar Bhavan next to Sagar Villa. The chief minister of Kashmir, Sheikh Abdullah, was felicitated by Papaji, with other chief ministers in attendance. The whole family including his Begum (wife) and son Farooq, stayed for two days enjoying the hospitality of Papaji, a son of the soil of Kashmir. The Chopra family had cordial relations, from as early as the 1940s, with the Abdullah family and Sheikh saheb.

Sagar Villa witnessed marriages of four of Ramanand Sagar's children. His oldest two sons Subhash and Shanti got married in the 648-square-foot flat in Mahim. For Subhash's marriage, the wedding procession extended from Shanmukhanand Hall to Arora Cinema in Matunga. For Shanti's marriage, a whole procession took off to Delhi by train. Sarita, our only sister and the youngest in the family, was married off in grand style in Sagar Villa. VIPs, politicians, top stars, distributors, and the entire film fraternity attended different functions. Papaji was on top of his game of his film career, having delivered superhit after superhit. Anand's, Moti's and my marriage followed in succession. All were very grand affairs with receptions held at the Sun-n-Sand Hotel.

After Sarita's marriage, Papaji's film career graph never reached the same heights of success as before. Papaji was very particular about choosing traditional girls to be his daughters-in-law who would look after the home and hearth. Before my eldest brother's marriage, he called all of us and made it very clear to us what principles he lived by. If someone desired a dowry, he was free to ask for it, but then he would also have to move out. If they wanted to stay with him, only a token of one and a quarter rupee would be accepted as shagun. He also believed that his five bahus should come from families that were equal in financial stature so as to avoid any comparisons in the future.

His wisdom told him that comparisons of any kind could break a family and be the root cause of separations in a joint family. His life mantra proved to be absolutely right, and it kept his children, grandchildren and even great-grandchildren all bound together, happy and content till he lived. Shanti's marriage to a princess from Rajasthan had to be turned down due to Papaji's no-dowry policy. Anand's marriage to a top industrialist's only daughter was accepted after extensive negotiations and only after the dowry money went into a trust for awards to science and scientists. Moti's marriage was predicted by an astrologer who read only three hands in a day, indicating to the girl's parents that the boy they were looking for was staying in a flat (Bhatia Builiding) in the opposite building on the second floor.

Sagar Villa also witnessed the rise of many film stars in the making. Hrithik Roshan used to play underarm cricket in the driveway of Sagar Villa. I had even sent a message to him that if he ever got into acting, I had the role of 'Aladdin' for him in our TV show *Alif Laila*. But he was very sure that he only wanted to join his father Rakesh Roshan and learn film direction from him. Rakesh was a leading man in Sagar Art's film *Pyara Dushman*. As a teenager, Bobby Deol too would zoom in with his sports car at high speed in a lane near Sagar Villa. One day my wife picked up a stone and smashed the windscreen of Bobby's car. He never again passed by that lane. Sagar Villa had over a dozen wild kids playing on the road, and Bobby's driving was dangerous.

Pushpavalli, the actor associated with Gemini Studios, once brought her daughter to Natraj Studios to meet Papaji to cast her as a heroine. The daughter later became the famous Rekha who starred in our home productions *Ram Bharose* and *Prem Bandhan*.

Papaji wanted to launch Anand as a director. Anand and I were regulars at the Sun-n-Sand swimming pool. As a cameraman I would suggest, day after day, one particular girl in a swimsuit to be cast as the film's heroine. She had a photogenic face and a great figure. Before we could approach her, we were told she had been signed by Raj Kapoor for a small budget film *Bobby* opposite his son Chintu. Her name was Dimple Kapadia and she belonged to a rich family.

During the shooting of *Prem Bandhan*, starring Rajesh Khanna, I had the pleasure of taking a few candid shots of the now Mrs Dimple Khanna. My daughter Ganga, who is a painter and photographer, had done a portrait of Dimple, which is now put up on our wall in our Karjat farmhouse. During the making of *Arzoo*, Mallika (cast opposite Mehmood) would bring her sister along, requesting Papaji to give her a chance. The sister turned out to be Mumtaz, the superstar of the '60s and '70s, before she got married to Mayur Madhwani, a millionaire, and settled in Africa.

During the shooting of *Hum Tere Ashiq Hain* in Madras, the local financier distributor Chota Manu brought a young girl to Hema Malini's Chola Hotel birthday party and introduced her as a leading artist in south India wanting to enter Hindi cinema. As the years passed, the young Tamil actor flowered into the glamorous Sridevi. A struggling actor used to wander about aimlessly in Natraj Studios, visiting the Sagar Art office repeatedly. Papaji knew his mother Nirmala Devi, an actor and Hindustani classical music vocalist. The young actor's determination made him the famous dancing star Govinda. Similarly, a struggling young boy aspiring to be a music director used to visit our office and for hours would drum tunes with his hands on the glass table, who later went on to become the famous Anu Malik, son of the legendary Sardar Malik.

When Papaji visited the FTII he saw a student film *Unto the Void*. He decided to give the young action star a break in *Ankhen*. The young actor demanded a role bigger than that of the main villain, the veteran actor Jeevan. As time passed, the aspiring young actor became a well-known villain-turned-hero to be reckoned with, named Shatrughan Sinha. Papaji also gave the first break to Tom Alter as an actor in *Charas*, playing an Interpol officer in Europe. Natraj Studios was a haven for struggling newcomers.

One day my cabin door opened with a bang and in walked a hefty six-foot-tall Jat, with the dense beard of a dacoit. He had a huge suitcase in his hand and asked for me. He then swung the heavy suitcase on to my glass table and opened it. I was shocked to see wads of notes amounting to a few crores. He pushed the money towards me and said, 'Make a film for me. This is for you. I will be your hero!' He could have well been robbed of all that hard cash in the Natraj compound itself. Papaji had warned us of such sharks roaming around in film studios ready to exploit innocent, struggling newcomers.

Hence, we were instructed to never say no to a newcomer and to keep the doors open. All attendants and staff were warned, as a policy, against stopping a struggler from meeting us. I offered the young man some food and locked him in Papaji's cabin, then called his home in Ludhiana. His worried parents came down and took him back. He had fought with the family, taken his share of the family land in Punjab, sold it and brought the suitcase full of cash to become a hero! In another incident, a young frightened teenage girl ran into Sagar Villa and hid herself from people in the flesh trade who were chasing her. Papaji called his junior artiste supplier, Mr Suri, who took her away to a safe place. Many years later, we were told that the junior artiste supplier had married her.

The outdoor shoot of *Prem Bandhan* was in Kashmir. Rajesh Khanna was very fond of food and it was his weakness. Even while shooting in the biting snow of Pahalgam, he wanted the food to be piping hot. There had to be a full-size onion included, on which he would bang his fist and break it, calling it 'muth maarke pyaaz'.

Ravi Thakur was an assistant on *Prem Bandhan*. He was so fed up of these starry nakhras that one day after pack up, he drank himself silly, got completely sloshed, got up like a stud and marched into Rajesh Khanna's hotel room, spouting a barrage of abuses. For over half an hour, it was a one-sided barrage of the choicest Punjabi expletives.

Tom Alter's debut film was Ramanand Sagar's *Charas*.

Photo collection: Ramanand Sagar Foundation

The superstar of his time, Rajesh Khanna just kept quiet. Papaji knew the implications of such incidents. At the dinner table there was pin-drop silence. No one spoke, worried about the next day's shoot and the film. In walked Rajesh Khanna—jovial, smiling and joking—and went straight to Ravi, hugged him and made him have a sip from his whisky glass. That was the greatness of Rajesh Khanna. In my film life journey of seventy years, no one till date has been able to reach such heights of stardom, with crazy fans and girls painting his portraits with blood. There are countless anecdotes about Rajesh Khanna, the real superstar of the Indian film industry.

In the film industry, if you want to work with a superstar, their minutest demands have to be accommodated and have to be part of the deal. Mala Sinha wanted an apple every day in her make-up room. The shoot would not start until the apple reached her. At times due to production problems there would be a delay of a few hours, but she would not appear on the set. One day, on the sets of *Geet*, a morning shift turned into a 4 p.m. one, but she was still in her make-up room, ready and dressed up. Papaji finally went to her to find out what had happened. He realised that she was waiting for an apple she had requested for in the morning. The production-in-charge had somehow undermined the importance of the apple.

Once when Papaji was in Bangalore shooting for *Charas*, he desired to meet his friend N.T. Rama Rao (NTR). He sent word to his secretary, who confirmed a four o'clock meet at NTR's bungalow. We were all excited about the opportunity to meet the biggest star of south India. Our local distributor R.N. Mandre advised Papaji to confirm if it was 4 a.m. or 4 p.m. We laughed it off.

However, when we enquired with NTR's secretary, we were shocked to learn that it was to be at 4 a.m.! Later, we learnt about the professionalism of the actor who, for a 7 a.m. shift, got up hours early to work on his make-up and dialogues.

Once the watchman of Sagar Villa came up to Papaji saying that there was a man sitting on the entry steps of Sagar Villa refusing to say who he was but wanted to meet him. It was the legendary tabla player Ustad Alla Rakha Khan sitting on the marble steps with his fingers playing on them. Papaji stood there watching the maestro lost in his taali and khali, and then greeted and hugged him. On one occasion, the Ustad was visiting Sagar Villa for a party. Hearing his own music being played in the hall when he reached there, he sat outside for an hour without letting anyone know, enjoying his own music. That was the devotion and mutual admiration between the two legends in their respective arts. Papaji would often ask him to teach him to play the sitar while he would teach Alla Rakha to sing.

Papaji's hospitality was as legendary as his intensity and sensitivity for his tribe of creative artistes. On one of his trips to India the legendary ghazal singer Mehdi Hassan called Papaji with a request, wanting to spend an evening with him. Papaji insisted that he and his team first enjoy a home-cooked meal. Mehdi saab landed up at Sagar Villa around 2 a.m. at night, drank till five in the morning, after which a lavish dinner with tandoori chicken and mutton rogan josh was served, among other delicacies. Around six in the morning, Papaji let him go after many hugs and memories. Imagine the ladies of the house all locked up in the kitchen cooking and serving the respected guests and at the same time enjoying Urdu shayari and gayaki. It was an unforgettable meeting. There were two more memorable mehfils or Urdu poetry sessions with Arshi Hyderabadi, and with the qawwali queen Shakila Bano Bhopali. The guests who attended the mehfil refused to leave even after sunrise.

On Sundays and holidays the entire clan made it a point to eat together shift-wise, since the dining table could accommodate only a maximum of twelve chairs at a time. Usually, it started with the gang of grandchildren eating makki di roti (Indian bread made with corn flour), with fresh, homemade white butter, jaggery and sarson ka saag (a dish cooked with mustard greens). A variety of dishes always followed—chicken, mutton, fish, sukhi sabzis, dal, curries and biryanis. Papaji, Mummyji, the five sons and a couple of guests would sit next, followed by the daughters-in-law, who would be sweating it out in the kitchen and personally serving the large family. Guests, friends, neighbours and extended family members would often be part of the Sunday lunches. One day, a guest was quietly eating to his heart's content. After he left, Papaji casually asked who he was, and much to our shock, we found out none of us knew him. He had walked in just for a hearty meal.

Sagar Villa was a favourite haunt for everyone in the film industry. Raj Kapoor often came to see his friend from the *Barsaat* days. He would narrate childhood stories of his son Randhir Kapoor (Daboo) and how he would mix up dialogues of his two hit films *Andaaz* and *Dastan*. Balasaheb Thackeray would often spend an evening with Papaji. One of his favourite exercises was to paint with colour dips, fold the paper and make a mirror image and then sign it, saying, 'One day it will bring you big money.' He especially loved to do this for my daughter Shabnam.

Dr Dharamvir Bharati and his litterateur wife had many intellectual sessions with Papaji in Sagar Villa. The Progressive Writers' group including Krishan Chander and Ali Sardar Jafri had their conferences sitting on the floor of the Sagar Villa hall. Two of our films *Hum Tere Ashiq Hain* and *Salma* were shot extensively inside the hall and dining room of our bungalow. In short, the 10,000-square-foot Sagar Villa never slept, and was a hub of various activities round the year. Even spiritual gurus like Acharya Rajneesh and Prabhupada, founder of ISCKON, have visited Sagar Villa. International figures from around the globe like Michael Solomon of Warner Brothers, Hollywood producer Ashok Amritraj, the president of Cinema Products Corporation, Ed Di Giulio, and Andrew Carnegie of Star TV have all graced Sagar Villa at some time or the other.

During informal evenings at Sagar Villa, brothers Govindrao Adik and Ramrao Adik, Maharashtra's heavyweight politicians, Y.B. Chavan, Vasant Dada Patil, Shalinitai, etc., would discuss non-political and personal issues as friends. Ramrao Adik introduced Papaji to Gagangiri Maharaj in Khopoli. Maharajji was the siddha purusha who had mastered the knowledge of jalastambhana, whereby you can live on the oxygen dissolved in water, like fish do. This is how Duryodhana is believed to have stayed under water for days, as mentioned in the epic Mahabharata. Once Maharajji spiritually charged a rudraksh (bead) mala with mantras and put it around Mummyji's neck, curing her of her breathing problem!

Meanwhile, *Prem Bandhan*, starring Rajesh Khanna, did not fare well. Papaji then decided to cast the teenage sensation Kumar Gaurav and filmed his next film *Romance* in the UK and India. This would be Papaji's third film to be shot overseas at Lake District, London, and Newcastle-upon-Tyne in the UK. By the time *Romance* hit the silver screen, Kumar Gaurav had had a string of flops. *Romance* too bit the dust. Never to give up, Papaji picked up his camera and took off to the Himalayas to shoot a very low-budget film, *Kohinoor*, with complete newcomers and a dozen artistes and technicians. It was a spy thriller that was to be shot at Haridwar, Rishikesh and Badrinath. During Papaji's stay at Parmarth Ashram in Badrinath, the head Swamiji had assigned a dedicated personal servant to Papaji.

One day, while pressing Papaji's feet, the servant narrated his life's story about how he had landed in the ashram. Apparently, he was a big businessman, but having failed in business, he had decided to go to the Himalayas in search of peace and to escape from his creditors. Soon he met a couple of sadhus who practised bhoot vidya (knowledge of ghouls). Slowly, he not only gained knowledge of bhoot vidya but also became an exponent of it. As he demonstrated the so-called little miracles with the help of ghosts, a small group of followers started accompanying him. A few ghosts walked along with him, whom only he could see. His miracle ghost-knowledge fame spread all around. He was now in a commanding position with blind followers singing his praises and making offerings to him which boosted his ego. Once there was a big summit of a council of Hindu spiritual leaders where he decided to challenge the religious leaders and their spiritual powers.

As soon as the fake guru entered the gates of the camp, the spiritual head gave one look of disgust, saw the invisible ghosts surrounding him, briskly walked up to him and slapped him tight in front of his slogan-shouting loyal followers. He fell on the ground. The spiritual head then pulled off all his garlands and yelled, 'Do you know what you are doing? All these spirits walking around you ... you fool—you will die the most horrible death! Leave this at once before it is too late.' He fell at the spiritual head's feet, begging for forgiveness and pleading guidance for the way forward. The spiritual head took him to the banks of Maa Ganga, made him sit under a particular tree, drew a twelve-feet wide circle around him and forbade him from leaving the circle for one complete year. For one whole year, people would come and leave fruits, milk and food for the silent sadhu who did not speak or leave his circle. After one year of complete silence and penance, the head of the Parmarth Ashram in Badrinath had taken him under his wings. Papaji was so touched and taken aback by this story that he refused to get any seva done by this spiritually elevated soul, and saluted him for his tapasya.

Papaji had accepted river Ganga as his real mother. He would often visit Haridwar by road or by train. He bought the Nepal kothi built by the Nepal royal dynasty, on the banks of the Ganga and converted it into a hotel. It even had its own private river bank, with water from Har Ki Pauri flowing over it. He would spend days sitting in the balcony, talking to Mother Ganga. He even bought a few acres of land right on the banks of the Ganga river, opposite the town of Kangri, to set up an ashram and spend the rest of his life in seva of his mother. In due course, almost all the railway guards in the trains between Delhi and Haridwar knew him and would spend their free time in his company. One day, a guard brought a twenty-year-old young Nepali boy, requesting Papaji to take him with him to Bombay as he had run away from home and had no one to take care of him. Papaji brought him to Bombay and helped him join the video editing department. His name was Raju Bisht. In course of time, Raju learnt the videotape craft and was put in charge of the edit unit of our production company. He soon managed to trace his parents in Nepal. Today, he is married and has a child. He still works for Sagar Art. Papaji never turned the needy away, perhaps because he had a rough childhood.

Papaji would often collect objects of spiritual significance in the form of shankhs and shaligrams (they are considered the dwelling places of Bhagwan Vishnu and, thus, are auspicious). Once an astrologer in Delhi told him that the food he ate was cooked by a man with only one eye. Papaji came to Bombay to realise that

Kumar, his cook for the last twenty years, had one artificial eye. His temple was filled with photographs of different deities, among other spiritual things. Shaligrams are normally collected from riverbeds and are characterised by the presence of a discus of Bhagwan Vishnu created by a river worm or insect (vajra keeta) that has a diamond tooth that cuts through it.

Shaligrams of different shapes are often associated with different incarnations of Bhagwan Vishnu. Shaligrams have marks of the shankh, chakra, gada and padma. The purest shaligrams are found in the Gandaki river in Nepal. Lakshmi Shankhs are sacred to Hindus around the world. They have a very rare reverse-turning spiral. All shankhs have spirals that twist rightwards, but a Lakshmi Shankh's spiral twists leftwards. These shankhs are found only in the Indian Ocean between Myanmar (Burma) and Sri Lanka.

After the release of *Ghunghat*, Papaji drove back from Madras to Bombay in an ambassador car with Mummyji. In Kolhapur, some students had organised a seminar with him. In the front row, a divine-looking young lad was in attendance. After the show, the parents of the teenage boy introduced their son, Dattabal, to him. He had a visible halo around him. His divinity just shone through, and Papaji felt spiritually drawn towards him. The two would discuss spirituality at length. Even today, Dattabal's samadhi is worshipped by his followers at Sri Dattabal Mission, Kolhapur. I have gone there a few times to pay my obeisance, and I feel at peace there.

Baghavat, a costume period love story between a gypsy and a princess, starred Dharmendra, Hema Malini, Reena Roy and Amjad Khan. Hema looked ethereal in the royal attire of a princess designed by Bhanu Athaiya. Free-spirited Dharmendra was perfectly cast as a gypsy, who protected the delicate princess. Amjad Khan as a tyrannical ruler provided the action. Reena Roy as the silent lover was the twist in the tale, who would reveal that the gypsy was actually a prince born to overthrow the tyrant king. It was a complete masala film with outdoor shoots at Jaipur's forts and palaces. It had shades of the short story 'Wazir-e-Alam', written by Papaji as early as 1939.

The Kumar Gaurav film *Romance* had, for the first time ever, Papaji's name, not as a writer, but only as the producer and director. The story was written by the Mirza Brothers. Papaji had cast Shammi Kapoor in a significant role and deliberately hired the entire team of Kumar Gaurav's debut hit *Love Story*, including R.D. Burman.

Kumar Gaurav was Rajendra Kumar's son, Papaji's friend and the star in his earlier hits—*Zindagi, Arzoo, Geet* and *Lalkaar*. After the first trial in Natraj Studios, the distributors brought a sack full of money to buy the distribution rights. Sensing the craze, Papaji shot two more song sequences. He raised extra money by selling off a part of the prized family property of Sagar Bhavan next door. But before *Romance* could hit the theatres, Papaji's fortunes took a nosedive. The monetary loss was so huge that one day, a financier arrived with a proposal to pawn Sagar Villa against dues owed to him, but finally drove off with Papaji's personal car as interest paid. The babus of Doordarshan spread the word that Ramanand Sagar's 10,000-square-foot Sagar Villa had been bought out of the money he had earned from *Ramayan*. They conveniently overlooked the fact that *Ramayan* was telecast in 1987, whereas Papaji had shifted to Sagar Villa in 1970. With such heavy losses, Papaji decided to remake a Pakistani hit film—*Salma*—with Gulshan Nanda as the writer. He shot practically the entire film in Sagar Villa, with different period settings.

However, the lead pair of Raj Babbar and Salma Agha failed to connect with the audience. With repeated failures at the box office, destiny seemed to be nudging Papaji towards making *Ramayan* for television. After all, the TV show did prove to be Padma Shri Ramanand Sagar's crowning glory.

9

RAMAYAN

Ramanand Sagar, a Ram bhakt, could be said to have been born to rewrite the epic Ramayana for the electronic medium. Many events in his life had already indicated that.

In 1942, when Papaji was twenty-five-years-old, a Kashmiri mystic, Pandit Nityanandji, had predicted that the Ramayana would be retold by Papaji. In 1976, film producer Mr Mohla, on reading Papaji's astrological horoscope chart, had said that Ramanand Sagar would cause a spiritual awakening globally through the medium of cinema. Mohla launched the film *Yogeshwar Shri Krishna* to be directed by Papaji, starring Shashi Kapoor as Krishna. The then BJP supremo L.K. Advani had given the muhurat clap for the film. However, he could not foresee that Papaji was destined to make the *Ramayan* for TV rather than *Shri Krishna* for cinema.

In 1970, Papaji had the divine darshan of the spiritual incarnation of Maha Avtaar Babaji at the Kamakhya Temple, Guwahati, Assam. This was an unusual meeting of a commercial filmmaker like Ramanand Sagar and a highly evolved spiritual soul like Babaji.

Babaji blessed Papaji to fulfil the divine yojana (grand plan) of bringing the tenets and ideals of the Ramayana back to a decaying society through television, a modern medium of mass communication. The reason for this very uncanny and unusual meeting between the two was revealed in 1984 by Swami Ramanuja Saraswati, an atomic nuclear-scientist-turned-spiritual-seeker.

There were many other events like the birth of a calf at Sagar Villa that seemed like a divine sign of the things to come. It looked like Papaji had already taken off on his destined path to make his greatest work.

Born as Chandramouli and being named Ramanand could by itself be considered a divine pointer to the making of *Ramayan*. Once a mendicant came to Sagar Villa and presented Papaji a rare ek-mukhi (single-faced) rudraksha (a seed traditionally used in prayer beads in Hindus) and said, 'You have to do a divine job. My guru in the Himalayas has sent this to you to accomplish this mission.' Without any further word, he immediately left. Papaji got a gold chain made with a tiny Lakshmi Shankh hook to hold the rudraksha and wore it religiously for the rest of his life. After Papaji passed away, my sister Sarita gave the gold chain with the rudraksha to me when Papaji's personal wealth was being distributed. Someone wanted silverware, another, his diamond ring. But I only wanted that rudraksha. Sarita just picked it up and gave it to me.

After having worn the rudraksha for some time, somewhere inside me, I had a nagging doubt whether or not such an invaluable rudraksha would accept me. On my next trip to Haridwar, I decided to do the shudhi (purification) of the rare spiritual wealth, with the holy waters of the Ganga. Sitting on the steps of Hotel Sagar Ganga's banks, I bathed the ek-mukhi rudraksha in milk and honey and, finally, some Gangajal. Suddenly, the rudraksha freed itself from the gold chain and fell into the fast-flowing waters of the Ganga. The way the goldsmith had hooked the rudraksha to the gold chain with the Lakshmi shankh, there was no way this should have happened, but I realised that this was perhaps what the rudraksha was meant to do after its mission with Papaji was over. By the time I came to my senses, much water had flown. I still put my hand into the rapid waters, and lo and behold, the rudraksha just came back into my empty palms! It was beyond me to know what I had been blessed with. The rudraksha is still with me and I am privileged to wear it with the gold chain.

In Hindu cosmology, Bhagwan Shiva is the presiding God of pralaya or cosmic dissolution. It is believed that during pralaya a tear from Shivji's eyes fell on the earth, and it was converted into a rudraksha. One of the names of Lord Shiva is 'Rudra', and 'Aaksh' means the eye. Hence, rudraksha in Sanskrit means the 'eye of Shiva'. Rudrakshas are available from one-faced to twenty-one-faced. Different mukhi rudrakshas are believed to have different qualities, and they nullify evil and confer blessings of the different nav grahas or nine astrological planets/deities. The rarest one-faced rudraksha is Shiva Bhagwan and stands for Surya Dev or the Sun God. Similarly, the three-faced is Agni and Mangal, seven-faced is Mahalakshmi and Shani Dev, eight-faced is Ganesh and Rahu, nine-faced is Durga and Ketu, and the twenty-one-faced is Omkar— the one with everything. Rudrakshas are worn for good health, mental well-being, stress reduction, blood pressure, etc. They are also believed to elevate the soul spiritually and help attain peace and realise aspirations. Scientifically, a rudraksha is believed to have electric, electromagnetic, para-magnetic and inductive powers, which vary for rudrakshas of different numbered faces. How to string rudraksha prayer beads is described in Devi Bhagwat Purana.

In 1943, Papaji saw the impact of the film *Ram Rajya*, directed by Vijay Bhatt, and starring actors Prem Adib and Shobhna Samarth, with crowds filling the streets, overcrowded theatres beholden by beloved 'Ram'. This could be a reason that made Papaji gravitate towards making *Ramayan*. Incidentally, *Ram Rajya* was the only film seen by Mahatma Gandhi. Papaji's entire writing journey from journalism to theatre plays, radio plays, scripts, stories and dialogues for films taught him to transcend emotions, emulate and imbibe the principles, values, morals and idealism and to perfectly adhere to one's dharma, despite the harsh tests of life and time—all portrayed in *Ramayan*. He made many box office hits only to learn the different aspects of mass media. The result was that globally, millions of people were glued to their TV sets mesmerised by Ram's story. Initially, Papaji actively participated, for over fifteen years (1950-65), in a Ram Mandali discussing and analysing Tulsidas's *Ramcharitmanas* in music director Anil Biswas's house, and later, in our tiny flat in Mahim. Papaji even recorded a song as early as 1954 in *Bazooband*.

'... *bina dosh Sita mata ko diya Ram ne ghar se nikaal* ...' written by Prem Dhawan. This song reflected his mind in the episode on the 'Luv-Kush' chapter he made for television *Ramayan*.

In 1976, during the course of shooting for the movie *Charas* in Switzerland, Papaji and the three of us—Subhash, Anand and me—were sitting in a very tiny roadside cafe in the French part of the Alps town Les Deblecaire. It was freezing cold. After a hard day's work, Papaji ordered a jug of red wine. Having served the wine, the French-Swiss man pushed a solid wooden rectangular cabinet of wood to face us and opened its front door to reveal a screen of glass. He switched on a button and soon, we were watching a French film in colour. It was unbelievable to see a solid wooden cabinet with no film tape or cassette playing a film on the screen. We were stunned! It was a colour TV—something we had never seen till then.

I recalled that back in the late 1960s, one day Rajendra Kumar had arrived in a van at Natraj Studios and proudly shown us a colour monitor attached to a video player. He had bought it in Europe during the shoot of Raj Kapoor's *Sangam*. The size of the video cassette was about two feet in length and the magnetic tape three to four inches broad. It was a television set with a magnetic tape video cassette player, where you switched on a film just by pressing a button. It was difficult to fathom how a magnetic tape could show visuals without an optical film print.

Papaji went into deep thought over his glass of red wine. The awakening had happened as ordained. He announced to the three of us, 'I am leaving cinema ... I am getting into television. My life's mission is to bring to mankind the virtuous story of Maryada Purushottam Shri Ram; followed by the one with sixteen virtues, Shri Krishna; and finally, the story of Maa Durga with infinite shakti.'

Papaji, like all commercial filmmakers, had always felt suffocated and trapped in the web of the worries of monetary returns on a film needed for survival on the one hand and pitted against the pulls of his creative side on the other. He always said that his cinematic work was a sugar-coated pill. In three hours of cinema, the ticket-paying audience wants complete entertainment, with Helen's dance and

Mehmood's comedy thrown in. The script has to check all the boxes that make the box office sing, woven with a story told creatively. Every film has to have big returns. One flop and all the financiers and distributors vanish. That's why it is called 'commercial art'. It is not like a painting or a book or poetry where only your talent and years of hard work are at stake. In filmmaking, if the cost of a film is not recovered, you may not be able to make another film. You are a slave and governed by box office returns. Your message as a thinker is hidden and has a minimum role to play. The audiences enjoy their three hours of entertainment since they have paid for it, but for doing that, they must also view five minutes of the maker's thoughts, philosophy and message. Papaji argued that television is free viewing and so you are free to express your philosophy. As a viewer, if you don't agree, you have the choice to switch off or change the channel. In cinema, you are bound in a dark room for a stipulated amount of time but TV viewing can be done from the comforts of your drawing room. Papaji realised that TV was the right medium for his creativity and the future of mass media communication. He was determined that he wanted to switch over to television, and soon. But he met a fair share of ridicule and criticism when he discussed his television plans with others.

The industry people thought that the Sagars had lost their mind. After all, we were a successful production house and things were going fine for us in cinema, so why would we even think of moving to TV? 'Who will watch a serial about mukut-mooch (crown and moustaches)?'

But Papaji was firm. He got pamphlets of *Ramayan* and *Shri Krishna* printed, announcing them to be launched through video cassettes; bought me a round-the-world air ticket, gave me contact letters to some of his richest overseas Indian friends and sent me off on a business trip to collect funds for his mammoth dream project.

Some of them stared at me in disbelief. A few politely instructed their secretaries to see me out of their office. Close friends advised me to put some sense into my father. After a month of hobnobbing, I came back empty-handed. There were zero buyers for Ramanand Sagar's vision and *Ramayan*.

Papaji would often discuss with me matters that he felt deeply about. He trusted me. I felt my father's mission had to be accomplished. I suggested doing test marketing, as they do in Hollywood. In Hollywood, a test marketing is carried out before a film hits the cinema halls. The entire creative unit, especially the director and the editor, view the film with the audience in a free road show in some remote township. They make notes, which are called clap traps, of the moments that had the people engaged, moments when they fiddled in their chairs or times when they were plain bored and took multiple loo breaks. Based on these notes, the entire final print negative would be re-edited and re-punched. Papaji was very happy with my thought process. I approached R.S. Agarwal of the upcoming cosmetic company Emami to fund us. He agreed to allot a silly budget of rupees one lakh for a half-hour episode.

Since I was both a film director and a cameraman, and had knowledge of special effects, Papaji put this responsibility on my shoulders. In the mid-Eighties, when TV had taken off in India, Sharad Joshi, scholar and columnist of the Indian newspaper *Navbharat Times*, and I got down to the roots of Somdev Bhatt's twenty-five stories of the Indian classic *Betaal Pachisi*, the foundation of the TV serial *Vikram aur Betaal*. The idea was to take a classic story and make it both engaging and deeply meaningful. The serial was designed for children and families, but the allotted time slot seemed to be a disaster. Doordarshan (DD), the national broadcasting network, gave it the worst slot of 4 p.m. on Sundays, a time when most children are usually at play.

But *Vikram aur Betaal* created history on Indian television with the *India Today* magazine talking about its '... electronic special effects coming to Indian television ...' and how '*Vikram aur Betaal* has unveiled an electronic era ...' Soon, the children's show took other forms like board games, books and comics, which reflected the wide success of the series. Tabloids like *Mid-Day* published political cartoons with Prime Minister Rajiv Gandhi as Vikram and senior lawyer Ram Jethmalani as Betaal perched on his back, questioning him about the Bofors scandal. Children and families all over India

THE COMPLETE FAMILY NEWSPAPER

MID-DAY

No. 2489 Published simultaneously from Bombay and New Delhi Bombay, Thursday, July 16, 1987

A cartoon from *Mid-Day* (16 July 1987), lampooning the Bofors gun scandal by showing India's top investigative lawyer Ram Jethmalani as Betaal questioning Prime Minister Rajiv Gandhi portrayed as Vikram.

were glued to the title track 'Vikram ... Vikram ... Vikram ... Betaal ... Betaal ... Betaal'. The punchline '... *tu bola aur main chala*' became part of watercooler conversations. Papaji was now confident that 'mukut–mooch' would work. The entire test-marketed star cast of *Vikram aur Betaal* was cast in *Ramayan*. Arun Govil, who played King Vikram, was cast as Ram; Deepika Chikhalia, the princess in many episodes of *Vikram Aur Betaal*, was Sita; Sunil Lahri, the prince in many episodes, became Laxman; and Dara Singh, who had played Virvar the warrior, was now the mighty Hanuman.

Another important reason that made Ramanand Sagar shift from cinema to TV was the increasing hold of the mafia in Dubai on the film industry. The dispute regarding the overseas rights of Feroz Khan's film *Qurbani* was settled by the mafia. Not only Papaji but also a number of other serious dedicated filmmakers considered the future of Indian film industry to be dark, what with the mafia in Dubai increasingly interfering in the film business. They were so right. In the coming decade or so, the conscientious filmmakers and single-film distributors slowly started taking a backseat. First the law of muscle and then the corporate invasion seriously debilitated meaningful commercial cinema.

Ramanand Sagar, as a thinker, realised early on that his independence as a creative filmmaker would henceforth be compromised by such elements, and as a result, he would become only a contractor. Switching to television was the only solution, so he took the plunge, defying the naysayers. He immersed himself into reading the different versions of the Ramayana in various Indian languages, including Goswami Tulsidas' *Ramcharitmanas* (Awadhi), *Valmiki Ramayana* (Sanskrit), *Ranganatha Ramayana* (Telugu), *Kamba Ramayanam* (Tamil), *Bhavarth Ramayana* (Marathi) and *Krittivasi Ramayana* (Bengali). He even researched the Urdu and Persian versions of the Ramayana. After going through more than fourteen versions of the epic, Papaji zeroed in on *Ramcharitmanas* as his main source. His next step was to put together a *Ramayan* committee of responsible Indian experts, scholars, researchers, gyaanis, pundits and thinkers, including Shivmangal Singh Suman, vice president of Kalidas Academy, Ujjain; scholar and Ramayana exponent, Dr Laxmi Mall Singhvi who was also a jurist and the former Indian High Commissioner in the UK; and writer Pandit Chandrasekhar Pandey, professor at Bhavan's College. The responsibility and credibility of the greatest Indian epic weighed heavily on Papaji. After all, it was going to draw a lot of media attention and there were going to be legal hassles too, once it was out on TV and in the public domain.

Meanwhile, DD called for a meeting of filmmakers to discuss partnerships to increase their advertisement revenue. They were looking at production houses that could deliver quality content on the one hand and advertisers and agencies who would like to use television to further their sales on the other. The meeting was chaired by the DD Director-General (DG) Harish Khanna, with the I&B ministry secretary, S.S. Gill, the controller of programmes, Madhukar Lele, and the additional DG Shiv Sharma comprising the core team.

Initially the think tank of the Government of India was averse to the idea of bringing the Ramayana and the Mahabharata on DD. But DD's officials argued that these were classical epics, purely depicting our culture, and not necessarily religious. Valmiki treated Ram as a human being, who is an ideal man—'Maryada Purushottam'. DD invited Ramanand Sagar and other head honchos of credible production houses and proposed the idea of producing the Ramayana and the Mahabharata for DD against telecast fees and Free Commercial Time (FCT), which the production house could directly sell to advertisers to recover their production costs and profits. Papaji proposed to write, produce and direct the televised version of the Ramayana, since he felt he was qualified, having done an in-depth study of the story of Ram. To impress the government babus, he rattled off names of Kamban, Krittivasi, Eknath, Ranganath—apart from Tulsidas and Valmiki—who had written their own interpretation of the great epic, thus making it sound like the greatest Indian mythology spanning the length and breadth of India. The government committee accepted his proposal and requested him to make an official application under the scheme named 'Private Producers Scheme', which reflected the partnership spirit of the public broadcaster, advertiser and producer. He was officially intimated to make a pilot episode. The official editorial team had okayed his concept with seventy-eight episodes in a forty-five-minute slot at 9 a.m. on Sunday mornings. The editorial team, comprising senior DD officials, including Shiv Sharma and Madhukar Lele, were to check the quality and content of the pilot episode submitted, as per government regulations. After discussion and suggestions by Harish Khanna, the pilot episode was approved, and Papaji was given a go-ahead to make a bank of four episodes. Meanwhile, Arvind Mafatlal from the corporate world had agreed to invest money for the initial production cost.

The authorities were concerned as to how a filmmaker would adapt to a small screen. Papaji argued for the length of the slot. He did not want a one-hour slot since he felt it would be difficult to hold attention for that long with distractions around. He also didn't want the half-hour slot since it was too short a time for an epic serial to take the story forward. He had his mind and heart set on a forty-five-minute slot for an epic like *Ramayan*. Thus, the required content would be for thirty-five minutes, with ten minutes of advertisement time, which was sustainable. Normally, TV doesn't have forty-five-minute slots in any part of the world, as it has inherent marketing and programming problems. For a broadcaster, the question is, what does one do with the remaining fifteen minutes of the one-hour slot? Globally, no TV station will accept such a slot. They will re-edit to standardise it for either half or one hour.

After a long creative battle, Papaji finally got the approval. In hindsight, his creative judgement regarding the length of each episode proved right. It was the thirty-five-minute content that kept the viewers glued to their TV sets. No one felt the content to be too little or too much to distract or divert their attention, and they came back next week for more!

Arvindbhai Mafatlal was a true Hindu at heart. He invited Papaji to his Peddar Road mansion for a cup of tea. It was quite an experience—driving up the long winding road to the white mansion. Arvindbhai personally greeted Papaji and our family. The two families sat chatting over hot cups of tea and Gujarati snacks. My mother spent time with the women of the house, while the men, especially Papaji and Arvindbhai discussed the Ramayana at length. I just looked around in awe at the grandeur of the mansion and how the people there were simple and followed the sanatan dharma.

Everything seemed to be going just fine, but a storm was brewing, gathering strength in the power corridors of Delhi. Many a power lobby in the Congress Party felt that broadcasting *Ramayan* on DD would topple the apple cart of politics and the ruling government. Apparently, a major objection came from the I&B minister V.N. Gadgil who felt a Hindu mythological serial on a public broadcaster would give rise to Hindu power and benefit the vote bank of the BJP. He feared that *Ramayan* would instil a sense of pride in the Hindu community and increase the possibility of the BJP coming to power. On the other hand, there were whispers that Prime Minister Rajiv Gandhi himself had suggested that the DD authorities telecast the great Indian epics like the Ramayana and the Mahabharata, and that these epics were our cultural heritage and needed to be shown with pride and in all their glory. The conjecture was that the judgement of the Shah Bano case was perhaps influencing his political decisions. The prime minister may have been advised that the judgement in the case had had a negative countereffect on the Hindu vote bank of the Congress Party. This was attributed to the Supreme Court's judgement in favour of Shah Bano, and the constitutional amendment that was perceived as appeasing the Muslim community and softening the impact of the court's verdict. So, in order to please the Hindus, and at the same time not antagonise the Muslims, the telecast of the greatest epics seemed a perfect political antidote.

A cat-and-mouse game had begun between the bureaucracy ruling Delhi and the cultural decision-makers in Mandi House, the DD headquarters in Delhi. The ploy was not to convey an outright 'no' but find some excuse or the other to delay the permissions and finally find faults or loopholes to not let the epics be telecast. For days and months together, Papaji was made to go around in circles. At times he would wait for hours outside the offices in Mandi House or the secretarial corridors. Many a time, he would park himself for over a week at The Ashok Hotel in Delhi, waiting for a phone call or an appointment, which if it materialised, lasted only a few minutes and yielded no positive results. At times he landed up early mornings at a bureaucrat's house, finding the husband and wife tending to their garden, excusing themselves for not having time for him. It all seemed like a dark tunnel with no light at the end. To add to this, the four pilot episodes were reduced to one. Finally, a peon in Mandi House, while handing back the video cassettes of the four-reduced-to-one episode, officially conveyed to Papaji what the babus at DD felt ... that he did not know how to write dialogues and his language needed to get better. It was humiliating for an author of Ramanand Sagar's standing, having written so many books and film scripts, to hear this. His writing, especially his novel, *Aur Insaan Mar Gaya*, was considered a classic and his dialogues for films like *Paigham* had fetched him honours and awards (Filmfare Award for Best Dialogue).

Without reacting to what the peon had just said, Papaji smiled and told him to convey to the authorities concerned that he would do the needful.

On Papaji's request, Nanik Rupani of Priyadarshini Academy, a heavyweight in political circles, took the Maharashtra cabinet minister Govindrao Adik to meet V.N. Gadgil in Pune with regard to the telecast of *Ramayan*. However, he refused to budge and did not greenlight the broadcast on the pretext of its likelihood of causing a political upheaval. Nanik then managed to rope in four members of parliament to watch *Ramayan* in private at his posh residence on Nepean Sea Road. All four of them pretended to doze off on the pretext of the production being very poor and boring.

Interestingly, the story goes that the I&B Secretary S.S. Gill personally viewed one edited episode and found it very interesting. Perhaps he quietly smuggled the video cassette to his residence and showed it to his deeply religious mother. Possibly, she, a very traditional old woman, was floored by the content that Ramayan offered and paid her respects to Lord Ram, thinking she was seeing God himself!

For her, this 'miracle' was beyond belief. It is said that she was lost and mesmerised after watching *Ramayan*. She felt that 'reading' the Ramayana was nothing compared to 'watching it come alive'. In the morning, at the breakfast table, she asked her son when the telecast was going to happen! Gill diplomatically explained to her the political embargo surrounding the show. At night when he returned home, he was shocked to see that his mother had not eaten a single morsel of food the whole day.

A devotee of Lord Ram, Gill's mother threatened her son that she would give up food and water if he didn't make sure that *Ramayan* was telecast. The 'divine yojana' was about to unfold. Devi Maa had bestowed her blessings on Ramanand Sagar through Gill's mother. In the Mahabharata, Bhishma Pitamaha was bestowed with the blessing of the capacity of 'swecha mrityu' (dying at one's own will) and conquer death by awakening the 'Svadhishthan chakra' in the 'kundalini'. In Jainism, one can opt to die at one's own will by giving up food and water to bring death upon oneself and this is called 'santhara'. I cannot vouch for the veracity of this happening, but this incident about Gill's mother was narrated to me by a highly credible source, who was very close to the family.

Coincidentally, there was a reshuffle in the bureaucracy. The anti-*Ramayan* group of secretaries, joint secretaries, etc., planted by the ministry were shifted to other portfolios. It seems four secretaries were shunted out in a single day. V.N. Gadgil had already been given a new ministry around November 1986. He no longer had any say in the I&B Ministry or DD. The new I&B Minister Ajit Kumar Panja was more cinema-friendly. After all, he had played the lead role of Ramakrishna Paramhansa in the Bengali film of the same name. Gill found the shunting of the secretaries as a perfect escape route. Seizing the opportunity, without any political consultations, he shot off a letter '... there is only one Ramanand Sagar ... there is only one *Ramayan* ...' Things started moving very fast thereafter, and Papaji received a call on 16 January 1987 from the ministry, enquiring whether he could confirm the telecast of *Ramayan* on Sunday, 25 January, a day before Republic Day. An almost impossible task stared at Papaji's face.

Every morning Papaji would feed pigeons on the terrace of Sagar Villa. There was a sack full of bajra (millet) kept for them in the store-cum-lift-room. Papaji believed that the pigeons were sages reborn. He would call the pigeons by the names of rishis—Bhrigu, Vashisht, Atri and Pulast. Before leaving for work every morning, Subhash, Anand, Moti and I would meet Papaji on the terrace for a few minutes before going to the studio office. The day's work, problems, suggestions including issues regarding production, editing, marketing, finance, etc., were sought to be sorted out during this brief meeting. On 16 January 1987, we were in for a surprise when Papaji asked us if we could confirm the telecast of *Ramayan* on 25 January. The instant answer was, 'No, it is impossible.' He quietly told us to meet him the next morning before sending his reply to DD. At night something divine seemed to have happened, as the next morning when we met Papaji on the terrace, both Subhash and

Anand were of the opinion that we should go ahead and make it because it was our dharma, our duty and an opportunity we couldn't and shouldn't miss. I told Papaji that it was his divine mission and we should take the first step and bring it to fruition. Papaji wasn't sure how we could do it. Moti said since each of us was specialised in a particular department of filmmaking, in seven days under the baton of five captains, we could execute it. It was like our minds had been wired to think alike. It was like a force above was nudging us in the right direction and transmitting a certain kind of divine power to do it. Papaji personally called up Gill and confirmed the telecast.

He then immediately shot off to Delhi to collect his letter of approval for the telecast of *Ramayan* on DD from 25 January 1987. On reaching Mandi House, an official of the level of controller of programmes met him and delivered the letter of approval in person. The official, being a Ram bhakt himself, advised Papaji to leave Delhi immediately without any delay. Papaji understood the explosive political implications of issuing such a letter, which normally is not issued due to the calculative manipulations in the hierarchy of Delhi's power corridors. He did not even visit his daughter's house in New Delhi, but instead rushed straight to the Delhi airport. His flight took off and Papaji's face bore a happy glow.

It took a few hours for the bureaucratic DD files to travel from one section to the other and finally to the I&B ministry and the prime minister's house. It created a huge storm and the officials of the ministry were furious. Telephones started ringing with only one command '... take the letter back ... find him!' The supernatural 'Brahmastra'—the mythical all-powerful weapon that never misses its mark according to Hindu mythology—had left its bow. The Brahmastra, with all the power of the universe, upholding dharma and satya, does not retract until it has met its target. *Adi Kavya Ramayan* was set to unfold—one of the greatest ancient epics in world literature, depicting the duties of relationships, portraying ideal characters like the ideal father, ideal brother, ideal husband, the ideal king and ideal servant. The nearly 24,000 verses divided into seven kaands or episodes with teachings of ancient Hindu sages in narrative allegory would soon spread the philosophical and ethical elements of the cultural conscience of India globally to the entire mankind.

The 'divine planning' that eventually led to the telecast of *Ramayan* was sought to be explained on Guru Prasad's portal dated 23 June 2018 titled, 'Rajiv Gandhi Was the Father of BJP'.

I reproduce below, partially, the views published in the press for readers to form their own opinion.

In mid-1980s, after Rajiv Gandhi came into power, some of his actions indeed helped the struggling BJP (still in a stage of infancy) get its first big break. The year 1986 was a landmark year in the history of India due to the communal politics played by Rajiv Gandhi which helped BJP take off.

A seventy-two-year-old divorced woman named Shah Bano was entitled for alimony (maintenance sum) as per Indian law from her ex-husband, but it was denied to her because she was from the Muslim community, which followed its own personal law that did not have such a provision of alimony for a divorced woman.

The case went up to the Supreme Court of India, which followed the rule book (Section 125 of the Criminal Procedure Code of India) and granted the verdict in her favour by ordering her ex-husband to provide her monthly maintenance money. This apparently did not go down well with the orthodox leaders of the Muslim community, who saw this as an attack on Islam (because the orthodox leaders did not want the state to interfere in their personal law). This, in turn, led to a mass outrage among Muslims who began protesting against the Supreme Court and the Rajiv Gandhi government. As an immature politician who had taken the position of the prime minister after his mother Indira Gandhi's death, Rajiv Gandhi lacked the political experience to handle such a situation and quickly slipped into a panic mode. He feared that if he did not intervene in the court judgement, the Muslim community would punish him in the next elections (by not voting for his party) and hence started looking at ways to appease them.

Since Rajiv Gandhi had won two-thirds majority (due to the sympathy wave after Indira Gandhi's assassination), he introduced a bill to modify the Constitution of India in the relevant sections, which, in turn, could nullify the Supreme Court's verdict and thus appease the Muslim community in the name of secularism. Now, this apparently did not go down well with the Hindu community who criticised Rajiv Gandhi for putting vote bank interests above national interests (by amending the Constitution just to satisfy one community). For the first time ever in the history of India, Hindus all over India felt intimidated due to the Congress surrendering itself to the minorities in the name of secularism, even at the cost of the nation. Sentiments were running high and they needed an organisation and a hardliner Hindu leader who could represent them and channelise their energies and sentiments to oppose the Congress party. This was precisely the moment when the BJP (Bharatiya Janta Party) pitched in, and L.K. Advani took a hard stand against it. He utilised the party resources and manpower to spread awareness about this to every nook and corner of the country through the party cadres at the grassroots level and to garner support in his favour. This was the beginning of the BJP's rise and prominence of the Hindutva movement. Now that the Hindus were enraged and the BJP was riding on the anti-Congress sentiments to consolidate its support base, Rajiv Gandhi feared that the Hindus would punish him in the elections and once again slipped into panic mode and started looking at possible options. The Ayodhya dispute, which was going on for more than thirty years, had begun to test the patience of Hindu fundamentalists who were demanding the gates of the disputed structure, the Babri Masjid, to be opened for worship by the Hindus.

The matter was within the scope of the judiciary, but Rajiv Gandhi intervened with an intention of appeasing Hindus, and an appeal was filed to unlock the doors. The swiftness with which the government and the judiciary worked on this matter had amazed everyone. Without wasting any time, the Rajiv Gandhi government testified that it would be safe (i.e., would not affect law and order) to open the gates for worship, and within hours of the verdict, the gates were opened. It was a historic moment for the Vishwa Hindu Parishad (VHP), which felt vindicated after decades of protests and patience. Also, it provided a platform for the BJP to launch its next mass movement in order to garner a much larger support base among the Hindus. This way, Rajiv Gandhi's Hindu appeasement tactic had laid a platform for the BJP to grow.

This was precisely the moment the BJP decided to launch its 'Ram Janmabhoomi Movement' (Ayodhya Temple Movement) demanding permission to build the Ram temple in Ayodhya. This issue had the potential to become a pan-India movement and, in turn, could help the BJP expand its Hindu support base. However, the problem was the lack of awareness among the people. Although Advani and his party were confident of building awareness among the major cities and towns in the form of 'rath yatras', something more was required to evoke the sentiments and to reach out to every corner of the country. Since Ram was one of the several Hindu deities, just using the name of Ram would not have the desired effect unless Hinduism became synonymous with Ram. The BJP needed a medium/platform that could evoke the sentiments of Hindus with respect to Lord Ram across the board—something that could strike a chord in the hearts of all Hindus, from children to their grandparents.[3]

Interestingly, this medium was handed to the BJP on a silver platter by none other than Rajiv Gandhi. In 1985, Rajiv had been contemplating on producing TV serials to be broadcast over DD that could depict the values of the Ramayana and the Mahabharata. He had discussed this with the concerned authorities who, in turn, ordered the Director-General of DD to take it up on priority basis, as it was very rare for a prime minister to discuss such initiatives related to TV serials. This was a great opportunity for DD to show their skills and obedience to the prime minister. This has been explained in great detail in the autobiography of Bhaskar Ghose, the Director-General of DD during Rajiv Gandhi's tenure.

It was decided to take up the DD *Ramayan* project on priority, and a contract was awarded to Papaji to produce the serial, which eventually took the nation by storm. During the telecast, streets were deserted as Indians were glued to their television sets. All those who

3. http://guruprasad.net/posts/rajiv-gandhi-was-the-father-of-bjp/

did not have a TV would gather in the neighbourhood and watch the serial with bated breath. Hindus who had only heard about or read the epic till then were mesmerised by the special effects in the TV serial. During the telecast, the TV set was perceived by some as a temple, and there were even instances of devotees applying tilak and decorating it with flowers and garlands during its broadcast. Being the first-ever television serial broadcast throughout the country, it had instilled devotion for Lord Ram in the Hindus, who had begun to identify him as the de facto deity/symbol of Hinduism. Thus, by the late 1980s, Rajiv Gandhi had successfully (but unintentionally) evoked the sentiments of the Hindus, and the religious context was set.

Advani and his party upped the ante to ride on this religious sentiment (revived due to the serial) and aggressively propagated the idea of the Ram temple at Ayodhya, which struck a chord with the Hindus all over India. In 1990, Advani hit upon the idea of embarking on a 'Rath Yatra', which would traverse through hundreds of towns starting from the Somnath Temple in Gujarat, all the way to Ayodhya in Uttar Pradesh (UP). The Rath Yatra was closely tracked and reported on by newspapers and the media, and there was a spurt of interest and feeling of oneness among Hindus across all castes which helped the BJP consolidate its support base. By the mid-1990s, due to the decisions of Rajiv Gandhi and the timely reactions of Advani, BJP had emerged as an alternative to the Congress, and the rest is history. Sociologists have done sufficient research to prove that *Ramayan* helped in the revival of religious sentiments. For instance, in the book *Politics After Television: Hindu Nationalism and the Reshaping of the Indian Public*, Arvind Rajagopal establishes the link between television, religion and politics during the late '80s and early '90s.[4]

Many years later, the foregoing perspective was endorsed by Arvind Rajagopal, professor of media studies, New York University, as follows:

---

4. Interview with the author of the book can be accessed here: http://www.frontline. in/static/html/fl1716/17160760.htm

Shri L. K. Advani embarked on a Rath Yatra from Somnath to Ayodhya, to ride on religious sentiments revived due to Ramanand Sagar's TV serial *Ramayan*.

(Images sourced from the internet)

... The weekly *Ramayan* tele-epic produced and directed by Ramanand Sagar was what established Doordarshan as a medium across north and south India, despite its reliance on the Hindi language.

Audience estimates grew from four crores to eight crores in a few months. City streets and marketplaces were empty at the time of the broadcast; it was not wise to schedule a public event during that time, as BJP leaders themselves found out when no one turned up for a party conclave held on a Sunday morning at the time of the show. For Doordarshan, the serial was a breakthrough. *Ramayan* won record audiences across Hindi and non-Hindi regions, and turned Sunday morning, which had been a 'soft spot', into primetime. More importantly, people who regarded television as a source of naach-gaana, and as morally dubious, came to regard it as acceptable and even auspicious. Thirdly, the Hindu mythological, which many people assumed was outdated, was shown to eclipse all other kinds of programming ...

... The fact that people across the country set aside their other duties and watched the show at the same time seemed like a celebration of their common heritage. It was often said, Muslims watched it too, as to prove the telecast's non-partisan nature ...

... No one predicted the response *Ramayan* generated. It should be remembered that it was the Congress that launched the serial, just as it was the Congress that launched the campaign to re-open the Babri Masjid. Arun Govil, who played Lord Ram in the serial, was brought out in full costume along with Deepika Chikhalia, who played Sita, to campaign for the Congress in a UP by-election, and Rajiv Gandhi offered Ram Rajya to voters as a campaign promise in 1989. Whatever gains accrued for the Congress from these moves, the net beneficiary was the BJP, who between 1984 and 1989 grew from two to eighty-five seats in the Lok Sabha, aided, of course, by its national campaign to wrest Ram Janmabhoomi away from the Muslims ...[5]

5. 'Our many Ramayanas: The Sunday mythology club' *The Indian Express*, 10 November 2015
https://indianexpress.com/article/lifestyle/art-and-culture/our-many-ramayanas-the-sunday-mythology-club/

The journalistic view was similar to the one expressed in a *Mumbai Mirror* article—'Rajiv Rewrote Ramayan'—by Mayank Shekhar, dated 11 July 2008. Shekhar wrote,

> ... Over twenty-three years since the birth of Indian television, the top billings still relate to the *Ramayan* and the *Mahabharata*. Rajiv Gandhi had just got back from what must have been a fairly tiring day at work. He sat on his couch and switched on his television at home. There were, of course, no channels to browse. For India's relatively young prime minister, as for his starved public in the '80s, there was only Doordarshan. He left it on for a while. Rajiv was clearly unimpressed with the dull affairs on his TV that evening. No one need be surprised. He urgently called to complain to his cabinet colleague, V.N. Gadgil, the minister for I&B then. Rajiv lectured Gadgil on how DD should broadcast serials that depict the values enshrined in our ancient texts and philosophy ... The kind of values that were contained in, say, the Mahabharata and the Ramayana. As is with bureaucracies, Gadgil copied this to the I&B secretary S.S. Gill. Gill may have passed it further down ...

Everyone took a casual suggestion to mean the prime minister wanted the Ramayana and the Mahabharata on DD. There was no time to spare, no tenders, no shortlisting. Two Bombay filmmakers, Ramanand Sagar and B.R. Chopra, were asked to immediately produce the epics. Rajiv Gandhi had asked for *Ramayan*! That is how the biggest moment in Indian television came about.

However, adversities never left Papaji. There was a continuous barrage from the press and the bureaucrats criticising the show and wanting to get the telecast truncated as early as possible, even during its unprecedented success as a cult classic.

Bhaskar Ghose refused to give Papaji an additional twenty-six weeks so that the show could be stopped midway. But the addiction to *Ramayan* in the country was so strong that if it had stopped, the whole country would have been hurt.

Despite Ghose's many efforts, the broadcast of the show did not stop. Papaji sought permission to continue with it, directly from H.K.L. Bhagat, who was the I&B minister at that time. Ghose's

The Ramayan Phenomenon

"BLOCK-BUSTER IN THE HISTORY OF INDIAN TELEVISION..."

"... It has set the Saryu on fire. Why only the Saryu, the Ganga, Yamuna, Narmada, Godavari, Krishna and Kaveri, even the mythical Saraswati, appear to have been affected.

Undoubtedly, "Ramayana" is a block-buster in the history of Indian television. On August 1, a crowd of over 40,000 waited patiently outside Jaipur's Birla Mandir to have a glimpse of Rama (Arun Govil) and Sita (Dipika) who were due to grace the shrine. Even ministers jostled with mesmerised fans for a "darshan". In Chandigarh, guests at a wedding ceremony were kept waiting as the bride failed to arrive at the "mandap" at the appointed hour. Inquiries revealed that she had refused to get married till the day's episode on television was over.

Whether it is Ahmedabad or Patna, Chandigarh or Jaipur, a large number of viewers, especially women, regard the serial as their main method of communion with God. Consequently, many bathe early and light sticks of incense or earthem lamps while the serial is telecast..."

—The Times of India, Bombay

"...Ramayan is a modern day miracle..."

Screen - Bombay

A brochure created by Sagar Art in 1988 about the phenomenal success of *Ramayan*.

dictatorship still did not end. He told Papaji that by reducing the Hindu element in *Ramayan*, it could be made a little more secular so that it could be watched by diverse viewers. This meant that there was no unity among the Hindus, and their ascendancy could not be in danger. But Papaji did not give up, despite all these conspiracies by Ghose. Nor did he agree to any kind of compromise in his direction of the show which he felt could not be stopped or changed. He was smart enough to send the video tapes to Ghose just at the time when there were only few hours left for the broadcast. Despite all the negativity, Ramanand Sagar had delivered the show with complete honesty.

Papaji had barely nine days before the telecast of *Ramayan* on 25 January 1987. The almost-impossible, Herculean job was to find a studio, erect sets, get costumes, etc. During the making of *Vikram aur Betaal*, I had worked very closely with Hirabhai Patel, the famous art director of yesteryears. He had ingenious ideas like miniature palace roofs, entire sets in miniature with background paintings and other cinematic tricks. I had managed to shoot the entire serial *Vikram aur Betaal* in Sagar Villa itself. As a classic costume drama, the script had required palaces, a set resembling the Mahakaal in Ujjain, etc., but the legendary Hirabhai, who had done a lot of mythological shows and fantasies for Wadia Movietone, managed all kinds of settings required on a shoestring budget.

Hirabhai was the owner of the abandoned sprawling Vrindavan Studios in Umargaon, Gujarat. The moulded palace pillars, thrones and settings were ready, all just waiting to be assembled. The creaking doors were opened, the cobwebs cleared and Hirabhai's Vrindavan Studios and Umargaon were about to enter the pages of history. An unknown small sleepy town, Umargaon, on the shores of Gujarat, would soon be recognised globally and find its place of pride on the world map. Even the BBC would speak about it. Papaji concentrated on the writing and research; Anand was the creative director; Moti took charge of editing; Subhash was in charge of production and I was in charge of technical matters, including camera, special effects and graphics. The team worked in total coordination. The star cast of *Vikram aur Betaal*, now in *Ramayan*, was a perfectly well-coordinated one—whether it was Ram, Sita, Lakshman or Hanuman. Sawant Dada and his team, who had earlier worked on multiple mythological episodes and fantasies with the Wadia brothers, were in charge of the make-up department.

On the morning of 25 January 1987, the first episode of *Ramayan* was telecast at 9 a.m. to the whole nation. Papaji and his entire family and staff watched it quietly, sitting on the Persian blue carpeted floor of his bedroom. When the episode ended, there was pin-drop silence for a few minutes, and then the entire room echoed with claps. Despite all the hurdles, Papaji's *Ramayan* was now a reality. Week after week, for seventy-eight weeks, *Ramayan* was telecast without a break or hurdle, no one fell sick, the tapes reached Delhi, at times minutes before the telecast, which was by itself a miracle. Over a hundred unit members, technicians, actors and workers slept in shifts, at times just for a few hours, to complete the shooting and post-production in time. Day and night, the Bombay-Umargaon route had cars plying and trains loaded with the *Ramayan* team. Strictly no air travel was allowed, neither for the boss nor for the actors.

There were no call sheets or schedules. All actors were on twenty-four-hour red alerts. If Papaji finished writing a scene at 3 a.m., the actors immediately got ready with their make-up and costumes and shooting began. There were no shift timings, as it was round the clock. Actors like Dara Singh spent three to four hours in the make-up room. The Hanuman look—with his foam rubber-moulded mouth—involved painstaking effort and was time-consuming. Hundreds of junior artists had to get ready. In the mass monkey scenes, local ideas were adopted—coconut shells with a marble strung between the cut edge to hold between the teeth in the mouth. They were called 'goti bandars' or 'marble monkeys'. During the shot, they were instructed to hold the marble, and a hundred monkey soldiers would be ready in a jiffy. Sawant Dada worked his make-up magic on everyone, be it the gods or the demons.

The pressure of writing weighed very heavily on Papaji. Imagine writing day and night, scene after scene, sometimes on the set itself, while the shoot was on. The responsibility was immense as the viewership was huge and cut across all social strata.

I remember praying in the Hanuman temple at Connaught Place, Delhi. Once, Papaji felt as if a copper statue of Hanumanji in the opposite shop was speaking to him. He just walked across and bought the statue, without even bargaining. After that, he would tell me that whenever he had writer's block, he would talk to the statue kept in his private room about what the dialogues should be. Papaji told me that Hanumanji would 'speak' to him and sometimes even narrate the dialogues required for the scene.

As I recall, on 1 January 2003 Papaji met Ashok Singhal, chief of the Vishva Hindu Parishad (VHP), at Sagar Villa. Both of them exchanged their experiences of miracles during the making of *Ramayan*. Papaji confided in him about how he had been worried and burdened with self-imposed responsibilities. Early one morning, a sadhu came to Sagar Villa. Papaji was on the terrace with my mother, feeding the pigeons.

It was a normal practice for many sadhus to come home or to our office at Natraj Studios. They were all treated with reverence. Some would want a rail ticket, and others, a blanket, and so on. If they appeared genuine, their requests were complied with, and if anything was found suspicious about them, they would still be given a ten-rupee note, because Papaji always believed that a sadhu should never be returned empty-handed. That day, instead of my mother, Papaji decided to meet the sadhu.

He was a very young sadhu and had a brilliant aura around him. Papaji asked him how he could help him. He said that he had come to give him a message from his guru in the Himalayas. Suddenly, to Papaji's shock, the tone and volume of the sadhu changed into that of a command, 'Who are you? What is this pride—I will not do this ... I will not do that! What do you think ... you are making the *Ramayan*! Why are you worried? In the upper spiritual world, there is a yojana vibhag (planning commission). India is going to lead the world and a few of you have been sent to create awareness. Do your work and come back ...' The divine-looking sadhu did not look back, and walked straight out of Sagar Villa.

After that day Papaji knew *Ramayan* was being written and executed by higher powers, and he was only an instrument. One such example to support this feeling was the sequence in *Ramayan* in which Bharat, Ram's brother, refuses the throne. The entire sequence had been shot and canned. Late at night, Papaji got an inspiration to redo it to make it more contemporary and relevant. Before King Dashrath in his royal court, his council of ministers and the praja (people), Bharat first analyses that there are three affirmations required to crown a king. The vote of the people, the approval of the gurus and the acceptance of the king to crown his next heir. In the case of Ram, all three conditions were fulfilled. Why, then, was he sent to exile for fourteen years? If you have a right to vote, it is your duty to protect this right. Surprisingly, no one rebelled when Ram was banished, to live in the forest for fourteen years. In such cases where you do not protect your right, other factors like palace intrigues and secret plots will be forced and dumped on the citizens and the country. This was a commentary on the dynastic family rule prevalent in Delhi.

Ashok Singhal smiled at the incident of the 'miraculous' sadhu, since he knew this was the truth. He then narrated his experience of a similar unbelievable miracle connected to Ram Janmabhoomi. The five officials involved in the historic case were all coincidentally named 'Pandey'. The Faizabad district and sessions judge was Krishan Mohan Pandey, the collector was Indu Kumar Pandey, the lawyer of the petitioner was Umesh Chandra Pandey, and so on. Initially, the judge was about to write that the lock on the disputed structure cannot be opened, but with every sip of tea, an invincible human voice told him that if he did not do it then, it would never happen. Convinced by his inner voice, he passed a judgement, ordering the breaking of the padlock on the door and ordering that the broken padlock be brought to him by evening. Later, the judge went to see Deora Baba, who not only recognised him by name but also said, 'You are the judge who passed the judgement', and then started weeping, with tears rolling down his eyes.

Judge Krishna Mohan Pandey immediately recognised the voice that was pressing him to pass the judgement to break the lock as that of Deora Baba's. Then the Baba asked him to take thirty-one steps backwards, facing him, and then turn and go away without looking back. Within a week, the judge was transferred from Faizabad to a higher post as chairman of the transport department, Lucknow, and then later as a judge in the Allahabad High Court. The divine forces took him away from a communally sensitive town to keep him safe and sound. Truly, this was divine intervention, as mentioned in the *India Today* magazine. In his autobiography, Pandey wrote that a monkey, which must have had some divine power, validated his decision.

The seemingly ageless Yogi Deora Baba was a siddha yogi. He lived atop a twelve-feet-high machan (wooden platform), supported by poles on the banks of the Yamuna river in Vrindavan. He was Indira Gandhi's spiritual guide after the Emergency. Sonia and Rajiv Gandhi took his blessings on the eve of the 1989 general elections. Deora Baba blessed his devotees by touching their heads with his feet from atop his perch. He wore a small deer skin to cover his semi-naked body. He was believed to have supernatural powers, and produced miracles. It was recorded that he lived for at least two hundred and fifty years, but many believed that he may have been five-hundred-years-old and may even have met Goswami Tulsidas,

Yogi Deora Baba

the author of *Ramcharitmanas*. He took samadhi after two years of the telecast of *Ramayan*. Papaji and Mummyji were blessed by him in the Mahakumbh of 1989 at Prayagraj (Allahabad). They were special guests, bathing in the private 'bajra', the royal wooden boat of Rajmata Scindia, which had a covered room with a bathing area for women. A special rectangle cut in the centre of the wooden platform of the room allowed access to the holy Sangam waters.

When my parents went to seek his blessings, Deora Baba was seated on his specially-constructed machan with his limbs and feet hanging out. He touched Papaji's head with his feet and whispered his blessings to him for carrying out the divine work entrusted to him—of reviving the values enshrined in our ancient texts and philosophy to a lost generation. Thereafter, Babaji jumped into the waters of the Sangam. His devotees told Papaji to leave, since for the next two hours Babaji would not resurface, and would go into an underwater samadhi, surviving on the dissolved oxygen of the water, having mastered 'jalastanbhana vidya'.

On 1 January 2003, Papaji further narrated to me that it was Ashok Singhal's view that *Ramayan* was like blowing off the fuse of a dynamite. What had been achieved by spreading the awareness of Ram, in India and globally, through the epic serial, could never have been achieved by thirty-odd 'rath yatras' taken out by the VHP. After the judgement in Faizabad, Singhal left for Badrinath with the first shila (brick) to be placed at Ayodhya's Ram Mandir. He met a sadhu in the Himalayan winters who knew their intentions. He advised them, ordered them in fact, and implored them to go and do the needful right away and place the shila in Ayodhya, since Bhagwan Ram wanted to build his house and no one could stop him. These were the words of the sadhu as told by Singhal.

A number of interesting incidents happened during the gruelling seventy-eight-week non-stop twenty-four hour shooting schedules. The *Ramayan* magic spread nationwide, like wildfire. In Umargaon, we had tribal women placing their newborn babies at the feet of Lord Ram for blessings. Scores of VIPs and visitors had to be catered to and looked after, while also keeping in mind to not delay the shooting schedules. Busloads of devotees and fans thronged Vrindavan Studios. Once three buses full of Ram devotees travelled for three days from Vijaywada, a thousand kilometres away, just to have a darshan of Ram. Not only were they allowed to meet Arun Govil, who played Ram, but we also gave them hot meals, bedding, milk for children and drinking water for the journey back. Their devotion and reverence for Ram had to be respected. The invisible hand of God's grace was evident during the making of *Ramayan*.

Halfway through the telecast of *Ramayan*, the character Sugreeva was to be introduced in the story. For months, the casting team had failed to find an actor to match the build of Dara Singh (Hanuman). Papaji rejected all the candidates suggested and continued shooting with a calm mind, very sure that Sugreeva would soon materialise. If nine days were enough to get *Ramayan* on the network, then seven days were enough for Sugreeva to appear, he thought.

Shooting in the adjoining jungle between the studio and the beach, one night, around 3 a.m., he called for pack up. As soon as the lights were switched off, in pitch dark, a silhouette of a tall figure appeared. It was scary, as there was not a soul around. The hulk of a figure came charging towards the unit. We were all very scared, but the big black ghost-like figure kept coming closer and finally leapt and fell at Papaji's feet. The lights were immediately switched on, and there, in front of us, was the perfect muscular human form of a wrestler. Papaji asked who he was, and he said, 'I am Sugreeva.' Everyone was stunned beyond belief as 'Sugreeva' turned out to be a pehlwan—a wrestler who did kushti (wrestling) in the akhadas (wrestling rings) of Indore. He had watched *Ramayan* and knew he had the build required to play Sugreeva. He was immediately sent to the make-up room and shooting for the Sugreeva chapter commenced. He had never acted, and he didn't know how to speak or memorise his lines. On the sets, he would speak the foulest language, used in wrestling combats. The foam rubber mask of the monkey and dubbing did the rest.

Then there was the case of Sushain Vaid, the ayurvedic doctor of the demon king 'Ravan'. He owned a betel nut shop in Indore and sold 'Ramayan paan' to diehard *Ramayan* fans during the telecast of the serial, just to boost his own ego. They convinced him that he looked like Sushain Vaid. He also had some basic elementary knowledge of Ayurveda. He approached Papaji, who immediately sent him for a look test. After *Ramayan*, he became a celebrity in Indore and started attending functions as a chief guest! He also would dispense medicines on the sly at a high price, exploiting the patients' belief that he was like the divine doctor who had cured 'Lakshman'!

There were many interesting incidents during the telecast of *Ramayan*. Apart from powerhouses being set on fire by frenzied mobs if there was a power cut during the telecast, brides were said to have run away from the marriage mandaps, to not miss watching *Ramayan*, before completing the nuptials. Streets in Karachi (Pakistan) were said to have worn a deserted look on Sunday mornings during the telecast. Even funeral processions were said to have been halted, with the corpse made to sit on a chair with open eyes to watch *Ramayan* for one last time! In Delhi, ministerial swearing-in ceremonies had to be delayed for lack of attendance, political rallies had to be postponed and the Hindu-Muslim rioters in Muzaffarnagar were said to have found deserted streets. Such was the impact of *Ramayan*! As one newspaper put it, 'It was a revolution in those times.'

Every Sunday, the train from Patna to Delhi would be delayed by one hour. The railway inspectors who were sent to find out the mystery behind this phenomenon discovered that only on Sundays the long-distance train reached a station called Rampur at 9 a.m. All the passengers, guards and even the driver would get off the train and go straight to the waiting room. They would sit in front of a TV set, garland it, break a coconut, light incense sticks and shout 'Jai Shri Ram'. For forty-five minutes, no one would move, and there would be pin-drop silence. Thereafter, the train would leave, an hour late. It was revealed that all the regular passengers had pooled in money and bought a black-and-white TV set, only to watch *Ramayan* every Sunday morning.

Another incident was about journalist Ali Peter John (who worked for *Screen* then), who was recouping at the Holy Spirit Hospital in Marol, Bombay. Next to his bed in the common ward was a fifteen-year-old who had lost his memory. His mother and sister would visit him regularly and try to jog his memory, but in vain. One Sunday morning, someone brought a TV set and put it in the common ward for everyone to watch *Ramayan*. Ali noticed a change in the boy's expression. After the episode ended, to the utter surprise of everyone, the boy asked everyone if Lakshman was alive after Indrajeet's arrow knocked him unconscious. The doctors rushed to the patient and the mother and sister hugged him, tears rolling down their cheeks. The entire ward was stunned at this miracle.

One day Papaji received a frantic call from a very prominent doctor from Madras. One of his senior citizen patients had gone into a deep coma, since he was unable to bear his icons Ram and Lakshman waiting for their deaths, caught in a 'Naagpash' (snake trap). The doctor fervently requested if someone could be flown to Madras by the next flight with the next week's episode where Ram and the 'Sheshnag' avatar of Lakshman came alive. This was considered to be the only last hope medically. Papaji roughly edited the rushes and dispatched the next week's episode, showing Ram and Lakshman alive, saved by Garuda, the enemy of snakes. The Ram devotee bounced back to life, weeping profusely and paying obeisance with folded hands. Such was the impact of the serial ... nothing short of divine.

After the Sunday telecast of the Naagpash episode, another shock awaited Papaji. On the following day, a leading newspaper carried headlines about a nationwide revolt by pundits, Ram Katha Vachaks (narrators of the story of Lord Ram), diehard Hindus and scholars, that Ramanand Sagar did not know the Ramayana and that he had fictionalised the sequence of Naagpash since there was no mention of it in the classic tale. Immediately, Papaji shot off a press release giving the page number and the verse number detailing the deadly sequence and specifically mentioned the Sankat Mochan Hanuman Masthak, which spoke about the Naagpash sequence. This clarification cleared the air and the whole nation rested easy. From there on, viewers had unwavering faith in the serial and its makers.

In another interesting incident, in Patna, there was an asylum with a central courtyard surrounded by cells secured with iron bars on all four sides. Several monkeys inhabited the surrounding trees. There was a continuous tussle between the inmates of the asylum and the monkeys over the food served to them. A psychiatrist suggested that if the inmates were shown the serial *Ramayan*, seeing the character of Hanuman on the screen, they might become more friendly towards the monkeys. The authorities placed a TV set in the middle of the open courtyard surrounded by the prison cells. Every Sunday, the inmates were let out and made to sit in front of the TV. Soon enough, Hanumanji, with his devotion and spiritual charm, had won over these inmates who then became friendly with the monkeys and even started sharing their food with them. Every Sunday morning, the monkeys would join the inmates in watching *Ramayan*.

It was a miraculous bond between man and animal. One day as soon as the title music came on, one of the older monkeys that had not yet made it to the TV set immediately started to swing from one branch of the tree to another, to make it in time for the show. The title song had become like a clarion call for the monkeys. Not wanting to miss the telecast, the monkey rushed and misjudged the last swing and fell with a loud thud on the ground. He died immediately. The inmates and the other monkeys not only buried him with honours but also built a little memorial for their 'Ram bhakt Hanuman'. Ramayan could make the adage 'Vasudhaiva Kutumbakam'—the whole world is one single family—ring true. ('Vasudha' means 'the earth', 'iva' means 'is' and 'Kutumbakam' means 'family').

On the day the killing of Ravan was shown on TV, the entire village where the actor Arvind Trivedi (playing Ravan) was born went into mourning. Every villager was sad at the 'death' of one of its sons of the soil.

Superstars Ram, Sita and Ravan finally got sucked into the political arena. They were offered tickets by the BJP for the Lok

Sabha elections. Deepika, who had played Sita, and Arvind Trivedi became MPs. Even Rajiv Gandhi used Arun Govil dressed as Ram to campaign in UP. In return, it is believed that he was given a show on DD.

An article published in the *The Sunday Times*, London, dated 31 January 1988, by Tavleen Singh, read as follows:

Hindu TV super soap brings nation to its knees in prayer

An ancient epic about the Hindu God Ram has become India's most successful television soap opera, watched by virtually the entire country's viewing population. When *Ramayan* is shown, life in cities, towns and villages across India comes to a virtual standstill. Conches are blown in celebration and incense sticks burned atop TV sets; after a power cut blacked out screens in the city of Jammu during transmission of the programme, riots erupted. And in Lucknow, distraught patients complained that doctors and nurses had abandoned them while the show was on the air.

Milk goes undelivered until *Ramayan* is over, telephones remain unanswered and political rallies have been postponed to avoid clashing with the series.

The director general of Doordarshan, India's state-controlled TV network, said that although *Ramayan* (the story of Rama) should have ended in December, the producer was allowed to extend it for another twenty-six weeks, to avert potential violent protests.

The story is among India's oldest and is believed to have been written more than 2,000 years ago. It tells the story of the God King called Ram, and his wife Sita, who are exiled from his kingdom Ayodhya by a stepmother with eyes on the throne for her own son.

Sita is abducted by an evil king of Lanka (Sri Lanka) called Ravana, and *Ramayan* tells of Rama's fight to get her back. Indian television-viewing has grown phenomenally in the past five years and now covers more than 70 per cent of the country, although there are believed to be only about 10 million sets with an estimated six viewers per set.

Since most viewers are semi-literate, deeply religious and Hindu, religion in the form of television soap opera is an obvious money-spinner. *Ramayan*, however, has created considerable controversy because many people feel it goes against India's supposedly secular grain.

Since *Ramayan* is considered one of the sacred Hindu texts, viewing it on television is treated by many as a rite of worship. Shoes are removed and offerings of flowers sometimes made to the TV. Religion has always been closely linked to theatre in India and religious films are big business. A few years ago, the Bombay cinema surpassed itself by inventing a Goddess, Santoshi Maa, who is now widely worshipped. For Doordarshan, Ramayan appears to be the first of many religious soap operas. Mahabharata, another Indian television epic, is already in the making, and others are bound to follow.

In an article 'Born to Make *Ramayan* in Kalyug … Jai Sagar Saheb', Ali Peter John, the columnist for the Indian film trade weekly, *Screen*, hailed Ramanand Sagar as one born to make *Ramayan*. He wrote: '… Ramanand Sagar, who was given up to die as a tuberculosis (TB) patient once, was born to fulfil the God-given mission. He was not born to make all those innumerable films which have made him Ramanand Sagar, the well-known writer and filmmaker. He was born to make *Ramayan* in Kalyug at a time when it was needed the most. Sagar who wore a crown once now wears a halo. Men, who used to touch his feet with respect, now touch them with reverence. He is treated like one of God's chosen ones …'

Born to rewrite and present *Ramayan* for the electronic era, Papaji's mission, according to the divine yojana, was now complete. He had to now move to the next chapters of Krishna and the shakti of Maa Durga.

10

SHRI KRISHNA
(1992–99)

Ramanand Sagar firmly believed that Maryada Purushottam Shri Ram would never banish his pregnant wife to the forest, that too, based merely on a washerman's hearsay who questioned the chastity of his wife when she had been forced to sleep for a night at a stranger's house when a flooded river prevented her from coming home, and passed sarcastic remarks about Lord Ram welcoming his wife back home after having been incarcerated in Lanka.

Doubts were earlier raised about the chastity of his pregnant wife, Sita. But she had already proven her chastity when she went through the Agni Pariksha (trial by fire). Yet the story went that the ideal Shri Ram was supposed to have requested Lakshman to leave Sita in the forest on some pretext. Papaji could never imagine his Ram ever doing anything like that. Such a conviction also seems to have been the dilemma before Sant Tulsidas while writing the *Ramcharitamanas*. Hence, he wound up his epic *Ramayan* with the establishment of Ram Rajya (the rule of Ram) on his return from the fourteen-year exile in the forest. He ended the story by merely mentioning that Ram had two sons. The rest of the story, 'Uttarkaand', with Luv and Kush, Ram's two sons, developed as narrated by other writers. Perhaps the original Valmiki Ramayana did not include 'Uttarkaand' at all. It was believed to have been added later by other narrators to spice up the story. Many staunch Hindus believed that preachers from other religions like Buddhism, Jainism and Islam did this calculatingly, so as to degrade the ideal character of Shri Ram and dilute the sanctity of the original Ramayana. Papaji wrote the script of the TV serial *Ramayan* according to *his* outlook and belief, with the climax of the crowning of Shri Ram establishing Ram Rajya. He made it clear to the DD authorities that he would end the serial with that last episode.

The telecast of the last of the seventy-eight episodes had the maximum viewership, followed by a total void the next week. It was understood that the Luv-Kush chapter would also be telecast. When it didn't happen, the Valmiki Samaj was the most hurt, since, for them, Bhagwan Valmiki was the main protagonist of the Luv-Kush chapter. The hurt slowly turned into anger; not showing the Luv-Kush chapter amounted to insulting their God. A storm started brewing. When cries for justice, appeals, strikes and rebellion did not work, anger turned into mob violence. It is believed that as a protest, streets were strewn with garbage, especially the Grand Trunk (GT) Road. The flesh of dead animals, carcasses of dogs and other animals were strewn on the GT Road from Delhi to Jalandhar. There was already a fear of a cholera epidemic breaking out due to the indiscriminate dumping of garbage. The rotting flesh of the dead animals would, as it was expected, give rise to the dreaded disease 'anthrax'. The disease caused fever, swelling and often death, especially of sheep and cattle. It could also affect humans due to exposure to infected animals. Crusading invaders to South America—such as Columbus in the fifteenth century—are believed to have conquered the native Americans by infecting them with deadly anthrax by strewing rotting flesh and carcasses of dead animals on their seashores.

Eventually, the Prime Minister's Office (PMO) got involved. Papaji started receiving telephonic requests to shoot the Luv-Kush chapter. But he stood firm in his belief. Calls from the PMO became frantic and desperate. Politically, it was difficult to hold back the tsunami of the Valmiki community. After intensive research for an alternative to Shri Ram banishing Sita to the forest, Papaji came across the

Radheshyam Ramayan. According to this, both Sita and Ram have their secret emissaries reporting to them about the sentiments of the praja, their subjects. The husband and wife meet them at night to take their briefs. Taking creative liberty, Papaji decided that Sita finally decides that she is Ram's ardhangini (other half) and thus has the right to decide to protect the image of her husband. She cannot accept or allow the subjects to point fingers at her husband and so she decides to leave Ayodhya on her own. To her, the rights and duties of a king are greater towards the subjects of the state than to his wife, son or father. At night, in their private chamber, she conveys to Ram that instead of him banishing her to exile, it would be her decision to leave Ayodhya. Papaji shot the episode with great sensitivity and presented it as righteously and morally as possible.

Before the Sunday telecast, out of nowhere, Dhirendra Brahmachari, the yoga yogi, stormed into the office of DD, authoritatively ordering a ban on the telecast of the episode of Sita's vanvas. The yoga yogi was a powerful political figure in the power corridors of Delhi. He had been extremely close to Indira Gandhi and, as alluded to by Khushwant Singh, '... one who had an hour with Indira behind closed doors every morning; yoga lessons may have ended up with lessons from the Kamasutra ...' Pupul Jayakar, known as the cultural czarina, maintained that 'the Indian Rasputin ... reportedly started to use her (Indira) name to pressure businessmen and officials ...' The 'Flying Yogi' owned an ashram at Mantalai (Jammu) with a private airstrip, and the Shiva Gun factory, apart from a Pitts S2 aircraft, expensive cars, etc. Nehru's private secretary, M.O. Mathai, described Dhirendra Brahmachari as 'very dangerous and powerful'.

As fate would have it, Papaji was at the DD office when the yogi, for reasons best known to him, nearly succeeded in derailing the Sita vanvas episode of the *Uttar Ramayan* (as the Uttarkaand was known on TV) telecast on DD. There was only an hour left for the telecast but Papaji refused to budge from his stand. He resisted powerful arm-twisting tactics used to pressurise businessmen and officials.

Who can be more powerful than Shri Ram? Papaji thought. The Sita vanvas episode was telecast as scheduled. But just imagine the network of the 'Flying Yogi'! The super-sensitive episode was kept a secret, flown to Delhi only on Sunday morning, delivered to DD just an hour before its telecast. And still, the Rasputin yogi was there to demand his pound of flesh. But this was not the end of Papaji's travails. After its telecast, there was a hue and cry across the length and breadth of India. 'How can Ramanand Sagar distort the *Ramayan*?' was the sentiment which culminated in a court case at the Allahabad High Court, which went on for a few years.

The diplomat-administrator and lieutenant governor of Delhi, Romesh Bhandari, negotiated for peace with the Valmiki Samaj for the telecast of the Luv-Kush segment on DD. He was instrumental in bringing about the meeting between Papaji, Prime Minister Rajiv Gandhi and the Valmiki Samaj. Rajiv Gandhi and Papaji garlanded a painting of Sage Valmiki, and the Luv-Kush telecast was cleared.

Finding child actors to play Luv and Kush was another story. Once, travelling by a private taxi in Delhi, the driver asked Papaji why he looked so hassled. Papaji told him, 'I cannot find actors to play Luv and Kush.' After watching *Ramayan*, the Haryanvi driver too, like millions across the country, had become a big Ramanand Sagar fan. With great hesitation, he asked Papaji if he would like to visit his home and meet his two infant sons named Luv and Kush. Papaji just smiled at the divine planning and the infants played Luv and Kush for an episode! Once Papaji told me that *Luv Kush* (*Uttar Ramayan*) was his best work on TV, and it would live long due to its deep philosophical and emotional content.

I must narrate a divine incident that took place on the sets of *Luv Kush*. As the story goes, Kakbhushundi, the king of crows, could not believe that the little child at King Dasharath's palace crying for milk was Ram, the avatar of Vishnu. So he snuck into the room of infant Ram crying like a human baby. Suspicious, Kakbhushundi hopped near the baby and snatched the roti from Ram's hand. Baby Ram started crying louder, as all babies do. Kakbhushundi was then convinced that the baby was a mere human and not a god, and could not protect himself. But while flying away, he realised that baby Ram was holding on to his feet and flying with him. A shocked

Kakbhushundi unsuccessfully tried his best to shake off the baby, traversing through different spiritual realms. He finally returned to Dasharath's palace to find to his utter disbelief that the baby was still crying! Realisation dawned upon him, and the enlightened Kakbhushundi bowed his head in complete surrender to Shri Ram. For the next day's shoot of the Kakbhushundi scene, many unit members and studio hands spent hours trying to catch a crow. After hard pursuit, they managed to catch four of them. The four were chained to prevent them from flying off or escaping at night. By the next morning, only one remained, and that one too was struggling with his sharp beak to break free.

The shot was readied. Baby Ram was placed in the middle of the room and the lone crow was chained next to him. The lights were switched on. Papaji prayed silently while the crow created a ruckus. He went to the restless crow, folded his hands in submission

The child artistes (Swapnil Joshi on the left and Mayuresh Kshetramade on the right) who played Luv and Kush.

Photo collection: Ramanand Sagar Foundation

to Kakbhushundi and pleaded, 'Kakbhushundiji, this episode has to be telecast this Sunday. I have come to your sharan. Please help me.' There was pin-drop silence—the ferocious crow had totally calmed down. It seemed Kakbhushundi had descended on the earth and into the body of the captive crow. Papaji started shooting, and the crow was unchained. For ten minutes, the camera was rolling. Papaji kept giving instructions, 'Kakbhushundiji, go to baby Ram and snatch his roti ...' The crow followed the instructions meticulously, snatched the roti, then gave it back to the wailing child and looked at him suspiciously, all the time acting and reacting to what was happening in the scene. After ten minutes of continuous filming, it just flew away. I was witness to this divine spectacle. There was no doubt that Kakbhushundiji—the king of crows—had come to fulfil Ramanand Sagar's mission!

The mission Papaji had undertaken, of following the telecast of *Ramayan* with *Shri Krishna* and completing the trilogy with *Shakti Maa Durga*, was about to be accomplished. It is worth recalling that the ruling Congress Party had lost eighty-six seats to the BJP after the telecast of *Ramayan*. The chatter in the ruling party was that if the *Shri Krishna* telecast was allowed, the Congress Party would surely lose again. And that is exactly what happened. From a mere two seats in 1984, the BJP rose to eighty-five seats in 1989 after the telecast of *Ramayan*. After the telecast of *Shri Krishna* on DD, the BJP won 161 seats and they came to power in Delhi. The forecast had proved to be right. Congress, the ruling party, had lost significantly after the telecast of *Shri Krishna* on DD.

Papaji had to cross bigger hurdles to bring *Shri Krishna* to TV. He not only blindly believed in, but had now also experienced, the omnipotence and omniscience of the Almighty, with the power to achieve anything, even the seemingly impossible. Normally, any TV channel, be it the BBC or CNN, would have laid down a red carpet to welcome Papaji after the legendary success of *Ramayan*, but DD was like a puppet controlled and run by dynastic political strings.

Papaji applied for producing *Shri Krishna* under the same scheme of 'Public broadcaster, Advertiser and Producer'—a partnership in spirit—as he had for *Ramayan*. Under the scheme, a producer had to buy a slot against Free Commercial Time (FCT). The application for *Shri Krishna* in this free-for-all auction scheme drew zero response. Having waited in the wings for months, Papaji started following up with letters of appeals, recommendations and requests by prominent personalities, including Opposition leader L.K. Advani, president of India R. Venkataraman, joint general secretary of VHP, Acharya Giriraj Kishore, I&B minister, Ajit Kumar Panja, industrialist scholar Ram Krishna Bajaj, Dr Shivmangal Singh Suman, the vice president of Kalidasa Academy, Ujjain, respected journalist Harindra Dave of *Janmabhoomi*, future prime ministers of India P.V. Narasimha Rao, Chandra Shekhar and V.P. Singh, Chief Justice P.R. Gopal Krishnan (also chairman of the advisory panel for *Shri Krishna*), prominent jurist Dr L.M. Singhvi, and Lok Sabha speaker Shivraj Patil. Despite support from such esteemed people, there was no response from DD. It was quite evident that the dynastic ruling family was perhaps not in favour.

Once the serial was underway, finding the right actor to play Krishna was another major hurdle. Papaji believed that God should be bigger than a star in TV serials, lest it affected or tilted the business scale. Even in *Ramayan*, he cast Arun Govil, who had no star image at all. The underlying philosophy was that the audience should 'see' and 'experience' Shri Ram and not be carried away by any star's image. Also, casting Arun as Shri Krishna was not an option, since people had now started looking at him as 'Ram', and they would have had trouble accepting him as Shri Krishna.

Many new faces were auditioned unsuccessfully. Finally, Papaji came across a Sanskrit film on the life of Adi Shankaracharya and found that the actor playing the lead fit the role of Krishna perfectly. Thus, Sarvadaman Banerjee was auditioned, and Krishna was found. Finally, as per Chakradhari Shri Krishna's plan, the video screening of *Shri Krishna* started on giant projection screens in Ujjain on 22 April 1992.

The battle lines were drawn. The war had begun. Papaji and I, as marketing directors of the Sagar Group, chalked out a strategy to take *Shri Krishna* to the masses. *Shri Krishna* video cassettes were launched in twenty-six volumes, each volume containing three

Video raths in Indore announcing the screening of Ramanand Sagar's *Shri Krishna* on giant screens.

Photo collection: Ramanand Sagar Foundation

episodes of forty-five minutes. I got the support of the corporates, Dabur, Amrutanjan and Mafatlal. Each of them bought twenty-six minutes of advertisement in the twenty-six volumes, with one minute in each cassette and twenty seconds of TV commercials after every episode. The idea was that every advertiser should get exposure across all seventy-eight episodes (twenty-six cassettes with three episodes each). The crowning glory was the buying of the remaining six minutes in all twenty-six VHS cassettes—a total 156 minutes of advertisements—by Hindustan Lever. At Rs 1 lakh a minute, the marketing team managed to garner twenty-six cassettes with nine minutes of advertisement in each cassette, a total of Rs 2 crore 34 lakh for the entire project. This came to Rs 3 lakh per episode. It was a marketing coup.

A *Times of India* article, 'Krishna enthralls crowds in Ujjain', carried the news of *Shri Krishna*'s video screening as regular evening slide shows. The crowds, instead of flocking to TV sets, as during the telecast of *Ramayan*, were now lining up in front of giant projection screens.

Photo collection: Ramanand Sagar Foundation

During this phase, I met the legendary marketing guru Shunu Sen, the marketing director of Hindustan Lever. During my very first meeting in his office at Lever House, Backbay Reclamation, I completely surrendered myself to his thinking. Sitting across him, I said, '*Ramayan* is the greatest Hindu epic.' Shunu retorted sharply, 'No, it is not the greatest Hindu epic!' I felt this corporate 'suit-boot babu' was insulting me—being a Hindu, insulting Hinduism, the oldest and the greatest religion in the world. The war of words escalated, and I rose to leave before retorting, 'If *Ramayan* is not the greatest Hindu epic, then what is?' He replied calmly, '*Ramayan* is the greatest Indian epic. We want everyone to view it ... Hindus, Muslims, Parsis, Buddhists, Jains ... all those who consider themselves Indian.'

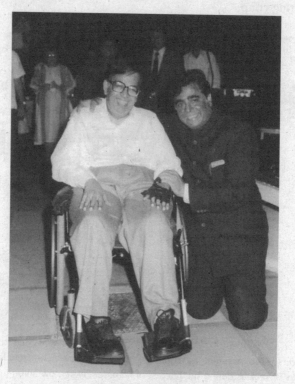

Shunu Sen and me.

Photo collection: Ramanand Sagar Foundation

I bowed down before him. Shunu accepted my proposal instantly and wanted the remaining six minutes in each of the twenty-six cassettes. He even coaxed me to remove Mafatlal, Amrutanjan and Dabur. I refused to budge. Not only was I committed to them, but it was also against my ethics and dharma. He saw my point.

To put my second strategy into place, with the help of my friend Ali Peter John, I managed to enter *Shri Krishna* in the non-competitive section of Remini Cinema (Italy). It was awarded a silver medal, and the news spread like wildfire. It got wide coverage that created a furore in Delhi. It brought about a deep awareness about the *Shri Krishna* serial being honoured on foreign soil but not being telecast by the Indian public broadcaster, DD! The rebellious voices were getting louder. 'Krishna is an Indian God. Hindus revere him and have deep respect and admiration, pray to him daily. How can the government be so blind?' was the refrain.

The time was now ripe for launching my Brahmastra. Through the Mauritius Broadcasting Corporation (MBC), I sent a message to the prime minister of Mauritius, Anerood Jugnauth, and requested for the repayment of a favour done to the MBC earlier by the Sagar family. Ram Lakhan of MBC had approached us to help the Hindu population in Mauritius to retain their cultural roots and uphold their Hindu religion.

No one would have given the MBC Hindi serials at an affordable cost, but Papaji gifted the superhit series *Vikram aur Betaal* to Mauritius free of cost as a contribution to the Hindus living on foreign soil. Keeping this favour of Ramanand Sagar in mind, an overjoyed Jugnauth accepted the proposal of doing a world premiere of *Shri Krishna* in Mauritius. The actors, my brother Anand (who had directed the series) and I were sent free air tickets and flown as VIPs to Mauritius. While being driven around the capital city of Port Louis on arrival, we saw the streets were lined with enthusiastic, cheering crowds showering flowers from their balconies. The prime minister's wife, Sarojini Jugnauth, launched the world premiere by lighting the traditional oil lamp at a special function.

In my speech, I said that we had launched *Shri Krishna* on the soil of Mauritius for the world family (Vasudhaiva Kutumbakam):

'We are all here today to enjoy the divine pleasure of a historic day for my family, our family and the world family. My family's mission has been fulfilled today.'

This created a storm in India with headlines in newspapers asking why the show was premiered in Mauritius and not in India. Did Krishna not belong here? Vishnu incarnated into his Krishna avatar in India, not in Mauritius. The Congress government was questioned in the Parliament. Some members even went to the extent of labelling them anti-Hindu. In the Rajya Sabha, a starred question was asked by Krishnalal Sharma, Member of Parliament, Rajya Sabha, on 27 February 1992, as to why *Shri Krishna* was not being accepted for telecast in India on DD.

R A J Y A S A B H A

GOVERNMENT OF INDIA
MINISTRY OF INFORMATION
AND BROADCASTING   STARRED QUESTION NO. 50

(TO BE ANSWERED ON 27-02-1992)

TELECAST OF T.V. SERIAL 'KRISHNA' IN CANADA:

*50. SHRI KRISHAN LAL SHARMA:

Will the Minister of INFORMATION AND BROADCASTING

सूचना और प्रसारण मंत्री   be pleased to state:

(a) whether it is a fact that T.V. serial 'Krishna' is being telecast in Canada;

(b) whether it is also a fact that the same serial is still pending for approval in our country;

(c) if so, the reasons of the delay in this regard; and

(d) by when the same is likely to be cleared for telecast in the country?

In the Rajya Sabha, Krishnalal Sharma tabled a starred question, regarding *Shri Krishna*'s telecast in Canada and its not being approved in India.

Photo collection: Ramanand Sagar Foundation

Amidst all this, DD announced the start of a new channel, DD2. R.K. Swamy, head honcho of one of the top five advertising agencies in India—R.K. Swamy and Sons—was a hardcore Hindu. He applied for a Sunday morning slot, signed the contract and paid the necessary fees/advance as required. DD was only too happy to have him on board. They did not think it necessary to even ask him the name of the programme he proposed to telecast on the allotted Sunday morning slot. Meanwhile, Papaji got the serial on the video cleared by the censor board of India, knowing fully well that DD would find the flimsiest of excuses to stop its broadcast.

On Thursday, 20 August 1993, the DD babus asked Swamy the name of the serial he proposed to telecast. Swamy mentioned *Shri Krishna*. The I&B minister and DD heads were visibly enraged. They tried every rule in the book to avoid the explosive blunder. Swamy stuck to his guns and even threatened to take them to court and stop the launch of DD2. In the following Sunday newspapers, the DD2 schedule had the name of a different serial instead of *Shri Krishna*, but the show had broken all bureaucratic shackles. Nothing could now stop the destiny of *Shri Krishna*.

On 22 August 1993, Metro DD2 started the first telecast of Ramanand Sagar's *Shri Krishna*, basically targeting the four metro cities of Bombay, Delhi, Madras and Calcutta. Papaji had struggled for four years (1989-93) with DD for this miracle to happen.

The TV serial *Shri Krishna* became an overnight hit and a huge sensation. The ingenious marketing strategy of launching the serial in Hindi and other regional languages like Tamil and Bengali had paid rich dividends. Instantly, there was a clamour to re-telecast *Shri Krishna* on the national channel DD1 for an all-India viewership. The unprecedented popularity, all-India requests and protests, and the anti-Hindu label for the Congress Party forced the I&B ministry and DD authorities to re-telecast the show on DD1. Papaji re-edited and condensed 156 episodes that had aired on DD2 to only thirty-five episodes, to be followed by freshly-shot new episodes for national viewership. This gave the serial a totally new look. The game plan was laid out, but the game was not over yet. DD2 had started the telecast of *Shri Krishna* on 22 August 1993, which was to end on 21 April 1996. Meanwhile, the earlier DG of DD, Bhaskar Ghose, had now been replaced by Ratikant Basu. Prime Channel was a production house owned by Neerja Guleri, who had pitched for a TV serial called *Chandrakanta*, a period fantasy in the golden Sunday morning slot, which had acquired legendary popularity because of Ramanand Sagar's *Ramayan*. There were rumours about Basu's proximity to Guleri. Before the *Shri Krishna* telecast was switched over from DD2 to DD1, the profitable slot had gone to her for *Chandrakanta*, which started telecast in 1994 but had to be pulled off air by DD in 1996, due to a nationwide demand for the telecast of *Shri Krishna* on the national network (DD1).

The battle had begun. Papaji was in no way going to compromise on the slot. Sunday morning 9 a.m. was a dead slot before the *Ramayan* had taken over. He argued with the babus in Mandi House that this was his slot from which *Mahabharat*, and now *Chadrakanta*, had profited hugely. He argued that in principle, he had a total right on the slot, morally and ethically. There was a tug of war between Basu and Papaji. Neither would budge from their stand, and the case finally landed in the Supreme Court of India. Papaji hired the top lawyer of the country, Arun Jaitley (former finance minister of the BJP government). With the massive efforts of Papaji's close aide, Thomas Banon, the Supreme Court ruled in favour of the architect of the slot, Ramanand Sagar! And thus began a new telecast of the serial *Shri Krishna* on the national channel of DD, on 28 April 1996, close on the heels of the end of the earlier version on DD2 on 21 April 1996. From 1996–99, *Chandrakanta* had to take a break and was reinstated in 1999, after the telecast of *Shri Krishna* ended on 13 June 1999.

The unprecedented commercial success of *Shri Krishna* filled the coffers of DD by Rs 135 crore as only airtime earnings from a single weekly slot, at a time when the yearly revenue of DD was only around Rs 500 crore. *Shri Krishna* topped the television ratings for over 120 weeks, becoming the no. 1 programme, at times touching a Television Rating Point (TRP) of around 46. During festivals, a ten-second spot would fetch over Rs 1.60 lakh. In the Lok Sabha, Vijay Goel tabled unstarred question no. 255: 'Which is the top revenue earner for DD?' The then I&B minister Jaipal Ready replied, '*Shri Krishna.*' According to ORG-MARG (a marketing research group), in the period July-December, 20 per cent of the entire population was watching *Shri Krishna*. This amounted to a 134 million viewership. The show topped the rating charts of the Indian Relationship Survey 1997–98, with 522 towns and 1,112 villages in the sample survey. After such a rock-steady chart of topping TRPs and the spot buy rates going haywire due to such popularity, suddenly, the television rating per point started to decline with each passing week. It dropped drastically from 40-plus to around 16 TRPs. The main advertiser, buying a bulk of sixty to one hundred and twenty seconds (six spots to twelve spots) per episode, started complaining and forced me to renegotiate the rate.

Surprisingly, the TRP of a competing serial, *Om Namah Shivay*, was reported to have started climbing the chart to the top, crossing 40 TRPs in the same period. *Shri Krishna* was charging Rs 1.12 lakh per ten seconds, whereas *Om Namah Shivay* was available for as low as Rs 60,000 per ten seconds. Papaji and I smelt a rat—something was not right. I hired the services of the wife of a top FMCG managing director, who headed a consultancy firm. After spending a hefty amount on R&D, going right up to the CEO Ramesh Thadani and approaching the team of Indian Marketing Research Bureau (IMRB), the conclusion handed to me was that the word 'Krishna' had reached a fatigue level, and we were advised to change the name of the serial. I walked out of the office in the Nirmal building while the entire hired research team was still seated around the huge conference table. It was impossible for Papaji to accept the fact that the title 'Krishna', which was highly revered across the length and breadth of India for centuries, could ever reach a saturation point. I then found a person who promised to increase my television ratings week after week for a fee.

The deal was struck. The same *Shri Krishna* climbed up to 36+ TRPs in a few weeks. Every week I was accurately informed in advance, of the next week's rating to be released. The wheeler-dealer even discussed with me the foolproof method. He did not want *Shri Krishna* to cross the *Om Namah Shivay* television ratings, since he was aware that his manipulative method would be exposed. His circle of manipulators believed that the *Om Namah Shivay* television ratings were artificially boosted to break the rate structure and monopoly of *Shri Krishna* as the no. 1 rated television serial.

A scene from *Shri Krishna*.
Photo collection: Ramanand Sagar Foundation.

During that period, the top ad agency Ogilvy & Mather (O&M) had an internal survey of television ratings and placed *Shri Krishna* way ahead as no. 1 in the 2/3rd triangular chart, below the four main cities where IMRB meters were installed. I got hold of their internal memo, which got attention on the front page in film press. This totally falsified the very low 16 TRPs of IMRB based on just four metro cities, whereas the O&M survey covered 625 cities and towns. The CEO, Rodha Mehta, a personal friend, fired me on the phone for leaking the private internal data to the press. We had to pay a hefty compensation and issue an apology letter to settle the matter. *Shri Krishna* proved to be a bigger hit than *Ramayan* in many ways. However, DD refused to give the golden goose an extension after the 156-week telecast, just to continue with the telecast of the half-complete *Chandrakanta*. Zee TV was only too happy to continue the serial without a break, including the 156th episode with the chapter on Gita, the immortal song of God, the spiritual dictionary of Shrimad Bhagwat Mahapuran.

For his remarkable contribution towards reviving the cultural inheritance of our country, Papaji was honoured by the government of India with the Padma Shri, and that too (as rumoured) due to the recommendation and insistence of Suresh Prabhu, a politician from the Shiv Sena. Maybe it was also because Dr Ramanand Sagar refused to bow down to business dealings and the lobbying required to receive such honours.

The time had come for Papaji to move on to his next initiative, the last of his trilogy, *Maa Durga*. This was the last of his missions on earth, and he was ready for it.

11

THE FINAL PHASE:
MAA DURGA AND BEYOND
(2000–05)

The toughest part of Ramanand Sagar's divine mission was to present 'Shakti' because, according to him, it was not possible for the human species to fully fathom the mysticism of Shakti. The tantra, mantra and yantra associated with it were vidyas (knowledge) beyond human comprehension. A few yogis or sadhus who embarked on this path were able to scratch only the surface of the infinite. Many attained unbelievable powers—siddhis, just by a touch or feel of the unfathomable Shakti. On the other hand, in the pursuit of Shakti, many lost their minds and became unacceptable by the sansarik or worldly standards and measures. Papaji contemplated intensely on whether or not he should showcase whatever little the superpower Maa Durga had revealed to him. After months of contemplation, he decided to take the first step and gave me the go-ahead.

Around that time, the film *Jeans*, produced by Ashok Amritraj, Sunanda and Murli Manohar, with music by A.R. Rahman was released. Amritraj was a close friend of Murli Manohar and Sunanda, based in Chennai, and I had business dealings with them during the making of *Ramayan* and *Shri Krishna*. Murli invited me with other film luminaries to Chennai for the launch of *Jeans*, directed by

Shankar. The lead actor of the film, Aishwarya Rai, her mother and I, along with some other industry persons, were booked on the same flight.

A few years ago, I had sent a message across to Aishwarya with the offer of the lead role of Scheherazade in our serial *Alif Laila* (Arabian Nights). She had just been crowned Miss World, and I thought she would readily accept the offer. But she politely declined the offer, saying she wanted to first join films. She was very focused on her career and future.

It rained cats and dogs at the muhurat schedule of *Jeans*. All the decorations were either washed out or in tatters. Murli and Sunanda took it as a blessing from the heavens. Ashok and I met and decided to spend the evening together. I had no idea what destiny was about to unfold for me. Over a drink, I discussed Papaji's vision of *Durga*, starring Hema Malini, as well as *Rajput*, starring Dara Singh as Maharana Pratap, inspired from the book *Annals and Antiquities of Rajasthan* by Lieutenant Colonel Todd (1782–1835), an officer in the East India Company, who spent many years in the Rajputana region. Ashok jumped with excitement at the idea of Papaji's composition of the project. He believed, and was convinced, that Papaji's trilogy, *Ramayan*, *Shri Krishna* and *Maa Durga* would create new records. He rang up his partner, Michael Solomon, former president of Warner Brothers International Television, used the good offices of Murli and signed one of the biggest deals as a producer in the history of Indian television. A sizeable advance was also arranged and handed over to us. Amitabh Bachchan, who had just launched ABCL (Amitabh Bachchan Corporation Limited), sent word through his CEO Sanjeev Gupta (who was earlier with Hindustan Lever Limited), that no one else but ABCL would have the distribution rights to the show. A further advance was then given to us, in view of the unprecedented success of *Ramayan* and *Shri Krishna*. With these developments, Papaji seemed set to roll.

A launch party was organised at Centaur, the five-star hotel next to the airport. Special pottery and clay artisans from Kumortuli (north Kolkata) were invited to make the idol of Durga, killing the buffalo demon Mahishasur, in the central lawns of the Centaur Hotel. Dancers were flown in from Rajasthan and were to perform a welcome dance called 'Chari', with fire pots perched on their heads. The governor of Maharashtra P.C. Alexander gave the muhurat clap, with Jaya Bachchan and Dara Singh in attendance. Two elephants, royally decorated, were at the entrance to greet Michael Solomon and Ashok Amritraj. It was a grand muhurat shot. Michael had a whole wing of the seven-star Leela Hotel booked for himself. He signed the contract with ABCL using a collectors' Mont Blanc pen in the presence of Sanjeev Gupta and me. This was followed by a cocktail dinner at the Leela, where the who's who of the industry, advertisers and corporate honchos including Shunu Sen (HLL), Sam Balsara (Madison World) and Roda Mehta (Ogilvy & Mather) filled the expansive lawns. Political heavyweights like Balasaheb Thackeray mingled with the crème de la crème of Mumbai. Michael and Ashok were mobbed by the media and hounded by the TV crew, each wanting a line or two or a quick interview. Papaji and his family were on cloud nine.

The climax was the announcement of *Durga* and *Rajput* to the entire world. The International Market of Communications Programmes (MIPCOM), the global market for entertainment content, held annually at the French town of Cannes, had decided to explore the eastern globe market in Hong Kong under MIP. Held at the Hong Kong convention and market centre, every nook and corner resounded only with *Durga*. The loudspeakers at the exhibition centre announced the tie-up of Ramanand Sagar and Michael–Ashok repeatedly. All over the exhibition, posters and banners aggressively displayed Durga. Michael Solomon treated my wife Neelam and me to an exclusive dinner in the main restaurant with his entire entourage. Heavyweights of the Indian film and TV industry, including Manmohan Shetty and Amit Khanna, watched the goings-on from the tables across. *Variety*, the top Hollywood trade paper, carried a front page headline announcing the biggest TV venture between India and Hollywood. *Hollywood Reporter* flashed similar headlines.

Overwhelmed and excited, Papaji went to meet Pramod Mahajan, the then I&B minister in charge of the DD National network. Uttam Singh Pawar, a three-time member of parliament, and I accompanied Papaji, expecting a grand welcome with open arms by the I&B minister in the BJP government. Shockingly, Mahajan did not even offer a seat to the man who had made *Ramayan* and *Shri Krishna* for DD, which many critics felt were responsible for the BJP victory and its coming to power. Pawar and I were stunned at the arrogant behaviour of the BJP minister.

Papaji remained silent. Mahajan bluntly and rudely told Papaji that DD would not be able to give him a slot for the telecast of *Maa Durga*. Later, however, DD announced and also telecast *Durga* with Hema Malini in the lead, but by another production house. There were many whispers in the power corridors of Delhi alluding to the involvement and exchange of big money in the decision-making. Hema Malini as Durga on the national TV network of India was literally hijacked by another production house. Papaji perceived this as a karmic rebuff, a divine message that he had no right to reveal the mystics and secrets of the divine Shakti, the creator, observer and destroyer of the whole universe. The Adi Shakti—the primordial energy beyond form—has neither a beginning nor an end; only eternal truth. All the money was returned with folded hands by Papaji, who surrendered to Adi Shakti Maa Durga, the Supreme Being.

His last TV productions

JAI GANGA MAIYA (1998)

Ramanand Sagar believed that Ganga Maiya (Ganga) was his mother. He felt that his soul was connected with the Ganga, the holiest of rivers. In reverence, he started a TV serial *Jai Ganga Maiya* for Doordarshan. Together with his creative companion, Dadoo (Ravindra Jain), he composed the superhit title song, '*Ooh Ganga Maiya tere sharan mein jo bhi koi aaya, tune berah par lagaya Ganga Maiya—har har Gange …*' He pictured and edited every shot himself, and then left it to his sons to complete the serial.

JAI MAHALAKSHMI (2000)

For the serial *Jai Mahalakshmi*, Papaji was very particular about recording the pictures for the title track himself, before letting his children take over.

SAI BABA (2003)

In 2003, at the age of eighty-five, Ramanand Sagar worked meticulously on the research and script of *Sai Baba*, and personally canned the first fifty or so episodes. He left the responsibility for completing the rest of the serial to his children. Television viewers were highly impressed with the research that had gone into it. After all, it was written by Papaji who had earlier acquired a divine halo by making *Ramayan* and *Shri Krishna* for the electronic medium. Papaji realised that the real spiritual life story of Sai Baba—the intensity of his spiritual journey, the miracles, teachings and his biography—would be taken forward with the narration and illustration of incidents from Baba's life. Based on his research and conviction, he wanted to give Sai Baba an identity of birth by depicting his abandonment by his mother, owing to unavoidable circumstances. I had gone to Shirdi with a synopsis, including this feature, for the press release. I placed it at Baba's feet for blessings. A gentleman from the Shri Saibaba Sansthan, the trust behind the Samadhi Temple in Shirdi, met me at Swamy's south Indian cafe outside the temple. I was too naive to understand what he was trying to convey to me after having read the press release.

On Saturday night, a day before the Sunday morning telecast, a rebel inner group of the sansthan walked into Sagar Villa with some legal papers to stop the telecast. With a heavy heart, Papaji took them to the editing room in Sagar Villa's garage, and against his will, removed the objectionable sequences—including the one depicting Baba being abandoned on the roadside.

The seed for the making of *Sai Baba* for TV was sown by Ramrao Shilke, who was working in the administrative block of the Sai Baba temple. Shri Uttam Singh Pawar and Shri Jayant Sasane (chairman of the sansthan) were very cooperative and helpful in bringing *Sai Baba* to millions of TV homes. Ramanand Sagar gave all three their due recognition in the credits.

After the *Sai Baba* TV serial, pilgrims at Shirdi are believed to have increased by leaps and bounds. Some insiders felt that it almost matched the numbers visiting the Tirupati Balaji Temple as also the extent of the collection of donations.

MAHIMA SHANI DEV KI

Inspired by Robert Svoboda's *The Greatness of Saturn*, I worked on the idea and script of *Mahima Shani Dev Ki* in 1991, when my maha dasha (great period) started. My right leg had got shortened due to the accident on the sets of the movie *Charas*, and I was diagnosed with a vascular necrosis in my hip joint. My face had turned dark due to excessive pigmentation. All this was in sync with Shani (Saturn) Dev.

I narrated the script to Papaji. He said it was very good but no channel would touch it since it was not about one of the popular deities, like Shri Ram, Krishna or Hanuman. I stuck to my determination, and with the kripa (kind blessings) of Shani Dev, the TV serial saw the light of day on Imagine channel. Sameer Nair, CEO of the channel, on hearing the script, immediately signed the commissioning agreement on the spot. *Mahima Shani Dev Ki* had a very successful run for almost three years, at times topping the channel's rating chart. Miraculously, my shortened leg came back to its original size with total hip replacement. My face, too, came back to its original skin tone. All this, I believe, happened due to Shani Dev's grace, my devotion and my seva towards Shani Dev for nineteen years.

Ramanand Sagar attained mukti (deliverance) on 12 December 2005. Shani Dev is believed to be the mukti grah (the configuration of deliverance) when he (Shani Dev) comes on a vahan (vehicle) drawn by deer.

A few months later, on 22 June 2006, my mother joined Papaji.

THE LEGACY CONTINUES: TV SERIALS FROM THE SAGAR GROUP (1985–2015)

DOORDARSHAN

Ramayan
Shri Krishna
Luv Kush
Alif Laila
Vikram aur Betaal
Ankhen
Ganga Maiya
Mahalaxmi
Dada–Dadi Ki Kahani

STAR PLUS

Hatim
Sai Baba
Durga
Hotel Kingston
Hello Dollie
Gurukul

COLORS

Maa Durga
Vikram Aur Betaal

SONY

Bach Ke Rehna Re
Arslaan

SAB TV

Brahma Vishnu Mahesh

SAHARA

Bajrangbali

IMAGINE

Ramayan
Chandragupta Maurya
Prithviraj Chauhan Dharamveer
Shani Dev
Basera

BIG MAGIC

Narayan Narayan

DANGAL TV

Mahima Shani Dev Ki

ENTERR10 TELEVISION

Surya Puran

VRINDAVAN ASHRAM

Jai Mata Vaishno Devi Ki

ACKNOWLEDGEMENTS

My sincere gratitude to **Dr Ramanand Sagar** for his tape recordings starting from 9 August 2004 at Sagar Film City.

Thanks also to the following people:

Shiv Sagar, my son and Ramanand Sagar's grandson for research and photos.

Smt. Sarita Chowdhari, my sister and Ramanand Sagar's daughter who lives in Delhi for allowing me to do a telephonic interview of her.

Mr Vijay Chopra, the half-brother of Ramanand Sagar who lives in Srinagar for a valuable tape recording.

Mr Shyam Sunder Bery and Mr Om Prakash Bery, my uncles from Delhi (my mother Leelawati's brothers).

My aunt, Mrs. Premlata Bery, the wife of Mr Om Prakash Bery.

Mr Gopal Krishna Patuwar at Haridwar, the kul purohit of the Chopra khandan.

Mr Ranjit Chowdhary at Jammu.

Mr Amit Biswas, son of the music director Anil Biswas, a close associate of my father.

Ms Deepika Chikhalia, who played Sita in Ramayan.

Mr Chandra Shekhar who acted in Ramayan.

Mr Ajit Naik, the director of photography for Ramayan.

Mr Nepolian Maryan Pinto, Personal Assistant, Mr Prem Sagar.